NOISE AND N(

A Practical Approach

Melville S Adams
BSc (Hons), MSc, MIOA, Lecturer in Building Science, Napier University

and

Francis McManus
MLitt, LLB (Hons), MREHIS, Lecturer in Law, Napier University

Wiley Chancery Law
A Division of John Wiley & Sons
London • New York • Chichester • Brisbane • Singapore

Published in the United Kingdom by
Chancery Law Publishing Ltd
Baffins Lane
Chichester PO19 1UD

Published in North America by
John Wiley & Sons Inc
7222 Commerce Center Drive
Colorado Springs CO 80919
USA

Typeset by
Mackreth Media Services, Hemel Hempstead

Printed and bound in Great Britain by
Redwood Books, Trowbridge, Wiltshire

ISBN 0471 93708 8
A copy of the CIP entry for this book is available from the
British Library.

Library of Congress Cataloguing-in-Publication Data
Adams, Mel S.
Noise and noise law : a practical approach / Mel S. Adams and
Francis McManus.
p. cm.
Includes index.
ISBN 0-471-93708-8 :
1. Noise control—Law and legislation—Great Britain. 2. Noise pollution—Great Britain. 3. Noise. I. McManus, Francis, 1952- . II. Title.
KD3380.A93 1994
344.41'04638—dc20
[344.1044638] 94-15198
CIP

All rights reserved. No part of this publication may be
reproduced in any form or by any means, electronic,
mechanical, photocopying, recording or otherwise, or stored in
any retrieval system without the written permission of the
copyright holders and the publishers.

The moral right of the authors has been asserted.

©
Melville S Adams
Francis McManus
1994

Figures 3.2, 3.3, 3.4 and 3.5 are reproduced from, Burns, W, *Noise and Man* (John Murray, 1973), by permission of John Murray (Publishers) Ltd.
Figures 6.4, 6.5 and Table 6.2 are reproduced from, Nelson, P, (ed), *Transportation Noise Reference Book* (Butterworth-Heinemann, 1987), by permission of Butterworth-Heinemann Limited.
Tables 5.3 and 5.4 are reproduced from the *CIBSE Guide Section A1*, by permission of the Chartered Institution of Building Services Engineers.
Table 5.1 is reproduced from, Atkins Development Research, *The Control of Noise in Ventilation Systems: A Designers Guide* (E & FN Spon, 1972), by permission of WS Atkins Noise and Vibration, Epsom, Surrey.

Contents

Preface	vii
Table of Statutes	ix
Table of Statutory Instruments	x
Table of EC Directives	xi
Table of Cases	xiii

	Page
Introduction	1

Part I The Technical Aspects of Noise	4
1. Basic Acoustics	5
Introduction	5
Propagation of sound waves in air	5
Units of sound	8
2. Response of the Ear, Frequency and Weighting Analysis	25
Introduction	25
Frequency response of the ear	25
Loudness	26
Frequency analysis	28
Digital filters	32
Weighting networks	33
3. The Ear, Threshold Shifts, Assessment and Control of Hearing Risk	37
Introduction	37
The ear	37
Threshold shifts	39
TTS, exposure and recovery time	40

Permanent threshold shift (PTS)	42
Presbycusis (presbycusis)	44
Audiometry	44
Assessing and controlling noise induced hearing loss	47
Future developments	52

4. Statistical and Energy-Based Noise Parameters   55

Introduction	55
Statistical level (percentile parameters) (L_{AN})	55
Equivalent continuous sound pressure level ($L_{Aeq,T}$)	58
Noise pollution level (L_{NP})	61
Single event noise exposure level (L_{AX} or SEL)	62
Day/night equivalent sound level (L_{DN} or DNL)	64
Community noise equivalent level or day/evening/night level (CNEL or DENL or L_{DEN})	64
Measurement of statistical noise parameters	65

5. Internal Noise Criteria and Sound Insulation Requirements   67

Introduction	67
Noise criteria (NC), noise rating (NR) and preferred noise criteria (PNC) curves	67
Speech interference	73
Sound insulation requirements	74
Rating criteria	81
Building regulation performance criteria	84
Achieving the regulation performance criteria	86

6. Environmental Noise   91

Introduction	91
Noise complaints statistics	91
Effects of environmental noise	93
Task performance and communication	102
Transportation noise	104
Road traffic noise	104
Aircraft noise	111
Military aircraft	122
Helicopter noise	124
Railway noise	126
Industrial noise and BS4142	129
Construction and open-site noise	133

| Entertainment, leisure and sporting noise | 136 |
| Other forms of environmental noise control | 142 |

Part II The Legal Control over Noise — 150

7. Environmental Noise: Legal Control — 151

Introduction	151
Nuisance	152
Statutory control of noise	161
Other statutory controls over noise	177
Noise in the workplace	195

Index — 203

Preface

Interest in environmental matters continues to grow apace. Awareness of and public reaction to noise has also become more noticeable in the last 25 years. The number of complaints about neighbourhood noise unfortunately increases each year. However, noise is an esoteric subject for a variety of reasons. It is hoped that this book will give those who have to deal with this form of pollution a better understanding of both its nature, mode of assessment as well as an understanding of the relevant law. The approach throughout is practical. The book is intended for legal practitioners, environmental health officers, builders and surveyors. It will also be particularly useful to students who are studying noise as part of their degree courses. It is not intended to be exhaustive either by way of the technical aspects or the law relating to noise. References and discussion of appropriate EC Directives, government circulars and subordinate legislation have therefore been kept to a minimum as a concession to brevity.

Frank McManus would like to thank Dr Alexander McCall-Smith and Jeremy Strang for reading and commenting on drafts of the law section of the book. He thanks also the Secretary of State of Defence, Mr Malcolm Rifkind QC and Mr Patrick Lamb of the Ministry of Defence, Ms A J Easey of the Department of Transport, MV Alex Custerson of the Department of the Environment, Ms Jackie Drakeford of the British Airports Authority, Mr J Duck of the Civil Aviation Authority for assistance given. All mistakes however are his own.

Lastly, both authors wish to acknowledge the support given to them by their respective families during the course of the preparation of this book.

The law is considered to be up to date as on the 9 April 1994.

FRANCIS MCMANUS
MELVILLE S ADAMS
Edinburgh, 1994

Table of Statutes

United Kingdom
Building Act 1984 193
s 1 172

Cinemas Act 1985
s 1 194
Civic Government (Scotland) Act 1982
s 49(1) 180
s 54 180
s 54(1) 179
s 54(3) 180
Civil Aviation Act 1971 184
s 29 186
Civil Aviation Act 1982 184
s 3 185
s 60(2) 182
s 60(3)(r) 184
s 62 182
s 76(1) 182
s 77(1) 184
s 77(2) 184, 185
s 78 .... 185, 186, 187, 188
s 78(1) 185
s 79 .... 186, 187
s 80 187
s 81 182
Sched 14 186
Control of Pollution Act 1974 162
Pt III 166, 170, 171
s 58 .... 164, 170, 172
s 58(4) 166
s 58(6)(a) 172
s 60 .... 167, 171, 172
s 60(2) 171
s 60(3) 171
s 60(4) 171, 172
s 60(6) 172
s 60(7) 172, 173
s 60(8) 173
s 61 .... 167, 172, 173
s 61(4) 172
s 62 173
s 62(1) 173, 174
s 62(1)(a) 173

s 62(1)(b) 173
s 62(1A) 173
s 62(1B) 173
s 62(2) 173
s 62(3) 174
s 62(3A) 174
s 63 .... 174, 175
s 64(3) 175
s 64(4) 175
s 65 167
s 65(1) 175, 176
s 65(2) 175
s 65(4) 175
s 65(5) 176
s 65(6) 176
s 66 167
s 66(1) 176
s 67 167
s 67(1) 177
s 67(3) 177
s 68 177
s 69 176
s 69(2) 176
s 71 177
Sched 1 .... 174, 175
Countryside Act 1968
s 13(2) 191
Crown Proceedings Act 1947
s 11 188

Environmental Protection Act 1990 162
Pt III 163, 164, 170
s 79 164
s 79(1) 165
s 79(1)(a) 164
s 79(1)(g) 164
s 79(1)(ga) 165, 166, 167, 168
s 79(2) 165
s 79(6) 164
s 79(6A) 165
s 79(7) 165
s 80 165
s 80(1) 165
s 80(2) 165, 167, 168

ix

s 80(2)(b)	168	Noise Abatement Act 1960	162, 177
s 80(3)	166, 168	Noise and Statutory Nuisance Act	
s 80(4)	166, 167, 173	1993	163, 165, 168, 170, 173
s 80(5)	168	s 9	169
s 80(7)	166	s 80A	168
s 80(8)(a)	166	Sched 2	174
s 80(9)	167, 173	Sched 3	169
s 80A	165		
s 80A(1)	167	Public Health Act 1936	
s 81(1)(A)	168	s 92(1)(a)	164
s 81(1)(B)	168	Public Health (Scotland) Act 1897	
s 81(3)	167		164, 181
s 81(5)	167, 173		
s 81(6)	173	Road Traffic Act 1988	
s 82	169	s 41	189
s 82(10)	169	s 41(1)	189
		s 41(2)(C)	189
Health and Safety at Work Act 1974		s 42	189
s 2(1)	198	s 54	190
s 3	180		
s 6	202	Theatres Act 1968	
s 6(1)	202	s 12	194
		Town and Country Planning Act	
Land Compensation Act 1973	190, 192	1990	178
s 1(3)	193	s 55	178
s 18	193	s 55(1)	179
s 20	193	s 70	186
Licensing Act 1964		s 70(2)	178
s 4	181	s 72(1)	178
Licensing (Scotland) Act 1976		Town and Country Planning	
s 38(1)(f)	181	(Scotland) Act 1972	
s 38(3)	181	s 26	186
Local Government Act 1972			
s 235	178	**Tasmania**	
Local Government (Miscellaneous		Environment Protection Act 1973	
Provisions) Act 1982	195	s 1	163
Sched 1	195		
Local Government (Scotland) Act 1973		**Western Australia**	
s 201(1)	178	Environmental Protection Act 1986	
Lotteries and Amusements Act 1976		(No 87)	
s 16	195	s 79(1)	163
Magistrates' Courts Act 1980		**Victoria (Australia)**	
s 101	166	Environment Protection Act 1970	163

Table of Statutory Instruments

Regulations

Aeroplane Noise (Limitation of Operation of Aeroplanes) Regulations 1993 (SI 1993/1409)	184	Building Regulations 1985 (SI 1985/1065 as amended by SI 1989/1119)	193
Air Regulations 1991 (SI 1991/2439)		Building Standards (Scotland) Regulations (SI 1990/2170)	
reg 39	183	Pt H	194
		Sched 1	193

Table of Statutory Instruments

Civil Aviation (Notices) Regulations
1978 (SI 1978/1303) 185
Control of Noise (Measurement and
Registers) Regulations 1976
(SI 1976/37) 175

Household Appliances (Noise
Emission) Regulations 1990 (SI
1990/2179)
reg 3 192
reg 4 192

Motor Vehicles (Type Approval)
(GB) Regulations 1984
(SI 1984/981) 190

Noise at Work Regulations 1989
(SI 1989/1790) 199
reg 4 199
reg 6 199
reg 7 .... 199, 202
reg 8 .... 200, 201
reg 8(1) 201
reg 8(2) 202
reg 9 200
reg 10 .... 200, 201
reg 11 201
reg 12 202
reg 13 202
Noise Insulation Regulations 1975
(SI 1975/1763 as amended
by SI 1988/2000) 190, 193

Noise Insulation (Scotland)
Regulations 1975 (SI 1975/
460) 193
Road Vehicles (Construction and
Use) Regulations 1986 (SI 1986/
1078, as amended) 189
reg 54 189
regs 56-58 189
reg 97 189

Town and Country Planning
(Assessment of Environmental
Effects) Regulations 1988
(SI 1988/1199) 191

Orders
Air Navigation (Noise Certification)
Order 1990 (SI 1990/1514) 184
Aircraft Navigation Order 1989 (SI
1989/2004 as amended by SI 1990/
2154 and SI 1991/1726) 185
art 3 183
art 3(1) 182–183
art 95(1) 183
Sched 2, para 6 183

Civil Aviation (Designation of
Aerodromes) Order 1981
(SI 1981/651) 186

Table of EC Directives

Dir 80/51/EEC on the limitation of noise
emissions from subsonic aircraft (OJ
1980 L18/26 184
Dir 83/206/EEC (OJ 1983 L117/
15) 184
Dir 86/188/EEC on the protection of
workers from the risks related to
exposure to noise at work (OJ 1986
L137/28) 199
Dir 86/594/EEC on airborne noise
emitted by household appliances
(OJ 1986 L344/24)
Art 6(1) 192
Dir 92/14/EEC on the limitation of the
operation of aeroplanes covered by Part
II, Chapter 2, Volume 1 of Annex 16 to
the Convention on International Civil
Aviation, second edition (1988)
(OJ 1992 L76/21) 184

Table of Cases

Allen v Gulf Oil Refining Ltd [1981] AC 1001, 158, 192
Andreae v Selfridge and Co Ltd [1938] Ch 1, 152, 155
Ankerson v Connelly [1907] 1 Ch 678, 160
Attorney-General v PYA Quarries Ltd [1957] 2 QB 169, 189

Bellew v Cement Co [1948] IR 61, 153, 160
Bolton v Stone [1951] AC 850, 197
Bramford v Turnley (1862) 31 LJQB 286, 154, 155, 156

Cambridge Water Co v Eastern Counties Leather plc [1994] 2 WLR 53, 156
Chapman v Gosberton Farm Produce Company Ltd [1993] 1 Env LR 191, 166
Christie v Davie [1893] 1 Ch 316, 154

Dunton v Dover District Council (1978) 76 LGR 87, 160

Gillingham BC v Medway (Chatham) Dock Co Ltd [1992] JPL 458, 153, 155
Goldman v Hargrave [1967] 1 AC 645, 156

Halsey v Esso Petroleum Co [1961] 1 WLR 683, 152
Harrison v Southwark and Vauxhall Water Company [1891] 2 Ch 409, 153, 155
Heath v Brighton Corporation (1908) 98 LT 718, 156
Holywood Silver Fox Farm Ltd v Emmett [1936] 2 KB 468, 152, 154

Kennaway v Thompson [1980] 3 All ER 329, 161
Kingston upon Thames Royal LBC v Secretary of State for the Environment [1973] 1 WLR 1549, 187
Kruse v Johnston [1898] 2 QB 91, 178

Lambert Flat Management Ltd v Lomas [1981] 2 All ER 280, 164
Leakey v National Trust for Places of Historic Interest and Natural Beauty [1980] QB 485, 156
London Brighton and South Coast Railway v Truman (1886) 11 App Cas 45, 152
Lord Advocate v Reo Stakis Organisation 1982 SLT 140, 154
Lovell v Blundells and Crompton and Co [1944] 1 KB 502, 198

Metropolitan Properties Ltd v Jones [1939] 2 All ER 202, 157
Miller v Jackson [1977] 3 All ER 338; [1977] QB 966, 159, 160
Morganite Special Carbons Ltd v Secretary of State for the Environ-ment (1980) 256 EG 1105, 175

Naismith v London Film Productions Ltd [1939] 1 All ER 794, 196
NCB v Thorne [1976] 1 WLR 543, 153
Nolan v Dental Manufacturing Co [1958] 2 All ER 449, 197

Pape v Cumbria County Council [1991] IRLR 463, 197
Paris v Stepney Borough Council [1951] 1 All ER 42, 197
Peak Park Planning Board v Secretary of State for the Environment [1980] JPL 114, 187
Penwith DC v Secretary of State [1977] JPL 371, 179
Powell v May [1946] KB 330, 178
Pyx Granite Co Ltd v Minister of Housing and Local Government [1958] 1 QB 554, 179

Qualcast (Wolverhampton) Ltd v Haynes [1959] AC 743, 197-198

R v Secretary of State for Transport, ex parte Richmond upon Thames LBC [1994] I WLR 74, 185
R v Shorrock [1993] 3 WLR 698, 156

RHM Bakeries (Scotland) Ltd v
 Strathclyde Regional Council
 1985 SLT 214, 156-157
Rose v Miles (1815) 4 M and S 101, 189

Sedleigh-Denfield v O'Callaghan [1940]
 AC 880, 156, 157
Slater v McLellan 1924 SC 854, 157
Smith v Scott [1973] Ch 314, 152, 157
Southwark London BC v Ince *The Times*,
 16 May, 1989, 164
Speed v Thomas Swift and Co [1943] KB
 557, 196-197
Spicer v Smee [1946] 1 All ER 489, 156
St Helens Smelting Co v Tipping (1865) 11
 HLC 642, 154
Stagecoach Ltd v Mc Phail 1988
 SCCR 289, 166

Strathclyde Regional Council v Tudhope
 1983 SLT 22, 171
Sturges v Bridgman (1879) 11
 Ch D 852, 159

Tetley v Chitty [1986] 1 All ER 202, 157

Wagon Mound (The) [1961] AC 388, 160
Wallington v Secretary of State for Wales
 and Montgomeryshire District Council
 [1990] JPL 112, 179
Webster v Lord Advocate 1984
 SLT 13; 1985 SLT 36, 158, 159, 160, 161
Wellingborough BC v Gordon
 [1993] 1 Env LR 218, 164, 166, 176
Wilson v Tyneside Window Cleaning Co
 [1958] 2 QB 110, 196

Introduction

We have already alluded in the Preface to the rapid upsurge in interest in matters environmental which until recently had attracted but scant attention. Thus far the legal profession has made a positive response and more and more lawyers are taking an active interest in this many faceted subject. One hopes that such interest will be sustained and the subject is not destined to be shortly cast aside like the latest Paris fashion! The current popularity of environmental law should not obscure the fact that the second half of the last century witnessed intense legislative activity in this field only for the subject to wane into relative decline until after the Second World War.

The practitioner is most likely to deal with noise in relation to so-called neighbourhood noise which is a fertile source of complaint to local authority environmental health departments. Such noise may, of course, also be the subject of a private nuisance action. Again, public inquiries dealing with the siting of new roads, railways, aerodrome runways etc will invariable deal with noise issues. The practitioner will therefore often have to deal with the reports of expert witnesses in the course of such proceedings. It is hoped that this work will facilitate an understanding among those so involved of the nature of noise, its measurement as well as the relevant law.

Little is assumed by way of prior knowledge of the subject. Students such as building, surveying, environmental health, environmental engineering, transport engineering as well as life science students who are studying noise as part of their professional qualifications should find the book helpful. The authors have refrained from discussing how the law could be improved. Rather, a practical approach to the subject has been adopted. Furthermore, as a concession to succinctness we have avoided as far as possible the reproduction of statutes, statutory instruments, codes of practice etc.

The book is divided into a technical and legal section. The technical section introduces the reader to basic acoustic theory. This will facilitate an understanding of the methods of analysis and parameters used to assess noise in the environment. The legal section commences with a discussion of nuisance at common law and under statue and then goes on to deal with a variety of statutes which have a bearing of noise. It should be remembered that noise law has developed slowly and piecemeal. Indeed, it probably ranks as the most fragmented branch of environmental law. The majority of statutes which are discussed primarily deal with other matters. The subject of environmental noise indeed seems to cry out for a consolidating statute. The law discussed is UK law. Where there is a divergence between English and Scots law the latter is discussed separately. However, in order to avoid tedious repetition, such discussion is condensed as far as possible without, it is hoped, sacrificing clarity of expression.

Part I
The Technical Aspects of Noise

Chapter 1
Basic Acoustics

Introduction

Sound may be defined as the transmission of energy through gaseous, liquid or solid media via rapid fluctuations in the pressure of the medium. The pressure fluctuations originate from some vibrating object, e.g. human voice, loudspeaker diaphragm, machine tool etc.

Propagation of sound waves in air

For a sound wave to be established it is necessary to have a sound source (vibrating object) and a medium for transmission. This immediately distinguishes sound waves from electro-magnetic waveforms, e.g. light, radiant heat and radio waves which need no medium for transmission and which can travel through a vacuum.

Consider the air near some vibrating surface as shown in Figure 1.1. During the first outward movement of the vibrating surface the particles of air around the surface are compressed together thereby producing a region of increased pressure in the air around the surface. After reaching some maximum displacement to the right, the surface retreats through its mean position to some maximum displacement on the opposite side of its mean position. As the surface retreats from its position of maximum displacement a region of reduced pressure, or rarefaction, is created behind the retreating surface.

As the surface continues to vibrate a series of alternate regions of increased and decreased pressure will continue to be produced

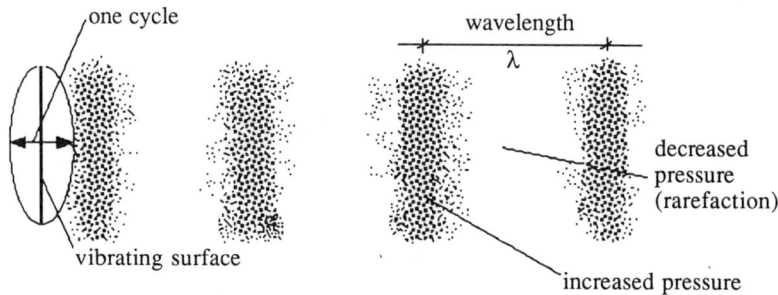

Figure 1.1 Propagation of a sound wave

in the air. The longitudinal movement of the pressure fronts through the air from the source to the receiver constitutes a sound wave.

Particle motion

If the motion of an individual particle of air under the action of a sound wave is considered, it will be seen that the particle is first displaced in the direction of propagation of the wave due to the compressive phase. The actual degree of displacement depends on the amplitude of vibration of the source. After reaching its maximum positive displacement (to the right) the particle will move back through its mean position to an equal negative displacement (to the left), due to the action of the rarefaction, and then back to its mean position. As long as the source continues to oscillate the particle will vibrate about its mean position with equal displacements on opposite sides of the mean position. This is shown on Figure 1.2. This type of motion is termed *simple harmonic motion*.

The motion of the particle from its mean position to the maximum positive displacement, back through the mean position to the maximum negative displacement, and then back to the mean position is termed *one cycle*. The time taken for one cycle is termed the *period* (T) of the vibration. The differentiation of the displacement of the particle with respect to time gives the *particle velocity*.

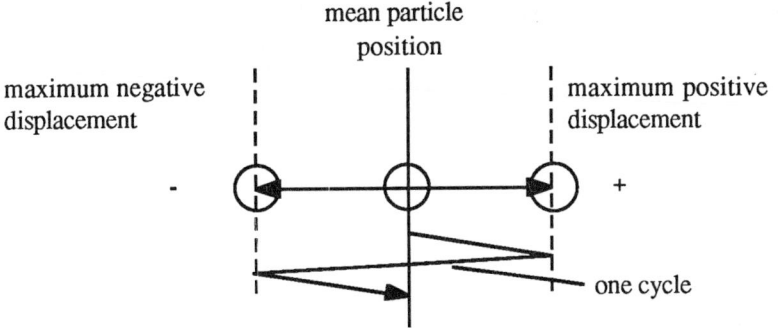

Figure 1.2 Particle motion

Frequency (*f*)

The frequency or pitch of a sound is the number of cycles, or pressure fluctuations, produced per second. The frequency is therefore the reciprocal of the period, *i.e.*

$$f = \frac{1}{T} \text{ Hz}$$

Frequency is measured in Hertz (Hz), 1 Hertz = 1 cycle per second.

The audible range varies from person to person but is normally in the region of 20 Hz to 20 kHz. Sounds below 20 Hz are termed *infra-sonic* and those above 20 kHz are termed *ultra-sonic*.

Wavelength (λ)

The wavelength, λ, is the distance between two successive pressure maxima or minima in a plane wave. The wavelength is illustrated on Figure 1.1.

Velocity or speed of sound (c)

The velocity of sound is the speed at which sound energy travels through a given medium. This value, which is constant for a given medium, is independent of the particle velocity and depends entirely on the characteristics of the medium. The speed of sound through a medium is given by the relationship :

$$\text{velocity} = \text{frequency} \times \text{wavelength}$$
$$c = f\lambda \text{ metres per second}$$

Since the velocity of sound is constant for a given medium it follows that if the frequency increases, the wavelength must decrease to keep the product of "$f\lambda$" constant, *i.e.* high frequency (high pitched) sounds have short wavelengths and low frequency sounds have long wavelengths.

The speed of sound in air at NTP is around 344 m/s. This means that the audible range of sounds from 20 Hz to 20 kHz corresponds to wavelengths of 17.2 metres to 17.2 millimetres.

It has already been stated that the speed of sound in a medium is determined by the characteristics of the medium.

The two most important physical characteristics of a medium with respect to the speed of sound are the elasticity and the density of the medium. The elasticity of air is found by experiment to be a constant, γ, multiplied by the atmospheric pressure.

$$\gamma = \frac{\text{specific heat of air at a constant pressure}}{\text{specific heat of air at constant volume}}$$

$\gamma = 1.4$ for normal calculations.

The speed of sound in air to be given by the relationship :

$$c = \sqrt{\frac{1.4 p_0}{\rho_0}}$$

where p_0 is atmospheric pressure and ρ_0 is the density of air.

Units of sound

Sound pressure (*p*)

A soundwave in air consists of a number of regions of increased and decreased pressure travelling longitudinally from the source

Basic Acoustics

to the receiver.

Sound pressure can be defined as force per unit area, *i.e.*

Pressure = force / area (Newtons per square metre)
N / m² or Pascals (Pa)

The pressure fluctuations produced when a sound wave travels through air are very small compared to static atmospheric pressure.

RMS sound pressure (p_{rms})

In a sound wave the number of positive pressure disturbances (compressions) balances the number of negative pressure disturbances (rarefaction). If the mean value of sound pressure disturbance were measured the value would therefore be zero. The mean value is therefore not a useful unit for quantifying the energy content of a sound signal with reference to sound pressure. A measure which adds (rather than subtracts) the effects of the rarefactions to the effects of the positive compressions must be adopted. Such a measure is the root-mean-square (rms) sound pressure, p_{rms}. The rms sound pressure is found by squaring the pressure disturbances at each instant of time, adding the squared values together, and then averaging over the sample time. (The squaring operation converts the negative rarefactions to positive values.) The r.m.s. sound pressure is the square root of the sum of the squares of the pressure disturbances over the sample time.

The relationship between peak pressure and r.m.s. pressure is shown on Figure 1.3

It can be shown for a sinusoidal waveform that the relationship between rms pressure and peak pressure is as follows ;

$$p_{rms} = \frac{p_{peak}}{\sqrt{2}}$$

i.e the rms pressure = 0.7071 times the peak pressure.

The ear is a pressure sensitive mechanism and hence it is

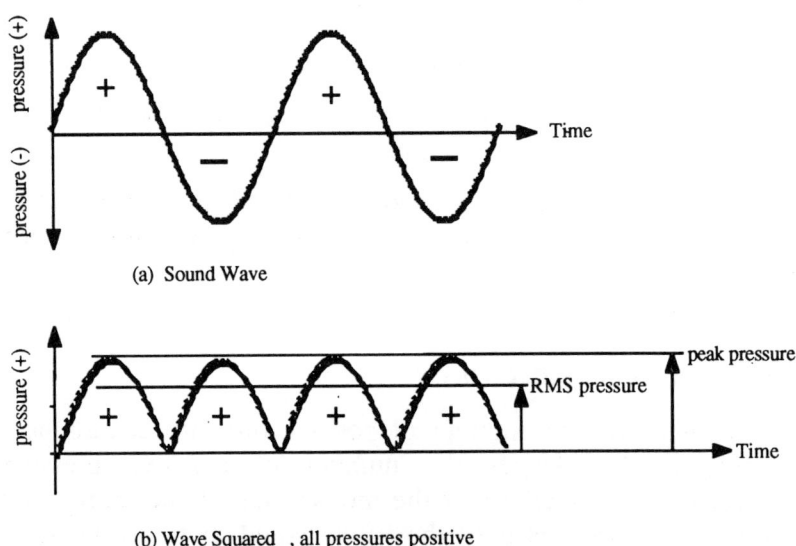

Figure 1.3 Peak and r.m.s. pressure (a) Sound wave (b) Wave squared

convenient to use pressure as a basis for the measurement of the magnitude of sound. For most types of sound the ear responds to the r.m.s. pressure. Sound pressures referred to in this book will therefore be rms pressures unless otherwise stated.

Impedance (z)

For a pure sinusoidal wave the ratio of the pressure (p) to the particle velocity (v) is termed the impedance of the medium.

$$z = \frac{p}{v}$$

It can also be shown that the impedance is the product of the density (ρ) of the medium and the velocity (c) of sound in the medium, i.e

$$z = \rho c$$

Impedance is measured in *rayls* (after Lord Rayleigh).

With the density of air taken as 1.2 kg/m³ and the velocity of sound in air as 344 m/s this gives an impedance for air of 413 rayls.

Sound intensity (I)

The intensity of a sound wave is the rate of flow of energy per unit area.

$$\text{Intensity} = \frac{\text{energy}}{\text{time} \times \text{area}}$$

Since energy per unit time is power (W), intensity can be expressed as,

$$\text{Intensity} = \frac{\text{power}}{\text{area}} = \frac{W}{A}$$

Intensity is measured in watts / metre² (W/m²).

The intensity is also equal to the product of pressure (p) and particle velocity (v), i.e.

$$I = pv$$

From the above impedance relationships

$$\frac{p}{v} = \rho c = z$$

the particle velocity, v, is given by;

$$v = \frac{p}{\rho c}$$

Hence the intensity can be written as ;

$$I = p\frac{p}{\rho c} \text{ i.e. } I = \frac{p^2}{\rho c}$$

Since the impedance (ρc) is constant for a given medium, the sound intensity is proportional to the square of the sound pressure.

Decibel scales (dB)

Although the measurement and calculation of sounds for acoustic and engineering purposes may consider the strength of a sound in terms of pressure (N/m^2 or pascals (Pa)) or intensity (W/m^2) it is generally more convenient to quantify sound levels in terms of decibels. There are two main reasons for adopting decibel scales:

1. The sensation produced at the ear varies with the *logarithm* of the intensity of a sound and not directly with intensity. Therefore a logarithmic scale should be used.
2. Logarithmic decibel scales compress the vast range of numerical values which result from using intensity or pressure.

If intensity is used as a scale for measuring sounds, the range of audible intensities, at a frequency of 1 kHz, varies from 10^{-12} W/m^2 at the "threshold of audibility" to 10^2 W/m^2 at the "threshold of pain". This gives a range of 10^{14}, *i.e.* 100 million million integer values in the scale!

The problem is not quite so severe if pressure is used. The range of audible pressures is from 2×10^{-5} N/m^2 ($20\mu Pa$) at the threshold of audibility to 2×10^2 N/m^2 at the threshold of pain. This still gives a range of 10^7, *i.e.* 10 million integer values in the scale.

The use of logarithmic decibel scales reduces the range of values down to 0 dB at the threshold of audibility and 140 dB at the threshold of pain, *i.e.* 140 integer values.

Three decibel scales are normally used in acoustics, *i.e. sound intensity level, sound pressure level* and *sound power level.*

Sound intensity level (L_I)

The sound intensity level is the decibel level of a sound relative to the sound intensity in W/m^2.

The sound intensity level is defined by ;

$$L_1 = 10 \log_{10} \left[\frac{I}{I_0} \right] \text{ dB}$$

where I is the intensity of sound being considered (W/m²) and I_o is the reference intensity = 10^{-12} W/m², i.e. intensity at the threshold of audibility.

If a sound at the threshold of audibility is considered ($I = 10^{-12}$ W/m²), the sound intensity level would be given by;

$$L_1 = 10 \log_{10} \left[\frac{10^{-12}}{10^{-12}} \right] \text{ dB}$$

i.e. $L_I = 10 \log_{10} [1] = 0$ dB

If a sound at the threshold of pain is considered (I = 10^2 W/m²), the sound intensity level would be given by ;

$$L_1 = 10 \log_{10} \left[\frac{10^2}{10^{-12}} \right] \text{ dB}$$

i.e.
$$L_I = 10 \log_{10} [10^{14}] \text{ dB}$$

i.e.
$$L_I = 10 \times 14 = 140 \text{ dB}$$

Sound pressure level (L_p)

The sound pressure level is the decibel level of a sound relative to the sound pressure in N/m².

Since the sound intensity is proportional to the square of the sound pressure, the sound pressure level is defined as:

$$L_p = 10 \log_{10} \left[\frac{p^2}{p^2_0} \right] \text{ dB}$$

i.e.

$$L_p = 20 \log_{10} \left[\frac{p}{p_0} \right] \text{ dB}$$

where p = pressure of sound being considered (N/m²)

p_o = reference sound pressure = 2×10^{-5} N/m² (20 µPa), i.e. the sound pressure at the threshold of audibility.

Inserting values of "p" of 2×10^{-5} N/m² and 2×10^2 N/m² into the above relationship would again give values of 0 dB at the threshold of audibility and 140 dB at the threshold of pain.

Microphones, which are the first stage of most sound level measurements, are pressure sensitive, and hence the sound pressure level is the quantity which is actually measured when a microphone is placed in a sound field. Sound intensity is a vector quantity, *i.e.* it has direction and magnitude considerations, and requires sophisticated techniques for measurement.

As has been previously stated, the ear is pressure sensitive and hence sound pressure level is generally a more useful parameter for noise considerations than sound intensity level.

Some typical sound pressure levels and sound pressures are illustrated on Figure 1.4.

Sound power level (L_w)

The sound power level is a measure of the energy output of a source independent of the environment in which the source is measured. This allows direct noise ratings of machines, machine tools, domestic appliances etc.

If a machine was placed in a room and sound pressure levels were measured at some distance from the machine, the measured levels would be a combination of direct noise from the machine plus reflected, or reverberant, noise from the room surfaces. The sound pressure level measurements would therefore be a function of the environment in which the measurements were made. If the machine was then placed in a different acoustic environment the measured sound pressure levels would be different. The sound power level relates directly to the source and therefore eliminates variation in measurement environments.

The sound power level is defined as ;

$$L_w = 10 \log_{10} \left[\frac{W}{W_0} \right] \text{ dB}$$

where W is the sound power of source being considered in watts and W_0 is the reference sound power = 10^{-12} W.

Basic Acoustics 15

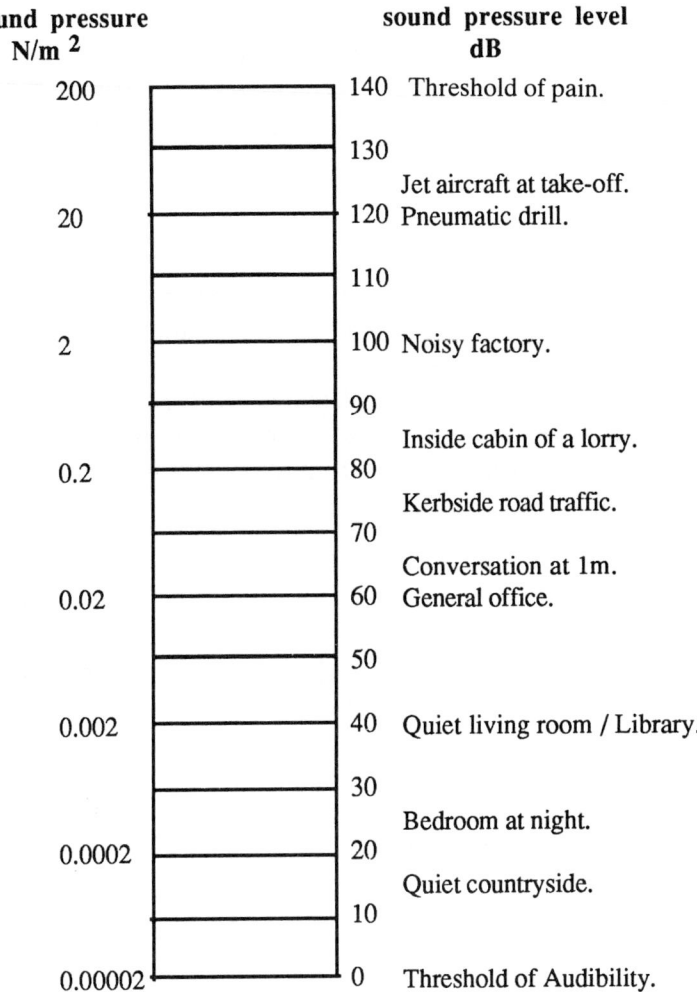

Figure 1.4 Typical sound pressures and sound pressure levels

For example, if a source radiates 0.2 W of acoustic power the sound power level would be;

$$L_w = 10 \log_{10} \left[\frac{0.2}{10^{-12}} \right] \text{ dB}$$

$$L_w = 113 \text{ dB}$$

If the sound power level of a source is known and the acoustic performance of the environment in which the source is to be placed is also known, accurate calculations of sound pressure levels at different distances from the source can be made.

Addition of decibel values

Since decibel values are based on logarithmic scales, decibel values are not directly additive, *i.e.* two sounds, each of sound pressure level 70 dB, would *not* give a combined level of 140 dB.

The addition of decibel values could involve the conversion of decibel values back to intensity in W/m² or pressure in N/m².

In terms of intensity, the total intensity (W/m²) is equal to the sum of the individual intensities, *i.e.*

$$\Sigma I = I_1 + I_2 + I_3 + \ldots + I_n$$

where I_1, I_2, I_3, I_n are the sound intensities from individual sources.

The total sound intensity level can then be found from the sound intensity level equation as follows:

$$L_I = 10 \log_{10} \left[\frac{\Sigma I}{I_0} \right] \text{ dB}$$

where L_I is the total sound intensity level, ΣI is the total sound intensity (W/m²) and I_0 is the reference intensity = 10^{-12} W/m².

Since intensity is proportional to the square of the pressure the total pressure can be found from ;

$$\Sigma p^2 = p_1^2 + p_2^2 + p_3^2 + \ldots + p_n^2$$

where p_1, p_2, p_3, p_n are the sound pressures from individual sources.

$$\Sigma p = \sqrt{p_1^2 + p_2^2 + p_3^2 + \ldots + p_n^2}$$

The total sound pressure level can then be found from the sound pressure level equation as follows;

$$L_p = 20 \log_{10} \left[\frac{\Sigma p}{p_0} \right] \text{ dB}$$

Basic Acoustics 17

where L_p is the total sound pressure level, Σp is the total sound pressure (N/m²) and p_o is the reference pressure = 2×10^5 N/m².

Both of the above methods require much in the way of calculation. A more convenient method of adding decibel values together, and one which does not require conversion to basic units of intensity and pressure is as follows:

$$L_{(total)} = 10 \log_{10} \sum_{i=1}^{n} 10^{Li/10} \text{ dB}$$

This expression can be modified to;

$$L_{(total)} = 10 \log_{10}[10^{L1/10} + 10^{L2/10} + 10^{L3/10} + \ldots + 10^{Ln/10}] \text{ dB}$$

If three sound pressure levels of 60 dB, 70 dB, and 80 dB, respectively, arrived simultaneously at a reference point, the total or combined sound pressure level would be given by;

$$L_{p(total)} = 10 \log_{10}[10^6 + 10^7 + 10^8] \text{ dB}$$

$$L_{p(total)} = 80.5 \text{ dB}$$

If two equal sound pressure levels are added together the resultant total sound pressure level is 3 dB higher than an individual sound pressure level, *i.e. if the sound energy is doubled the sound pressure level increases by 3 dB.*

For example, if two sound pressure levels, each of 70 dB, are added, the total sound pressure level is given by:

$$L_{p(total)} = 10 \log_{10}[10^7 + 10^7] \text{ dB}$$

$$L_{p(total)} = 73 \text{ dB}$$

Similarly, if the sound energy output of a machine were halved, the reduction in sound level would be 3 dB.

A quicker, though less accurate, method of adding two decibel values together is to use the relationship given in Table 1.1.

For example if two sound levels of 76 dB and 81 dB are to be added the difference in level is 5 dB and therefore the value to be added to the higher level is 1 dB. This gives a resulting level of 82 dB. The true overall level using the previous equations is 82.2 dB. The value of 82 dB derived from the table is accurate enough for most purposes.

Table 1.1

Difference between dB values to be added	dB value to be added to the higher level
0 or 1	3
2 or 3	2
4 to 9	1
10 or more	0

Subtraction of decibel values

Decibel values can be subtracted in a similar manner to the addition of decibel values. For example, if two machines operating together produce an overall sound pressure level of 79 dB at a reference point and one machine on its own produces 72 dB at the reference point, the level produced at the reference point by the other machine on its own would be 79 dB minus 72 dB. The answer to this subtraction is given by;

$$L_p = 10 \log_{10}[10^{7.9} - 10^{7.2}] \text{ dB}$$

$$L_p = 78.03 \text{ dB}$$

Again the problem can be simplified by the use of the values in Table 1.2.

In the previous example the difference in levels being considered is 7 dB and therefore the value to be subtracted from the overall level is 1 dB. This gives a value of 78 dB for the

Table 1.2

Difference between dB values to be subtracted	dB value to be subtracted to the higher level
10 or more	0
6 to 9	1
4 to 5	2
3	3
2	4 or 5

second machine. This value agrees closely with the calculated value.

Sound and distance

Sound intensity decays with distance from the source. The nature of the decay depends on the type of sound source.

Sound sources can be categorized as either (i) *point sources* or (ii) *line sources*.

Point sources

Consider a point source of sound power "W" watts radiating spherically through a sphere of radius "*r*" metres and hence surface area $4\pi r^2$ square metres, as shown on Figure 1.5. By definition the sound intensity at a point on the surface of the sphere would be:

Intensity = power / area

$$I = \frac{W}{4\pi r^2} \ (\text{W/m}^2)$$

If the distance from the source, "*r*", is increased the intensity would obviously decrease since the same source power "*W*", is

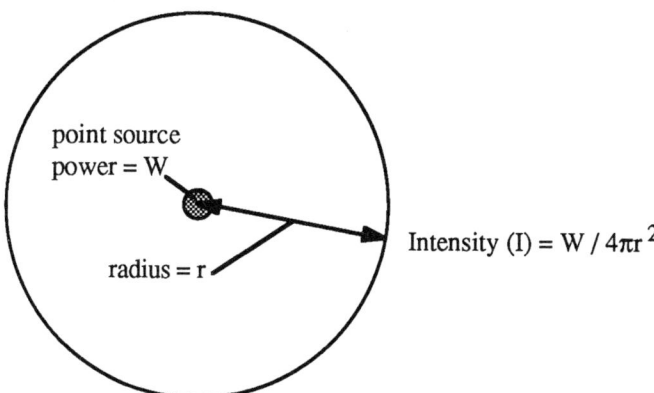

Figure 1.5   Spherical radiation from a point source

being dissipated over a bigger surface area.

Since the value of $W/4\pi$ will remain constant for a given source it follows that the intensity (I) varies inversely with the square of the distance (r) from the source, i.e.

$$I \propto \frac{1}{r^2}$$

$$I \propto \frac{1}{\text{distance}^2}$$

This is known as the *inverse square law*.

If the distance (r) from the source was doubled, the intensity (I, W/m²) would be quartered, i.e.

$$\frac{1}{2^2} = \frac{1}{4}$$

The effect of quartering the sound intensity is to bring about a 6 dB reduction in sound level, i.e.

$$10 \log_{10} \left[\frac{1}{4} \right] = -6 \text{ dB}$$

Thus, for point sources, the decay is often expressed as being a 6 dB reduction in sound level per doubling of distance from the source.

If a point source is located on a hard, reflective surface the sound power would be dissipated over the surface area of a hemisphere as shown on Figure 1.6. The intensity would be given by:

$$I = \frac{W}{2\pi r^2}$$

This is often the assumption made for equipment or machines mounted on or near the ground.

Often real noise sources are directional in their sound radiation but the inverse square law is still applicable. This is shown on Figure 1.7. The area over which the sound power from the source is being dissipated varies with the square of the distance from the source and hence the intensity of sound varies inversely with the square of the distance from the source.

Basic Acoustics

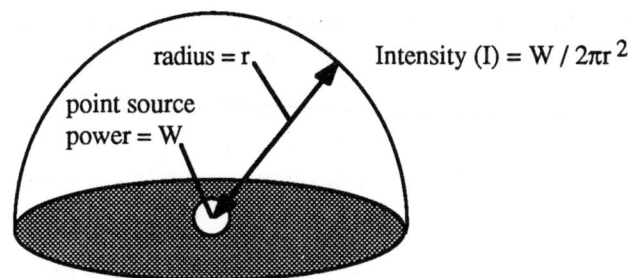

Figure 1.6 Hemispherical radiation from a point source on a reflective surface

As can be seen from Figure 1.7, the sound power is dissipated over 1 unit of area at distance "d" from the source, 4 units of area at distance "$2d$" from the source, and 9 units of area at distance "$3d$" from the source.

The most useful relationship for predicting the sound pressure level at a certain distance from a point source is:

$$L_p = L_w - 10 \log_{10} A$$

where L_p is the sound pressure level (dB), L_w is the sound power level of source (dB), A is the area over which sound power is

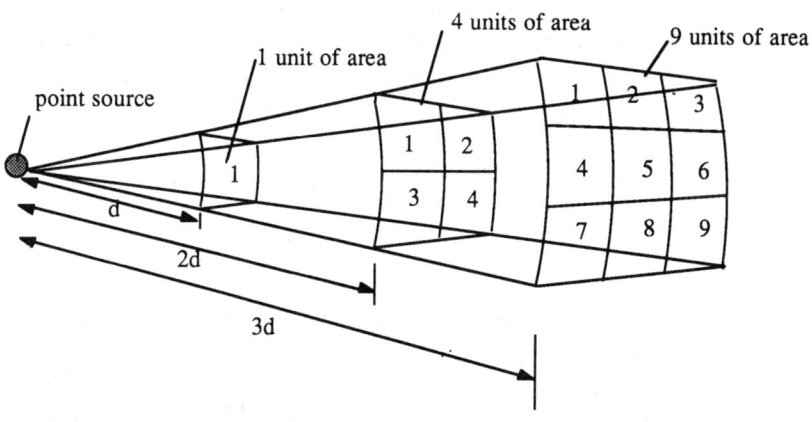

Figure 1.7 The inverse square law for a directional point source

being dissipated (m^2), = $4\pi r^2$ for spherical radiation, = $2\pi r^2$ for hemispherical radiation and r is the distance from source (m).

Example: A compressor on a construction site has a rated sound power level of 110 dB. Calculate the sound pressure level at a distance of 20m from the compressor assuming hemispherical radiation.

$$L_p = L_w - 10 \log_{10} 2\pi r^2 \text{ dB}$$

This modifies to:

$$L_p = L_w - 10 \log_{10} r^2 - 10 \log_{10} 2\pi \text{ dB}$$
$$L_p = L_w - 20 \log_{10} r - 8 \text{ dB}$$
$$= 110 - 20 \log_{10} 20 - 8 \text{ dB}$$
$$= 76 \text{ dB}$$

Line sources

For a line source, e.g. free-flowing traffic on a busy road, the sound power tends to be radiated over the surface of a cylinder, or part of a cylinder, rather than the surface of a sphere. This is illustrated on Figure 1.8.

If the distance from the source is doubled the surface area over which the source power is dissipated also doubles.

Thus the intensity of sound is proportional to the distance from the source rather than the *square* of the distance from the source, *i.e.* if the distance from the source doubles the intensity of sound (W /m^2) halves.

The corresponding reduction in sound level is given by:

$$10 \log_{10} \left[\frac{1}{2} \right] = -3 \text{ dB}$$

In other words, the decay for a line source is 3 dB per doubling of distance from the source.

Thus sound from a point source decays at twice the rate of sound from a line source. This explains why busy road traffic, heard at a distance, is fairly constant in level and very general in

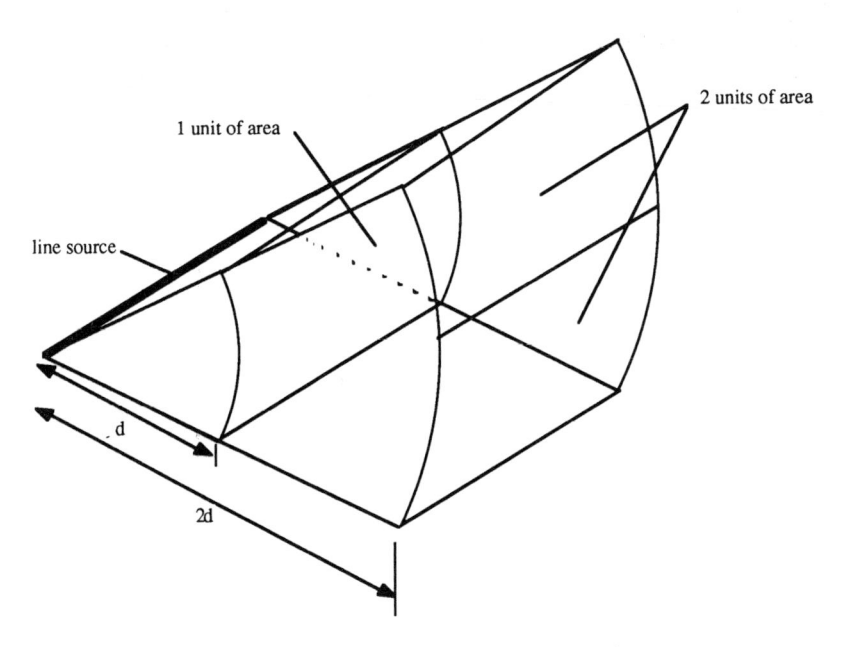

Figure 1.8 Radiation of sound from a line source

character compared to the same traffic heard from a point close to the road. Close to the road, individual vehicles (point sources) can be distinguished clearly. At a distance from the road, the noise from the individual point sources has decayed at twice the rate of noise from the overall line source of the traffic. Thus at a distance the sources have blended together to give a fairly bland, uniform noise.

Sound and distance, other factors

The relationships for sound and distance discussed above for point and line sources assume an unobstructed propagation path from the sound source to the reception point, and take no account of the additional reduction, or attenuation, of sound level resulting from the absorption of sound energy by soft surfaces such as grass, cultivated ground etc.

Obviously the effect of reflective surfaces, barriers to

propagation (noise barriers, walls, earth mounds etc.) as well as absorption, would have to be taken into account in the accurate assessment of the sound level at a given distance from a sound source.

Chapter 2
Response of the Ear, Frequency and Weighting Analysis

Introduction

The response of the ear to sound is very dependent on the frequency content of the sound arriving at the ear. Since the same sound pressure level (dB) will produce different responses at different frequencies, it is necessary to consider the frequency content of a sound if an estimation of the subjective effect on the ear is to be made. The frequency content of sounds can be considered by using *frequency analysis* or *weighting analysis*.

Frequency response of the ear

Figure 2.1 shows the threshold of audibility (hearing) for young people in the age range 18–25. As can be seen from the figure, the ear has peak response around 2.5–3 kHz and is highly responsive in the range 1–5 kHz. At low frequencies the ear has a relatively low response. It would take a sound pressure level of about 55 dB to produce audibility at 32 Hz compared to around 0 dB to produce audibility at 3 kHz. Therefore, sounds with frequencies around 3 kHz are going to be assessed subjectively as being much louder than sounds around 32 Hz even though the sounds may have the same sound pressure level. Therefore, for consideration of the subjective effect on the ear, the frequency content, as well as the sound pressure level, must be taken into account.

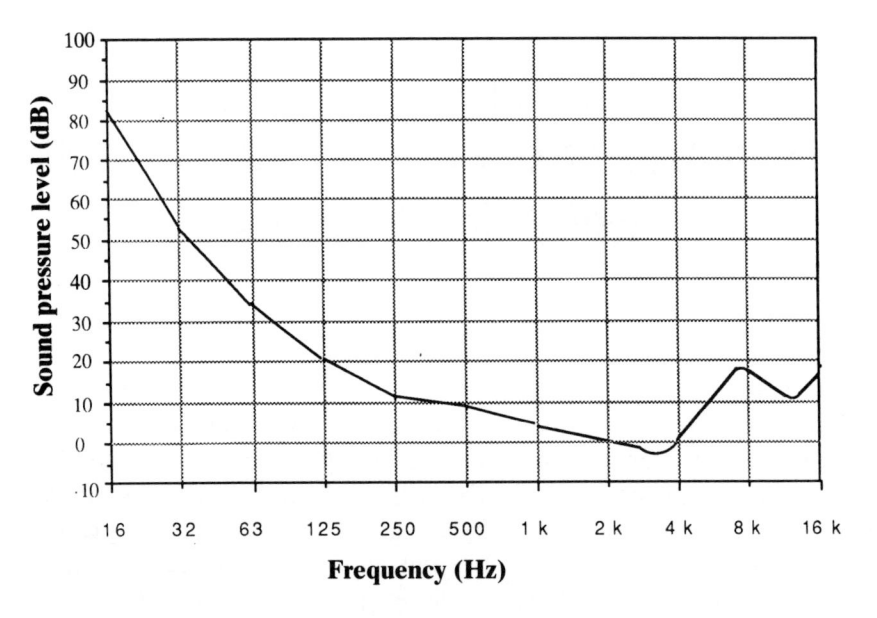

Figure 2.1 Threshold of audibility (hearing)

Loudness

Loudness is a function of the frequency content of a sound and the sound pressure level. Initial work into producing a scale for loudness used a 1 kHz pure tone as a reference. Pure tones of other frequencies were compared with that of the 1 kHz and by adjusting amplitude equal loudness contours, as shown in Figure 2.2, were produced. The unit of loudness was the *phon*. The loudness of a sound in phons is numerically equal to the sound pressure level (dB) of an equally loud 1 kHz pure tone.

From a given phon contour, the sound pressure level necessary to produce the same degree of loudness at different frequencies can be calculated. For example, to produce 40 phons of loudness the following sound pressure levels would have to exist at the stated frequencies:

Response of the Ear and Analyses

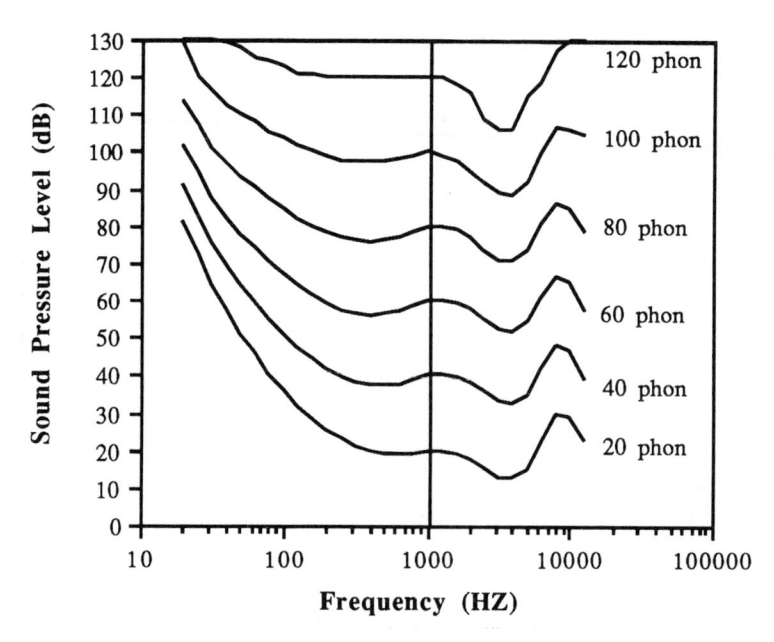

Figure 2.2 Equal loudness contours

Frequency (Hz)	Sound pressure level (dB)
30	78
50	66
100	52
200	44
500	35
1 k	40
2 k	38
3 k	30
5 k	32

From the values it can be seen that as the ear becomes more responsive around 3 kHz the sound pressure level needed to produce a given loudness in phons decreases. The phon scale had the disadvantage that it could only be used with accuracy for pure tones, but had some convenience in the relationship between phon value and the dB value at 1 kHz. From a subjective point of view, a doubling of loudness corresponded to an increase of 10 phons. In other words, a sound of loudness of 60 phons would appear to be twice as loud as a sound of 50 phons.

The phon scale of loudness is no longer used and has been superseded by the use of weighting networks which are discussed later in this chapter.

Frequency analysis

Most everyday sounds are complex in nature in that they contain many frequencies generated simultaneously at different sound levels. The process of splitting a complex sound into its component frequencies is termed *frequency analysis*. For most purposes it is not necessary to identify every component frequency. It is sufficient to group frequencies into band ranges for analysis. The two most commonly applied types of frequency analysis are *octave* and *third-octave* analysis. (In acoustics an octave represents a doubling of frequency.)

Although many filters used in modern acoustics equipment are digital, the concept of filter shapes and bandwidths is more easily understood from the consideration of analogue filters. The typical shape of an analogue filter is shown in Figure 2.3.

The bandwidth lies between two vertical lines drawn 3 dB (half-power) down from the top of the filter at each side of the filter. The following relationships exist for a filter:

$$f_c = [f_1 f_2]^{0.5}$$

$$f_2 = 2^a f_1$$

$a = 1$ for an octave filter, $a = 1/3$ for a third-octave filter.

If an octave and third-octave filter are considered, both with a centre frequency of 1000 Hz, the following limiting frequencies and bandwidths are obtained:

Filter	Lower limiting frequency	Upper limiting frequency	Bandwith
Octave	710 Hz	1420 Hz	710 Hz
Third-octave	891 Hz	1122 Hz	231 Hz

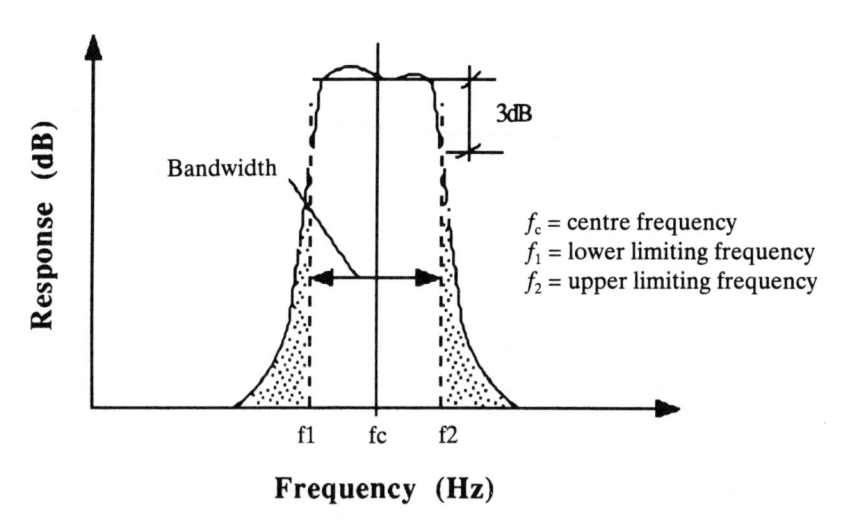

Figure 2.3 Typical analogue filter shape

f_c = centre frequency
f_1 = lower limiting frequency
f_2 = upper limiting frequency

In an octave filter centred on 1000 Hz all frequencies in the range 710 Hz to 1420 Hz are grouped into the one band for analysis. Thus octave analysis gives only a broad break-down of the frequency groups present in a complex sound. The one-third octave filter has a bandwidth of 231 Hz when centred on 1000 Hz. The use of third-octave analysis therefore gives a finer resolution of the frequency groups present in any sound. The following centre frequencies are used in octave and third octave analysis in the audible range. (Italic values are octave *and* third-octave centre frequencies.) 20 Hz, 25 Hz, *31.5 Hz*, 40 Hz, 50 Hz, *63 Hz*, 80 Hz, 100 Hz, *125 Hz*, 160 Hz, 200 Hz, *250 Hz*, 315 Hz, 400 Hz, *500 Hz*, 630 Hz, 800 Hz, *1 kHz*, 1.25 kHz, 1.6 kHz, *2 kHz*, 2.5 kHz, 3.15 kHz, *4 kHz*, 5 kHz, 6.3 kHz, *8 kHz*, 10 kHz, 12.5 kHz, *16 kHz*, 20 kHz.

Figure 2.4 shows the octave and third-octave spectrum of the noise from a machine. As can be seen from the figure the third-octave analysis affords a finer resolution of the frequency pattern of the noise. It is also important to notice that the centre frequency sound level is higher when using an octave filter. This is because the octave filter encloses more sound energy than a third-octave filter because of the greater bandwidth. For

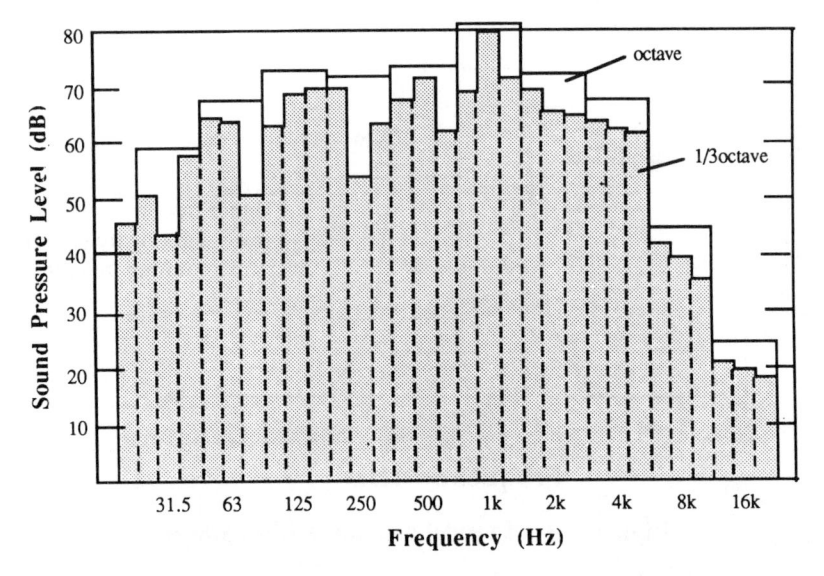

Figure 2.4 Third-octave and octave spectra of machine noise, histogram form

example, if the third-octave sound pressure levels at centre frequencies 400 Hz, 500 Hz, and 630 Hz were each 70 dB, the octave level on the centre frequency of 500 Hz would be given by;

$$L_{p(octave)} = 10 \log_{10}[10^{70/10} + 10^{70/10} + 10^{70/10}] \text{ dB}$$

$$L_{p(octave)} = 74.8 \text{dB}$$

It is therefore very important when stating the sound pressure level at a given centre frequency that the type of filter used is indicated.

The histogram form shown in Figure 2.4 is the correct method of illustrating spectra in terms of third-octave and octave analysis. Another commonly adopted method is in terms of straight lines joining the centre frequencies of the filters. When using this method it must be remembered that intermediate frequencies cannot be inferred from the gradient of the straight lines. Figure 2.5 shows the same spectra as Figure 2.4 illustrated by the straight line method.

Octave and third-octave filters are termed *constant percentage*

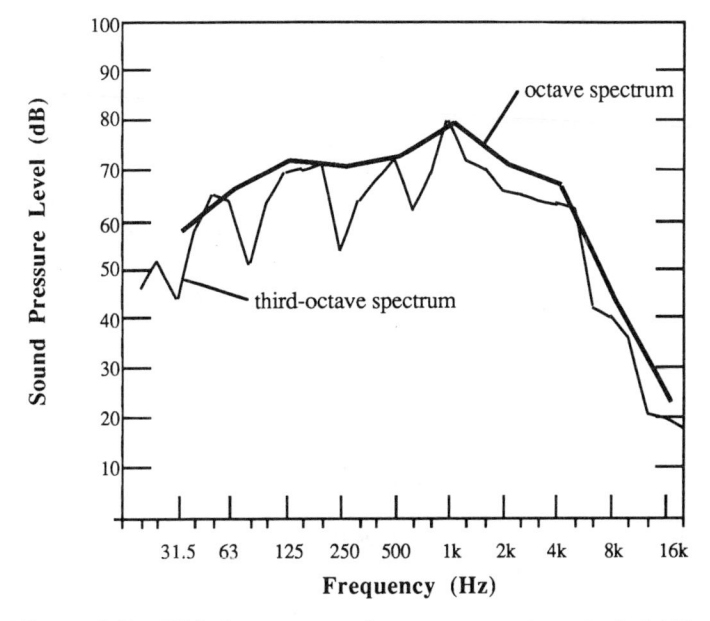

Figure 2.5 Third-octave and octave spectra, straight line representation

bandwidth filters since the bandwidth is a constant percentage of the centre frequency. For octave filters the bandwidth is 71% of the centre frequency of the band and for third-octave filters the bandwidth is 23% of the centre frequency of the band. As the centre frequency increases the bandwidth will also increase. For example, for a centre frequency of 4000 Hz (4 kHz) the bandwidth for the octave filter is 71% of 4000, *i.e.* 2840 Hz. In other words, all frequencies from 2840 Hz to 5680 Hz are included in this filter. For an octave filter centred on 63 Hz the bandwidth is 44 Hz (71% of 63 Hz), *i.e.* frequencies in the range 44 to 88 Hz are included in the 63 Hz octave filter. Constant percentage bandwidth filters therefore give a fine resolution of frequencies at low frequencies but only a broad resolution of frequencies at high frequencies.

If a more detailed analysis of sound pressure level against frequency is required it may be necessary to use narrow band analysis. Narrow band filters are often termed *constant bandwidth filters* because the bandwidth is independent of the centre frequency of the band. Commonly used bandwidths are 0.5 Hz, 2 Hz and 10 Hz. The bandwidth of 0.5 Hz, 2 Hz or 10 Hz will remain constant with increase in frequency. This type of analysis is often used in mechanical engineering to help locate noise sources associated with machine noise, bearing noise etc. Often pure tone components are related to the running speed of a machine. Such pure tones would not be revealed in octave or third-octave analysis. Figure 2.6 shows a typical narrow band analysis of machine noise.

Digital filters

Many modern frequency analysers use digital filters. Digital filters consist of a number of multipliers and adders and can perform filtering actions on digital signals. The centre frequency and bandwidth of a digital filter are governed by the sampling frequency, F_s, in samples per second. Altering the sampling frequency gives a new centre frequency and bandwidth. A digital filter can therefore be made to act as a number of filters simply by altering the sampling frequency.

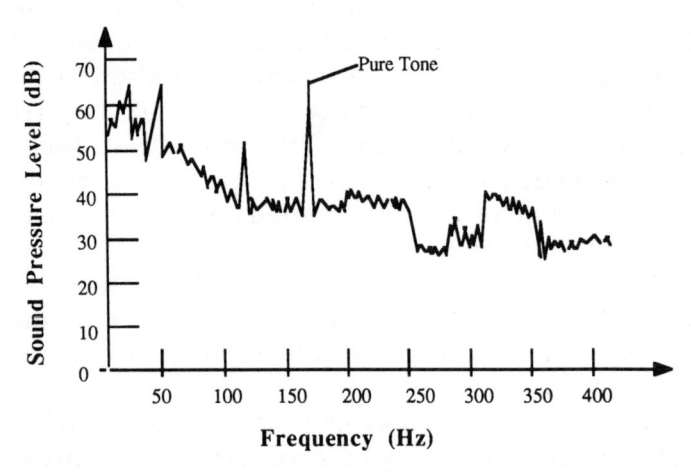

Figure 2.6 Narrow band analysis of machine noise

Weighting networks

Frequency analysis is essential from an engineering point of view to enable the appropriate noise control measures to be carried out for plant and machines etc. However, as far as the ear is concerned, it is useful to have a method of assessing the frequency components of a sound and producing a single figure level of the sound relative to the response of the ear. For this purpose weighting networks have been devised and incorporated into sound level meters.

Initially three weighting networks A, B, and C were used. The argument for the use of the three networks was that the response of the ear becomes more linear with frequency the higher the level of the sound. Initially A-weighting was used for loudness levels below 55 phons, B-weighting for sounds between 55 and 85 phons of loudness, and C-weighting for sounds with loudness levels higher than 85 phons. The D-weighting was introduced later for jet aircraft noise measurement for which the sensitivity of the ear around 4 kHz is important. Whine from jet engine compressors is around this frequency. The four weighting networks are illustrated in Figure 2.7.

It is now recognised that the A-weighting network is applicable to higher loudness levels than was previously thought and hence the A-weighting network has become used, universally, for most types of industrial and environmental noise, including aircraft. This weighting network is the approximate electronic inverse of the 40 phon loudness contour (Figure 2.2). The other three networks now find little use in noise analysis. The third-octave and octave band adjustments in terms of the A-weighting network are shown in Tables 2.1 and 2.2 respectively.

When a sound pressure level is measured using the A-weighting network the sound level meter analyses the sound in terms of the A-weighting curve and then gives a single figure value in dB(A) relative to the weighted energy.

The following example illustrates the principle of obtaining an A-weighted sound pressure level from an octave frequency analysis of machine noise. The octave band centre frequencies

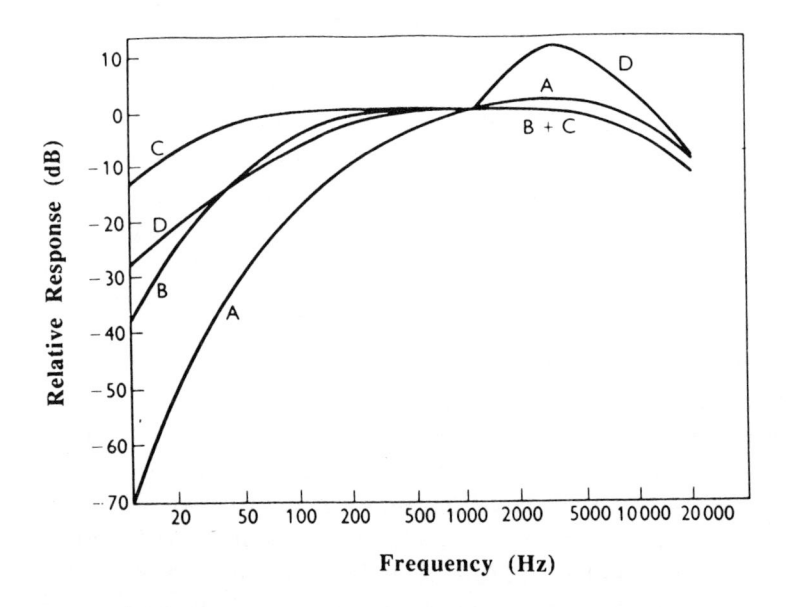

Figure 2.7 Weighting networks A, B, C, and D

and measured sound pressure levels are given in columns 1 and 2 of Table 2.3. Column 3 gives the A-weighting network adjustment or correction appropriate to each frequency. By making the corrections to the measured sound pressure levels, the A-weighted sound pressure level for each frequency is obtained (column 4). The overall A-weighted sound pressure level is then obtained by adding together, in decibel terms, all of the column 4 values.

The overall level in dB(A) of the machine noise is calculated from the equation for the addition of decibels given in Chapter 1. The overall A-weighted sound pressure level is therefore (addition of column 4 values);

$$L_p(A) = 10 \log_{10}[10^{50/10} + 10^{48/10} + ... + 10^{45/10} + 10^{26/10}]$$
$$= 86.3 \text{ dB(A)}$$

This machine noise example is illustrated graphically in Figure 2.8. The measured and A-weighted spectra are illustrated. The

Table 2.1 A-weighting adjustments, third-octave bands

Third-octave band centre frequency (Hz)	A-weighting adjustment (dB)	Third-octave centre frequency (Hz)	A-weighting adjustment (dB)
10	−70.4	500	−3.2
12.5	−63.4	630	−1.9
16	−56.7	800	−0.8
20	−50.5	1k	0
25	−44.7	1.25k	+0.6
31.5	−39.4	1.6k	+1.0
40	−34.6	2k	+1.2
50	−30.2	2.5k	+1.3
63	−26.2	3.1k	+1.2
80	−22.5	4k	+1.0
100	−19.1	5k	+0.5
125	−16.1	6.3k	−0.1
160	−13.4	8k	−1.1
200	−10.9	10k	−2.5
250	−8.6	12.5k	−4.3
315	−6.6	16k	−6.6
400	−4.8	20k	−9.3

Table 2.2 A-weighting adjustments, octave bands

Octave band centre frequency (Hz)	63	125	250	500	1k	2k	4k	8k
A-weighting adjustment (dB)	−26	−16	−9	−3	0	+1	+1	−1

overall level of 86.3 dB(A) is the addition of the energy under the A-weighted spectrum (shaded area). If the machine noise was measured on a sound level meter with the A-weighting network selected, the conversion process would be carried out automatically and the meter would indicate a single reading of 86.3 dB(A).

In subective terms, it is generally accepted that an increase of

Table 2.3 Conversion of octave levels to A-weighted levels

Octave band centre frequency (Hz) (1)	Measured sound pressure level (dB) (2)	A-weighting adjustment (dB) (3)	A-weighted pressure level (dB(A)) (4)
63	76	−26	50
125	64	−16	48
250	82	−9	73
500	78	−3	75
1 k	84	0	84
2 k	80	+1	81
4 k	44	+1	45
8 k	27	−1	26

10 dB(A) represents a doubling of loudness, *i.e.* a sound of 70 dB(A) would appear to be twice as loud as a sound of 60 dB(A).

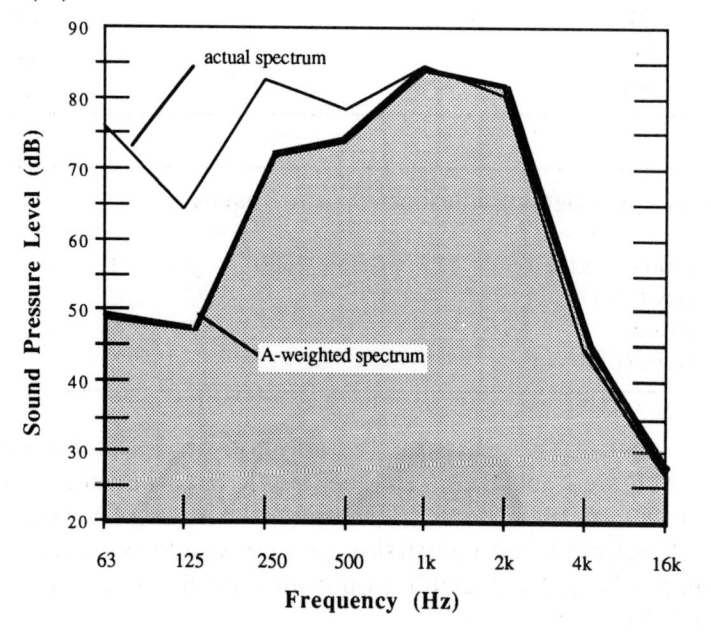

Figure 2.8 Machine noise example

Chapter 3
The Ear, Threshold Shifts, Assessment & Control of Hearing Risk

Introduction

The threshold of hearing for the ear was discussed in Chapter 2 and the typical hearing curve illustrated in Figure 2.1.
This chapter examines the basic hearing mechanisms of the ear, threshold shifts (hearing losses) which occur due to age and noise exposure, and audiometry, *i.e.* hearing assessment.

The Ear

The ear acts as a transducer converting sound energy into electrical energy which is sent to the receptive centres of the brain via electrical impulses.
Figure 3.1 shows a simplified diagram of the main hearing components of the human ear. Some of the non-hearing parts of the ear, *e.g.* semi circular canals (balance) have been omitted for clarity.
The ear comprises three main regions (i) the outer ear (air-filled), (ii) the middle ear (air-filled), and (iii) the inner ear (fluid-filled). Sound is directed into the ear via the auditory canal and strikes the ear drum (tympanic membrane) which is set into vibration. The vibration is transferred mechanically across the middle ear by three small bones, known collectively as the ossicles, which are suspended in the middle ear by ligaments. The small bones are individually termed the malleus (hammer), the

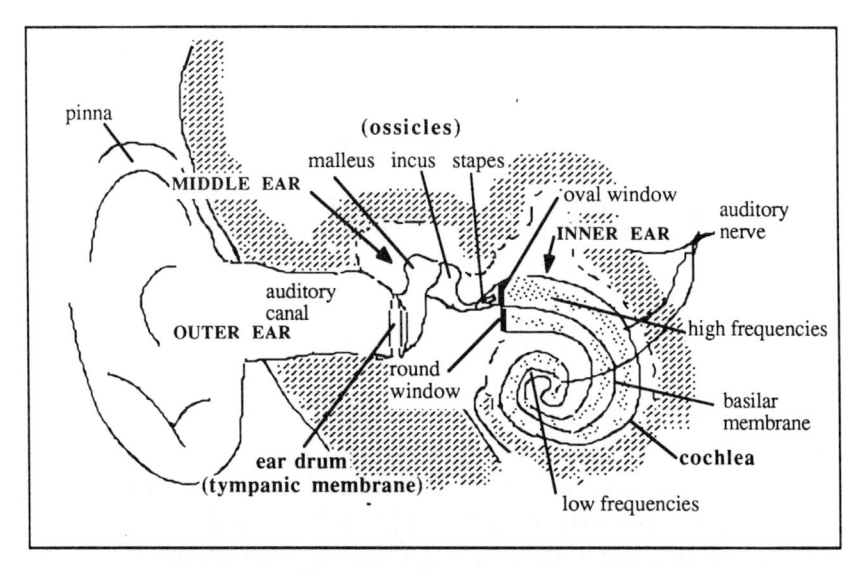

Figure 3.1 Hearing components of the ear

incus (anvil), and the stapes (stirrup). The ossicles act as a system of levers transferring the sound pressure acting on the ear drum to the oval window at the footplate of the stapes.

The ear drum has a pressure collecting area of about 70 mm² in comparison to 3.2 mm² of area of the oval window. This reduction in area gives a 22-fold increase in sound pressure from the ear drum to the oval window. The amplified pressure acting on the oval window is sufficient to cause the fluid in the cochlea (a snail-shaped organ) to move backwards and forwards. The round window bulges out to accommodate movement of the fluid in the cochlea.

Hair cells on the basilar membrane are set into motion by the fluid movement and detect the frequency content of the sound acting on the ear. Hair cells close to the oval window respond to high frequencies while hair cells further into the cochlea respond to low frequencies. Movement of the basilar membrane detects loudness. The movement of the hair cells and the basilar membrane produce electrical impulses which are transferred to the receptive centres of the brain via the auditory nerve.

Deafness

It is not the purpose of this book to elaborate on the hearing processes or the physiology of the ear and the perceptive mechanisms of the brain. However, it is felt that some mention of the subject of deafness should be made. The term deafness has no specific definition but is used universally to denote a variety of hearing defects. Although deafness is a large and complex area of study it is possible to classify deafness into three main types. The types of deafness are (i) conductive deafness, (ii) sensory neural deafness, and (iii) central deafness.

Conductive deafness

This type of deafness results from defects in the pathway from the exterior to the footplate of the stapes. Examples are perforated ear drum, otosclerosis (bone growth which makes stapes immobile), stiffening of the joints in the ossicles, and blocking of the auditory canal by wax. Usually this type of deafness can be eliminated by medical treatment or surgery.

Sensory neural deafness

This type of deafness is the result of defects in the cochlea or auditory nerve, *e.g.* degeneration of hair cells near the base of the cochlea resulting in loss of sensitivity to high frequency sounds.

Central deafness

This type of deafness refers to hearing defects which cannot be explained by abnormality of the cochlea or auditory nerve. Central deafness is due to defects in the hearing pathways and perceptive mechanisms of the brain.

Threshold shifts

The threshold of hearing for young people in the age range of 18 to 25 was shown in Figure 2.1. Most adults will have some deviation from the curve relative to age and noise exposure. At some frequencies it will require a higher sound pressure level to produce a sensation of hearing than indicated in Figure 2.1. The additional sound pressure level required to produce a sensation of hearing at a given frequency is termed a *threshold shift* (TS). For example, Figure 2.1 indicates that a sound level of around 0 dB should produce a sensation of hearing at 4 kHz. If it actually requires a sound pressure level of 25 dB to produce a sensation of hearing at 4 kHz for a given individual then that individual has a threshold shift of 25 dB at 4 kHz.

Threshold shifts can be classified as (i) temporary threshold shift (TTS), resulting from exposure to high level sound for a comparatively short period, and (ii) permanent threshold shift (PTS), due to prolonged noise exposure or age. Permanent threshold shifts which are due to years of exposure to high level industrial noise are termed *noise induced permanent threshold shifts* (NIPTS).

TTS, Exposure and Recovery Time

When a person with normal hearing is exposed to low level sound, say less than 70 dB, any threshold shift experienced is at the same frequency as the sound to which the person is exposed. If, however, a person is exposed to high level noise for some time the maximum threshold shift occurs at a frequency about half or more of an octave *above* the exposure frequency or frequency band. The reasons for this are not known precisely but a possible factor is an aural reflex which tends to protect the ear against high sound pressure levels at the lower frequencies in combination with the fact that the ear is most sensitive around the 1 kHz to 5 kHz region. TTS is therefore most common around the 4 kHz region even though the exposure is to noise of much lower frequency. The relationship between TTS, exposure time, and sound pressure level of the stimulus is shown in Figure 3.2. This shows the TTS at 4 kHz two minutes after exposure to

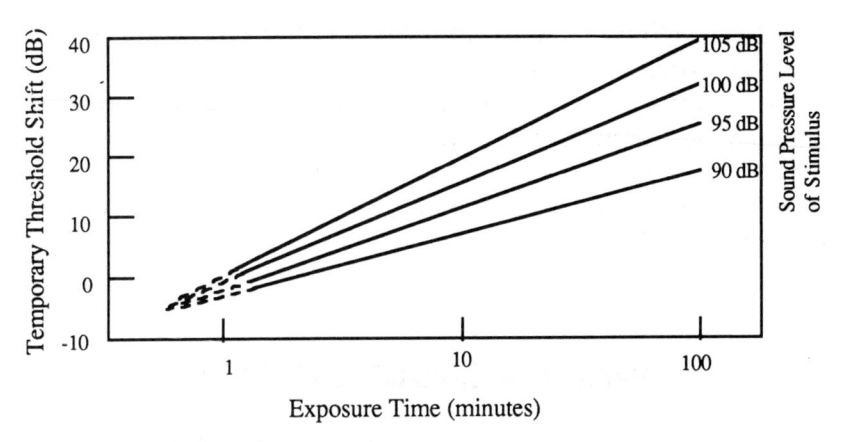

Figure 3.2 TTS, exposure time and sound pressure level of the stimulus

noise in the 1200 Hz to 2400 Hz octave band (old octave frequencies)[1].

As can be seen from Figure 3.2, the amount of TTS is a function of the exposure time and the sound pressure level of the stimulus. The TTS increases rapidly with sound pressure level of the stimulus for any given exposure time.

The relationship between TTS, recovery time, and sound pressure level of the stimulus is shown in Figure 3.3.

This shows the recovery time from TTS at 4 kHz at various intervals after the end of exposure to a band of steady noise in

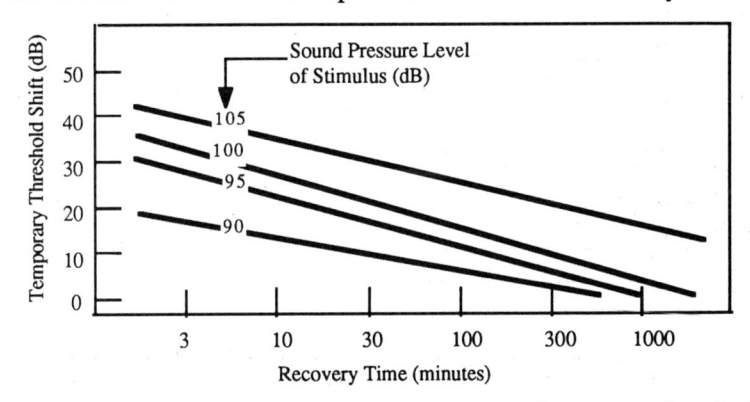

Figure 3.3 TTS, recovery time, and sound pressure level of stimulus

the 1200 - 2400 Hz band at various sound pressure levels and for the same exposure duration [2].

The important fact that Figure 3.3 illustrates is that recovery time increases greatly with increase in TTS. For TTS around 20 dB recovery time is comparatively short but for TTS in excess of 40 dB the recovery process is delayed greatly, *i.e.* in excess of 1000 minutes (16.7 hours).

Permanent threshold shift (PTS)

For a worker exposed to high level occupational noise, with a high TTS, the condition often occurs where the TTS has not completely recovered before further exposure to noise the next working day. In such conditions a PTS may develop as hair cells in the cochlea degenerate. PTS generally starts around the frequency of 4 kHz (remember that for high level noise exposure the threshold shift occurs at frequencies above the exposure frequency). With continued noise exposure, the 4 kHz drop in sensitivity increases and spreads to other frequencies. This is shown in Figure 3.4.

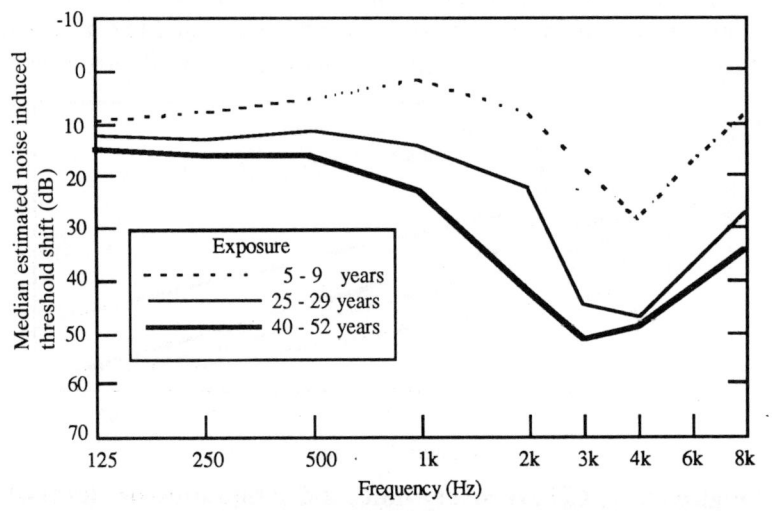

Figure 3.4 PTS with increasing years of exposure (Ref 3.3)

Eventually loss of hearing in the speech range of frequencies may occur. This will result initially in signs of dullness of hearing and often *tinnitus* (ringing in the ears) after exposure to high level noise at work.

Figure 3.5 shows the results of some research carried out into occupational hearing loss [3]. The research was carried out using workers in the textile industry. The control group had not been exposed to noise. Spinners and weavers had spent, on average, ten years in their respective occupations. The loss in sensitivity at 4 kHz for the weavers (noisy industry) is characteristic of noise induced permanent threshold shift (NIPTS).

Although there is a definite correlation between hearing loss and noise exposure it must be borne in mind that individuals have widely varying degrees of susceptibility to hearing loss. Some people who have spent years working in noisy industry exhibit little hearing loss other than that which would be expected due to age, whilst other people employed in the same

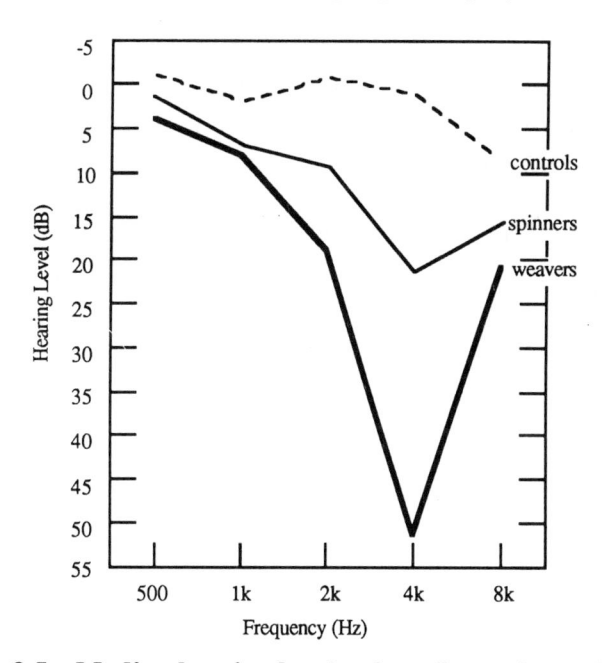

Figure 3.5 Median hearing levels of textile workers after 10 years noise exposure (Ref 3.3)

industry, with the same noise exposure, exhibit considerable noise-induced hearing loss.

Presbycusis (presbyacusis)

Presbycusis is hearing loss due to increasing age. Hearing loss due to age starts in the higher frequencies and gradually moves to the lower freqencies. Typical presbycusis hearing loss curves are illustrated in Figure 3.6.

The curves are a generalization with many individuals actually exhibiting little hearing loss with age. Any study into noise induced hearing loss must take typical presbycusis losses into account.

Audiometry

Audiometry is the measurement of a person's hearing sensitivity and threshold of hearing at selected frequencies. The instrument used for this purpose is termed an audiometer and the record of threshold of hearing against frequency is called an audiogram. The audiometer presents a variable level pure tone sound in the earphone and measures, at each frequency, the minimum sound

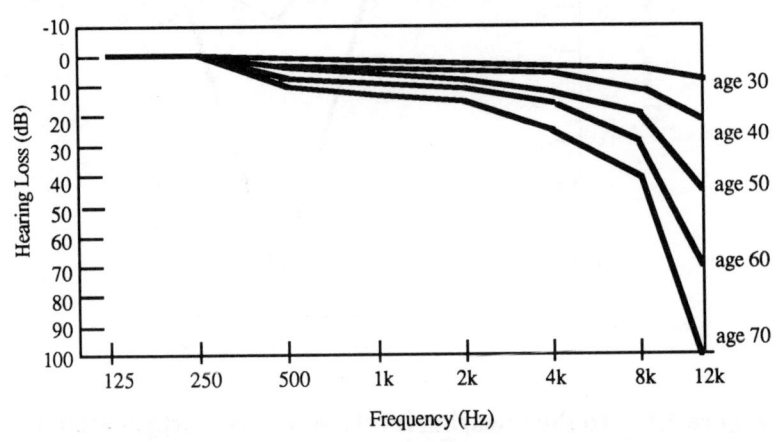

Figure 3.6 Typical presbycusis hearing loss

pressure level that the person can just detect. This level is then compared to the average threshold for young persons with no hearing defects (Figure 2.1). The dB difference between the test subject's threshold and the ideal threshold is reported as the hearing level, or hearing loss, at each frequency and for each ear. Typical audiograms are illustrated in Figure 3.7(a) and 3.7(b).

There are two main types of audiometer, *i.e.* manual and automatic. Automatic (Bekesy) audiometers are faster for group

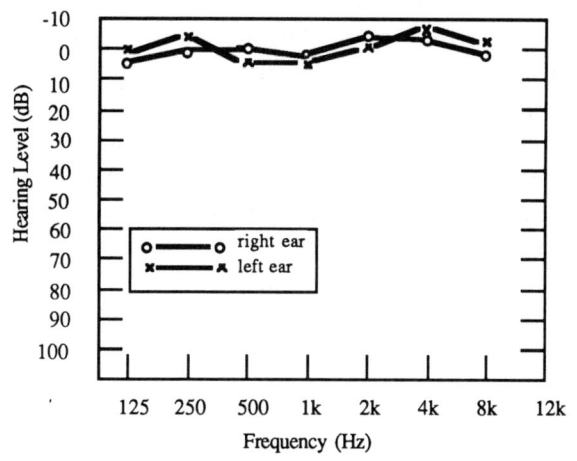

Figure 3.7(a) Audiogram showing hearing within normal limits for a young person

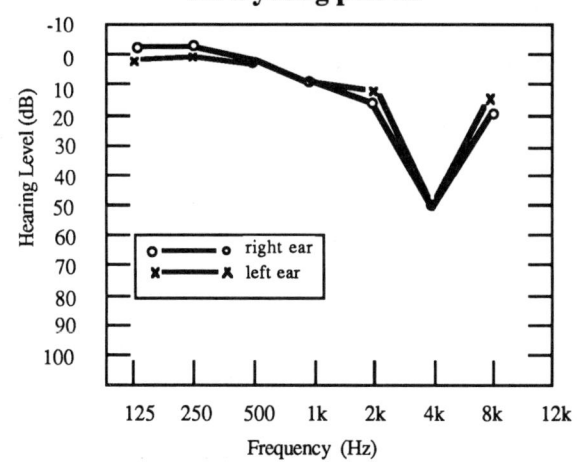

Figure 3.7(b) Audiogram showing hearing loss at 4 kHz

testing and are preferable for claims purposes since the test subject, himself or herself, controls the test using push-button controls. This type of audiometer also allows automated record keeping and computer print-out of audiograms. For large scale testing, multiple stations can be controlled by one operator and one computer. For reliability of results audiometric tests must be carried out in a very quiet environment to ensure that ambient noise does not adversely influence the test results. For best results audiometric tests should be carried out in a specially designed audiometric booth. Mobile audiometric units in the form of vans and trailers are convenient for on-site industrial audiometric screening.

For industrial audiometry to be of an acceptable standard the test has to be supervised by a suitably trained operator. The test must be precise enough to detect small changes in the hearing of a worker over a period of time and be reliable enough for the results to be acceptable for medical and legal purposes. R. D. Wright [4] lists the following requirements for an acceptable standard of basic industrial audiometry.

1. The measurement should be for pure tone hearing thresholds for each ear.
2. The precision of the test should be valid within 5 dB.
3. The test-retest reliability should be within 10 dB.
4. Tests should be across the frequency range 250 Hz to 8 kHz at no more than one octave intervals.
5. The audiometer should meet the air-conduction testing requirements of a Type 3 audiometer in accordance with IEC 645, Part 1.
6. The audiometric tests should be carried out in an adequate test room or booth in accordance with ISO 8253, Part 1.
7. A written record of the test and audiogram should be produced.
8. The tests should meet all relevant standards including IEC standards on equipment, ISO standards on procedures, the requirements of the International Organization of Legal Metrology (OIML), and any additional national or industrial requirements.

9. While meeting all of the above conditions the time per test should be a minimum.
10. The tests should make the most efficient use of the time of the person administering the test.

Assessing and controlling noise induced hearing loss

Much work has been carried out to assess the risk of occupational hearing loss. Burns and Robinson [5] identified the fact that a person's age corrected hearing level was related to the sound energy of exposure. This sound energy was a function of the level of noise and the duration of exposure. The sound energy could be associated with a high level of noise for a short period of time, or a lower level of noise for a longer period. The exposure sound energy was termed by Robinson as the *Noise immission level* (NIL). This was expressed as;

$$E_A = L_A + 10 \log_{10} \frac{t}{t_0}$$

where E_A is the A-weighted noise immission level, L_A is the daily occupational noise exposure level, t is the duration of exposure in years and $t_o = 1$ year.

When the noise immission level has been calculated the hearing risk for otologically normal people can be estimated using tables in BS 5330:1976 [6]. More recent work by Robinson *et al* has been carried out for and published by the Health and Safety Executive (HSE) into the assessment of hearing risk for otologically normal persons due to long-term noise exposure. A significant hearing loss has been defined as a 30 dB hearing loss averaged over the three frequencies of 1 kHz, 2 kHz, and 3 kHz. The percentage of the population suffering a hearing impairment for increasing long term noise exposure is shown in Figure 3.8. The data in Figure 3.8 and the tables published by the HSE [7] form a basis from which employee noise exposure can

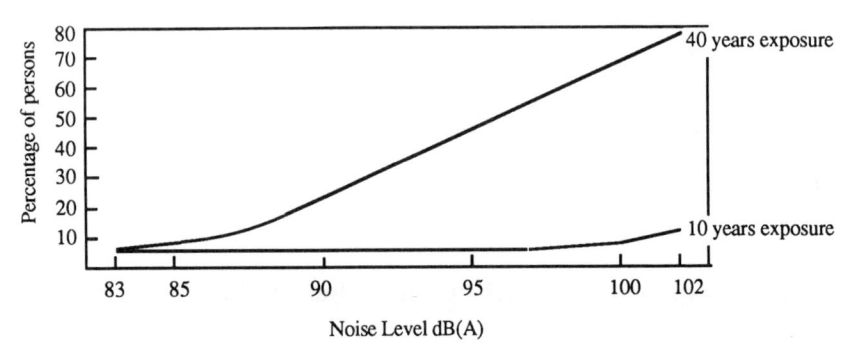

Figure 3.8 Percentage of persons attaining or exceeding a mean hearing loss of 30 dB

be assessed and the appropriate noise control and hearing protection measures taken.

The earlier work of Burns and Robinson was used to develop the 1972 Code of Practice [8] which recommended a maximum acceptable exposure noise level of 90 dB(A), for the unprotected ear, where the noise was reasonably steady and continuous for 8 hours. For fluctuating sound levels and for periods of exposure other than 8 hours an *equivalent continuous sound pressure level*, normalized to 8 hours on an energy basis, was to be calculated. This A-weighted, 8 hour, equivalent continuous sound level, denoted by $L_{Aeq,\ 8\ hour}$ (see Chapter 4 for a more complete definition), was not to exceed 90 dB(A) for the unprotected ear. If the exposure sound level doubled then the permissible exposure time would be halved, *i.e.* 93 dB(A) for 4 hours is equivalent to a sound level of 90 dB(A) for 8 hours.

The Noise at Work Regulations 1989 [9], which came into force on 1 January 1990, were introduced in response to the European Communities Council Directive [10] on the protection of workers from risks relating to exposure to noise at work. The Regulations use the parameter of $L_{Aeq,\ 8\ hour}$ for assessing daily personal noise exposure. In the Regulations the daily personal noise exposure of an employee is symbolized as L_{EPd}. For workers exposed to fluctuating sound pressure levels during the working day, L_{EPd} can be calculated from:

$$L_{\text{EPd}} = 10 \log_{10} \frac{1}{T_0} \sum_{i=1}^{n} t_i \, 10^{L_i/10} \text{ dB(A)}$$

where : T_o = 8 hours, t_i is the the exposure time in hours and L_i is the exposure sound pressure level in dB(A).

Example: during an 8-hour working day a worker is exposed to the following steady sound pressure levels:

2 hours at 76 dB(A)
1 hour at 80 dB(A)
3 hours at 88 dB(A)
2 hours at 83 dB(A)

The worker's L_{EPd} would be calculated as follows:

$$L_{\text{EPd}} = 10 \log_{10} \frac{1}{8} [2 \times 10^{7.6} + 1 \times 10^{8.0} + 3 \times 10^{8.8} + 2 \times 10^{8.3}] \text{ dB(A)}$$

$$= 84.9 \text{ dB(A)}$$

This type of calculation can quite easily be undertaken with modern electronic calculators which have a memory facility and a "10^x" button.

For workers exposed to rapidly varying sound pressure levels over short periods of time the above type of calculation becomes impossible and to assess the L_{EPd} such workers may have to be equipped with personal logging noise dosemeters for a trial period to assess typical daily noise exposure.

The Noise at Work Regulations 1989 specify three action levels with respect to noise exposure.

The *first action level* is equivalent to a daily personal noise exposure (L_{EPd}) of 85 dB(A).

The *second action level* is equivalent to a daily personal noise exposure (L_{EPd}) of 90 dB(A).

The *peak action level* is equivalent to a peak sound pressure of 200 N/m² (pascals), *i.e.* 140 dB re 2×10^{-5} N/m². (20 µPa).

For daily personal noise exposure values between the first and second action levels, *i.e* L_{EPd} equal to or greater than 85 dB(A) but less than 90 dB(A), the employer shall ensure, as far as is practicable, that the employee is provided, *at his request*, with suitable and efficient ear protectors.

For employees exposed to the second action level or above, or to the peak action level or above, *i.e.* L_{EPd} equal to or greater than 90 dB(A) or peak sound pressure equal to or greater than 200 pa, the employer shall ensure, so far as is practicable, that employees are provided with suitable personal ear protectors which, when worn properly, can reasonably be expected to keep the risk of damage to an employee's hearing to below that arising from exposure to the second action level or, as the case may be, to the peak action level.

The peak action level is provided to protect the hearing of workers exposed to impulsive noises such as loud impact or explosive noises which often cause the peak action level to be exceeded even though the L_{EPd} is below the second action level.

The Noise at Work Regulations 1989 are discussed further in Chapter 7. The requirements of the Regulations can be summarized here as follows:

Requirements of employers :

(1) To make, and up-date when required, assessments of noise exposure of employees. Such assessments have to be carried out by a competent person and an adequate record of the assessment must be kept.
(2) To reduce the exposure of employees to noise. Reasonable steps (other than the provision of hearing protectors) have to be taken to reduce noise exposure, *e.g.* engineering solutions to reduction of machine noise, when any employee is likely to be exposed to the second action level or above, or to the peak action level or above.
(3) To provide personal ear protectors for their employees as discussed above. Employers also need to provide information about the protectors and how to obtain them at the first action level and ensure that they are used at the second and peak action levels.
(4) To demarcate and identify ear protection zones. Zones where ear protectors must be worn have to identified by signs. In

such areas, *i.e.* where employees are likely to be exposed to the second action level or above or the peak action level or above, ear protectors must be worn and no employee should be allowed to enter the zone unless wearing personal ear protectors.

(5) To maintain and use properly equipment provided under the Regulations. Regular checks need to be made to find out if noise control equipment, *e.g.* silencers and enclosures, is in good condition and in proper use. Proper provision must be made for the clean storage of re-usable protectors and cleaning materials for protectors should be kept available to users.

(6) To provide information, instruction and training for employees relative to noise at work. Information should be made available on the likely noise exposure and hearing risk, how to report defects in noise control equipment and ear protectors, and where and how ear protectors can be obtained. Instruction and training on the use of protectors, the identification of hearing defects, the identification of noisy machinery and ear protection zones should be given.

Requirements of employees :

(1) To co-operate with noise exposure assessments.
(2) To use noise control equipment such as silencers and enclosures in accordance with the employer's instructions.
(3) To wear personal ear protectors at or above the second or peak action levels (it is in an employee's own interest, though not a statutory duty, to use ear protectors between the first and second action levels).
(4) To report to the employer any defect found in ear protectors or other protective equipment or difficulty in using them.

Requirements of makers, designers and suppliers of machines :

To provide information on the noise likely to be generated by a machine if the machine is likely to cause pesons at work to receive an L_{EPd} at or above 85 dB(A), or at or above a peak pressure of 200 Pa(140 dB re 20 µPa).

The fact that the Noise at Work Regulations 1989 identify a first action level at an L_{EPd} of 85 dB(A) does not necessarily imply that no risk to hearing exists for exposures below this level. A small residual risk exists for exposures below this level and so it must be a long-term aim of the EC, national governments, employers and machine manufacturers to reduce noise exposure as far as is practically and economically possible.

Future developments

Future developments in the control of noise in the workplace lie in the Commission of European Communities' draft proposal for a Directive on Physical Agents [11]. The general approach on which the physical agents proposal is based defines three zones of risk:

(1) A black zone corresponding to an exposure involving unacceptable risks.
(2) A white zone where the residual health risk does not deserve specific measures and which is a target for long-term efforts.
(3) A grey zone where appropriate measures must be gradually introduced to reduce exposure.

The main proposals of the Commission's draft are:

(a) The introduction of five action levels based on personal daily noise exposure which will be renamed $L_{EX,8h}$. The action levels are :

- 75 dB(A) ; the upper limit of the white zone.
- 80 dB(A) ; the level for informing workers on the existing risk, making protectors available, opening the right to health surveillance.
- 85 dB(A) (and 112 Pa) ; the level for the provision of

information on noise produced by work equipment and the application of a programme of engineering and administrative control.

- 90 dB(A) (and 200 Pa) ; the lower limit of the black zone and the level for the identification of areas requiring the mandatory wearing of ear protectors.
- 105 dB(A) (and 600 Pa) ; the significant increase in hearing risk justifies that such cases are reported and that equipment producing such levels is marked so that workers in the vicinity are aware of the increased hazard.

(b) The introduction of special rules which would apply to workers at particular risk, *i.e.*

- Workers with a disease or deformity of the ear or those who use ototoxic substances.
- Pregnant women. The draft proposal indicates that the exposure of pregnant women to noise above 85 dB(A) may affect the hearing of the foetus and that the risk increases for exposure at frequencies of 500 Hz and below.

Ultimately the reduction of workplace noise levels to the white zone of the CEC Directive can only be achieved by the reduction of noise at source for machines, equipment, power tools and plant. Currently much work is being undertaken to quantify and limit noise emission levels of machinery. EC Directives 89/392 [12] and 91/368 [13] on machinery safety specify the following requirements with respect to noise emission:

(i) Noise reduction is an integral part of machinery safety.
(ii) Machinery must be so designed and constructed that risks resulting from the emission of airborne noise are reduced to the lowest level taking account of technical progress and the availability of means of reducing noise, in particular at source.
(iii) Specified quantitative information on airborne noise emitted by machinery under defined operating conditions must be made available by manufacturers (noise declaration).

References

1. Ward WD, Glorig A, and Sklar DL, "Dependence of temporary threshold shift at 4 kc on intensity and time", *Journal of the Acoustical Society of America*, 1958, 30, 944.
2. Ward WD, Glorig A, and Sklar DL, "Relationship between recovery from temporary threshold shift and duration of exposure", *Journal of the Acoustical Society of America*, (1959), 31, 600.
3. Burns W. *Noise and Man*, (John Murray, 1973).
4. Wright RD, "Screening for noise related hearing loss", *Proceedings of the Institute of Acoustics*, Euronoise, (1992), Book 1, 207.
5. Burns W, and Robinson DW, *Hearing and Noise in Industry*, (HMSO, 1970).
6. BS 5330 : 1976, *Method of Test for Estimating the Risk of Hearing Handicap due to Noise Exposure*.
7. Robinson DW, "Tables for the estimation of hearing impairment due to noise for otologically normal persons and for a typically unscreened population as a function of age and duration of exposure", *HSE Contract Research Reports No. 2, and No. 29*, (1991).
8. *Code of Practice for Reducing the Exposure of Employed Persons to Noise*, (DoE. 1972).
9. *The Noise at Work Regulations 1989*, SI 1989/1790.
10. Council Directive on the Protection of Workers from the Risks Related to Exposure to Noise at Work, 86 / 188 / EEC.
11. CEC Working Document, 1991, 05 / 4578EN91L10 sw.
12. Council Directive on the Approximation of the Laws of the Member States Relating to Machinery, 89 / 392 / EEC.
13. Council Directive amending Directive 89 / 392, EEC, 91 / 368 / EEC.

Chapter 4
Statistical and Energy-based Noise Parameters

Introduction

Statistical and energy-based noise parameters are used to produce a single figure assessment of some noise signal which varies with respect to time, *e.g.* road traffic noise, construction site noise, industrial noise. For environmental impact purposes the parameter is usually based on the energy content of the noise being analysed. To be useful, there must be a good correlation between the parameter selected and the subjective response to the noise from the point of view of annoyance and noise intrusion.

For most types of environmental noise analysis statistical parameters are measured, or calculated, for positions close to the facade of buildings affected by the noise. Although it may be argued that levels of noise within buildings are more relevant from an annoyance point of view, the calculation of internal noise levels originating from an external noise source would require detailed knowledge of the sound insulation characteristics of the outer fabric of each building affected by the noise. Such calculations would not be practical for the large number of buildings affected by a new road, a new railway line, a new airport, or by a new factory or industrial estate.

Statistical level (percentile parameters) (L_{AN})

A convenient way to describe environmental noise, *e.g.* road traffic noise, is in terms of percentile points on a cumulative distribution of the noise. The points of interest in the distribution are designated by the levels which are exceeded for a given percentage of the time and are written as subscripts to the sound level designator "L_A". L_A is the A-weighted sound pressure level in dB(A). The percentile points normally of interest are as follows :

L_{A10}: this is the level exceeded for not more than 10% of the time. This parameter is used as a "not to exceed" criterion for noise.

L_{A90}: this is the level exceeded for not more than 90% of the time. This parameter is often used as a descriptor of "background noise" for environmental impact studies.

L_{A50} : this parameter is the median noise level.

The parameters are shown for a normal distribution of noise in Figure 4.1. For a normal distribution the parameters L_{A10} and L_{A90} are situated equally on either side of the median level at a distance of 1.28 standard deviations from the median.

For a normal distribution the difference in noise level between L_{A10} and L_{A90} is 2.56 standard deviations, *i.e.* $(L_{A10} - L_{A90}) = 2.56$ s.

Figure 4.2 shows the record of a 1 hour sample of road traffic noise with the parameters L_{A10} and L_{A90} indicated.

The L_{A10} value of 68 dB(A) means that the noise level was above 68 dB(A) for 6 minutes in the hour (*i.e.* 10% of 1 hour),

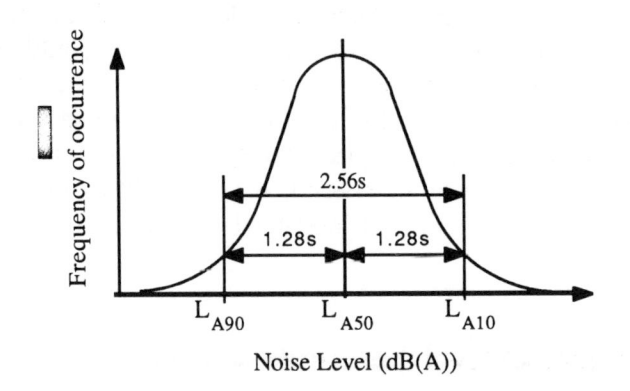

Figure 4.1 Percentile parameters for normal distribution of noise

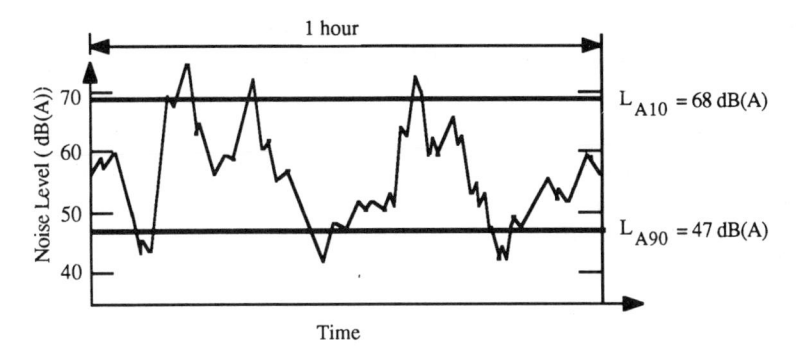

Statistical and Energy-based Noise Parameters

Figure 4.2 1 hour sample of road traffic noise

and equal to or less than 68 dB(A) for the remaining 54 minutes. The background noise level, L_{A90}, of 47 dB(A) was exceeded for 54 minutes in the hour (*i.e.* for 90% of 1 hour).

It has been known since the early 1970s [1] that a good correlation exists between public dissatisfaction with excessive road traffic noise, from freely flowing traffic, and the hourly L_{A10} values averaged arithmetically over the 18-hour period from 0600 to 2400 hours. The parameter produced is termed the *eighteen hour L_{A10} value* and is measured or calculated for a position 1 m in front of a relevant building façade.

$L_{A10,18\,hour}$ or $L_{A10,18\,h}$ = the arithmetic average of the hourly L_{A10} values in the period 0600 to 2400 hours.

The $L_{A10,18\,h}$ value is the parameter which is generally used in the prediction of road traffic noise for proposed new roads, or altered roads, to assess the environmental impact of the road scheme on the community.

Currently, dwellings which are newly subject to $L_{A10,18\,h}$ values of 68 dB(A) or above, due to a new or altered road, and for which the $L_{A10,18\,h}$ value has increased by at least 1 dB(A) due to the road, have entitlement to noise insulation treatment, *e.g.* acoustic double glazing, under the Noise Insulation Regulations 1975.

Traffic noise index (TNI)

Although $L_{A10,18\,h}$ is the most widely used parameter in determining the environmental impact of road traffic noise, one of the arguments against its use is that the parameter takes no account of background noise level. A given value of $L_{A10,18h}$ may cause far more dissatisfaction in a rural area, where the background noise level is very low, compared to a busy urban area where the background noise level is comparatively high. A parameter which takes L_{A10} into account as well as the background noise level, L_{A90}, is the traffic noise index (TNI). TNI is calculated as follows:

$$\text{TNI} = L_{A90} + 4(L_{A10} - L_{A90}) - 30$$

TNI is generally based on 24-hour L_{A10} and L_{A90} values.

TNI was derived by Griffiths and Langdon [2] using roads with heavy traffic flows in the London area. To obtain the correct correlation between dissatisfaction and TNI the fluctuation between L_{A10} and L_{A90} had to be multiplied by a factor of 4. In rural areas, with low traffic flows, where the differential between L_{A10} and L_{A90} is great, the use of the factor of 4 produces very high TNI values. It is now widely believed that the use of TNI, as quantified above, over-estimates dissatisfaction with traffic noise in rural areas. Griffiths and Langdon emphasized the fact that TNI may not extrapolate sensibly outside the range of noise conditions from which it was derived, *i.e.* urban areas with heavy traffic flows. From the London survey it was suggested that building façade values of 74 TNI represent a reasonable standard of amenity in urban conditions.

Equivalent continuous sound pressure level ($L_{Aeq,T}$)

The equivalent continuous sound pressure level is the level which, if generated continuously, would give the same energy content as some fluctuating signal over a given time period. The ISO definition of the parameter is:

$$L_{eq} = 10 \log_{10} \frac{1}{T} \int_0^T \frac{p^2_t}{p^2_0} \, dt \text{ (dB)}$$

Statistical and Energy-based Noise Parameters

where T is the time period under consideration, p_t is the instantaneous sound pressure N/m² and p_o is the reference sound pressure level = 2×10^{-5} N/m² (20 µPa).

For calculation purposes the A-weighted L_{eq} can be found from:

$$L_{Aeq.T} = 10 \log_{10} \frac{1}{T} \sum_{i=1}^{n} t_i \, 10^{Li(A)/10} \; dB(A)$$

where T is the total time period under consideration and t_i is the time period during which the sound pressure level was at a value of L_i dB(A).

Example: In an 8-hour environmental noise study the following steady noise levels were observed for the periods indicated,

1 hour at 66 dB(A)
2 hours at 58 dB(A)
2 hours at 50 dB(A)
1 hour at 45 dB(A)
2 hours at 63 dB(A)

The L_{Aeq} for the 8-hour period would be given by:

$$L_{Aeq.8h} = 10 \log_{10} \frac{1}{8} (1 \times 10^{66/10} + 2 \times 10^{58/10} + 2 \times 10^{50/10} + 1 \times 10^{45/10} + 2 \times 10^{63/10}) \; dB(A)$$

$$L_{Aeq.8h} = 10 \log_{10} \frac{1}{8} (1 \times 10^{6.6} + 2 \times 10^{5.8} + 2 \times 10^{5} + 1 \times 10^{4.5} + 2 \times 10^{6.3}) \; dB(A)$$

$$L_{Aeq.8h} = 60.7 \; dB(A)$$

i.e. if 60.7 dB(A) had been generated continuously over the 8-hour period the energy content of the noise would have been equivalent to that of the fluctuating noise pattern given.

This example is shown diagrammatically in Figure 4.3.

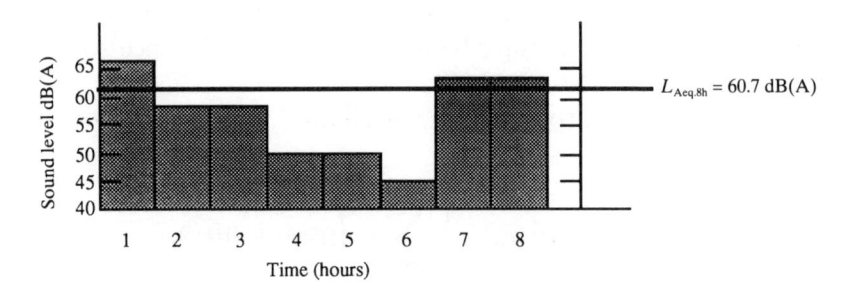

Figure 4.3 Example showing L_{Aeq} calculated for an 8-hour period

Example: A local authority have set a 12-hour (07.00 to 19.00 hours) L_{Aeq} limit of 75 dB(A) on the boundary of a construction site near residential flats. Typical site activities produce a current $L_{Aeq,12h}$ of 70 dB(A) on the site boundary. The contractors require to bring on to site a piece of plant which will produce a sound pressure level of 78 dB(A) at the site boundary. For how many hours during the 12-hour working day can this piece of additional plant be permitted to operate assuming other site activities continue at the previous level?

The $L_{Aeq,12h}$ value available for the additional piece of plant can be calculated by the subtraction of dB values as indicated in Chapter 1, *i.e.* 75 dB(A) (permissible) minus 70 dB(A) (current value)

$$L_{Aeq,12h} \text{available} = 10 \log_{10} (10^{75/10} - 10^{70/10}) \text{ dB(A)}$$

$$= 73.3 \text{ dB(A)}$$

This value enables the time period "t" for the plant to be calculated:

$$L_{Aeq,12h} \text{available} = 10 \log_{10} \frac{1}{12} (t \, 10^{78/10}) \text{ dB(A)}$$

$$73.3 = 10 \log_{10} \frac{1}{12} (t \, 10^{7.8}) \text{ dB(A)}$$

Dividing both sides by 10 gives :

$$7.33 = \log_{10} \frac{1}{12}(t\, 10^{7.8})\ dB(A)$$

taking antilogs of both sides gives :

$$\text{(antilog } x = 10^x)$$
$$10^{7.33} = \frac{1}{12}(t\, 10^{7.8})$$

therefore:

$$t = \frac{12 \times 10^{7.33}}{10^{7.8}}$$

$$t = 4.07 \text{ hours}$$

$L_{Aeq,T}$ has become the most widely used parameter for the assessment of environmental noise and is now used for aircraft noise, rail noise, industrial noise, and most other types of environmental noise. For environmental considerations, the 24-hour day is often split into two periods, *i.e.* a 16-hour day period of 07.00 to 23.00 and a night period of 23.00 to 07.00. The corresponding designation of the L_{Aeq} values is $L_{Aeq,16h}$ and $L_{Aeq,8h}$.

Noise pollution level (L_{NP})

Although $L_{Aeq,T}$ has become the most widely used parameter in the assessment of environmental noise, one of the arguments against its use is that it takes no account of the fluctuation in noise level. This fluctuation may be important from the point of view of annoyance, *i.e.* noise which fluctuates between high and low levels is generally more annoying than noise which is at a fairly constant level. Figure 4.4 shows two samples of noise over the same time period. Although both samples have the same L_{Aeq}, sample (b) is likely to be more annoying because of the greater fluctuation in noise level.

A parameter which takes account of the energy content of the noise and the fluctuation in noise level over time is the noise

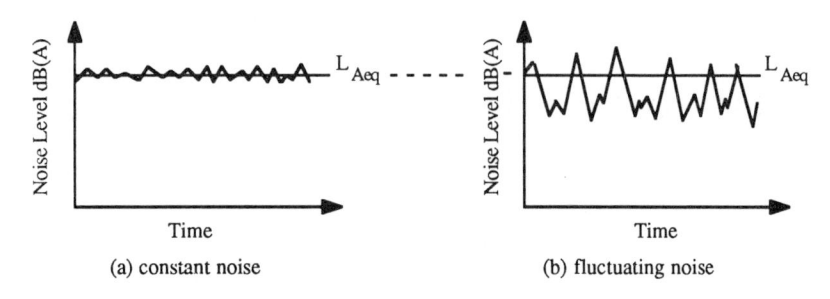

Figure 4.4 Samples of noise with the same L_{Aeq} but different degrees of fluctuation

pollution level (L_{NP}). L_{NP} is defined by :

$$L_{NP} = L_{eq} + 2.56\,s$$

where s is the standard deviation of noise level.

For a normal distribution of noise $2.56\,s = (L_{10} - L_{90})$ (see Figure 4.1), hence,

$$L_{NP} = L_{eq} + (L_{10} - L_{90})$$

Generally noise levels for the calculation of the noise pollution level would be made in dB(A).

Although the two samples of noise shown in Figure 4.4 have the same L_{Aeq} value sample (b) would have a higher L_{NP} due to the greater standard deviation of the fluctuating noise.

The parameter noise pollution level has been around since the late 1960s [3] and would appear to be an ideal parameter for assessing community noise, but it has found limited use in reality. Perhaps this is because of the difficulty in measuring the parameter when it was first introduced. Many modern integrating sound level meters and environmental noise analysers have the capability of measuring the parameter for time-varying noise.

Single event noise exposure level (L_{AX} or SEL)

In many cases community reaction to noise is governed by a

single noisy event or by a series of identifiable noisy events, *e.g.* blasting operations. A parameter is needed to quantify the effect of such events on the overall noise climate. The parameter used is the single event noise exposure level (L_{AX} or SEL).

L_{AX} is the the level in dB(A) which, if it lasted for one second, would produce the same A-weighted energy content as a specified noise event, *i.e.* the logarithm of the total noise energy contained in the event normalized to one second.

$$L_{AX} = 10 \log_{10} \frac{1}{1 \text{ sec}} \int \frac{p^2}{p_0^2} \, dt$$

where p is the sound pressure above threshold (Pa) and p_o is the reference sound pressure (20 µPa).

To measure the L_{AX} it is necessary to set a threshold detection level above which only the event will produce noise. This distinguishes the event from general background noise. Whenever the noise level is above this threshold the instrument treats the signal as a significant event and logs data for the calculation of the parameter.

L_{AX} can be converted to a period L_{Aeq} by the relationship:

$$L_{Aeq} = L_{AX} - 10 \log_{10} T$$

where T is the number of seconds in the time period under consideration.

Example: The 1-hour L_{Aeq} for a reference position is 72 dB(A). What would be the new 1-hour L_{Aeq} if 8 events each of L_{AX} 96 dB(A) were superimposed on the existing noise within the 1 hour period?

$$\begin{aligned}\text{event } L_{Aeq} &= L_{AX} - 10 \log_{10} T \\ &= 96 - 10 \log_{10} 3600 \\ &= 60.4 \text{ dB(A)}\end{aligned}$$

The contribution of eight events to the hourly L_{Aeq} would be given by:

$$\begin{aligned}L_{Aeq \, (8 \text{ events})} &= 10 \log_{10}[8 \times 10^{6.04}] \text{ dB(A)} \\ &= 69.4 \text{ dB(A)}\end{aligned}$$

The new 1-hour L_{Aeq} would be given by adding the contribution of the eight events to the existing level:

$$L_{Aeq, 1h} = 10 \log_{10}[10^{7.2} + 10^{6.94}] \text{ dB(A)}$$
$$= 73.9 \text{ dB(A)}$$

This example illustrates the benefits of being able to quantify single event contributions to the overall period L_{Aeq}.

Day/night equivalent sound level (L_{DN} or DNL)

In this parameter, which originated in the USA, the energy is averaged over a 24-hour period but the noise level during the night-time period of 22.00 to 07.00 receives a 10 dB(A) penalty to emphasize the greater disturbance of noise during this period. L_{DN} is defined by:

$$L_{DN} = 10 \log_{10} \frac{1}{24} [15 \times 10^{Ld/10} + 9 \times 10^{(Ln+10)/10}] \text{ dB(A)}$$

where: Ld = L_{Aeq} over the day-time 15-hour period 07.00 to 22.00 in dB(A)
Ln = L_{Aeq} over the night-time 9-hour period 22.00 to 07.00 in dB(A)

The 10 dB(A) penalty for the night-time period is empirical rather than based on scientific evidence. The parameter is in widespread use in the USA for noise assessment, including road traffic and aircraft noise, but is not in general use in the UK although reference is sometimes made to the parameter in environmental noise reports.

Community noise equivalent level or day/evening/night level (CNEL or DENL or L_{DEN})

This is a variation on the day/night equivalent level in which the

Statistical and Energy-based Noise Parameters

evening noise in the period 19.00 to 22.00 receives a 5 dB(A) penalty and the night-time noise in the period 22.00 to 07.00 receives a 10 dB(A) penalty. The parameter is defined by:

$$L_{DN} = 10 \log_{10} \frac{1}{24} [12 \times 10^{Ld/10} + 3 \times 10^{(Le+5)/10} + 9 \times 10^{(Ln+10)/10}] \text{ dB(A)}$$

where: $Ld = L_{Aeq}$ over the day-time 12-hour period 07.00 to 19.00 in dB(A)

$Le = L_{Aeq}$ over the evening 3-hour period 19.00 to 22.00 in dB(A)

$Ln = L_{Aeq}$ over the night-time 9-hour period 22.00 to 07.00 in dB(A)

Again this parameter is not in general use in the UK although it does occur from time to time in noise reports. It is used in some EC countries, *e.g.* Denmark and Holland.

Measurement of statistical noise parameters

The parameters discussed in this chapter are generally measured at a reference point close to the façade of an affected building, *e.g.* 1 m from the façade of the building for road traffic noise. The parameters would be measured using an integrating sound level meter (ISLM) or noise analyser. This type of meter or analyser measures sound pressure levels at selected intervals, *e.g.* every 0.1, 1, or 10 seconds, stores the measured values in a memory and calculates the selected parameter or parameters at the end of the relevant survey time. The integrating sound level meter or analyser can be connected to a printer to download the calculated parameters at set intervals during the survey or at the end of the survey. Most modern ISLMs are very versatile and offer the convenience of being left unattended, if secure, to carry out long-term surveys.

References

1 Scholes WE and Sargent JW, *Designing Against Traffic Noise*, MPBW Building Research Establishment, Garston, 1970.
2 Griffiths ID and Langdon FJ, "Subjective Response to Road Traffic", *Journal of Sound and Vibration*, (1968),Vol. 8, 16.
3 Robinson DW, *The Concept of Noise Pollution Level*, NPL Aero Report, Ac.38, National Physics Laboratory, (1969).

Chapter 5
Internal Noise Criteria and Sound Insulation Requirements

Introduction

This chapter examines the criteria used for assessing the effects of, and setting design targets for, internal noise within buildings. It also examines the building regulation requirements for sound insulation with respect to residential buildings and the methods of measuring the sound insulation of building elements for compliance with the appropriate regulations.

Noise criteria (NC), noise rating (NR) and preferred noise criteria (PNC) curves

Perhaps one of the simplest ways of rating noise within buildings is by means of a dB(A) value. This method has merit in the fact that the noise level will relate, broadly, to how the ear perceives the noise, but has the disadvantage as a design criterion that it gives no real indication of the frequency content of noise. It also has the disadvantage that it discriminates against low frequency noise and may fail to adequately assess the problems of low frequency noise associated with such items as centrifugal fans used in mechanical ventilation systems.

To provide more suitable methods of assessing internal noise, rating curves have been developed based largely on equal loudness contours. The curves are based on octave sound pressure levels.

Noise criteria (NC) curves were developed in the USA, in the 1950s, mainly for use in the heating and ventilation industry. Similar *noise rating* (NR) curves were developed in Europe, mainly for community noise assessment. Following observations that NC and NR curves were not rigorous enough at the low and high ends of the spectrum and tended to produce spectra with low frequency "rumble" or high frequency "hiss", *preferred noise criteria* (PNC) were developed in the USA in the 1970s. PNC curves provide a spectrum which is more acceptable from a subjective point of view by reducing permissible noise levels at the high and low ends of the spectrum for a given rating value. Although PNC gives more acceptable spectra, the PNC system has not been widely adopted in the UK in comparison to the NC and NR systems. NC and NR curves are both used in the UK for assessing noise from building services origins, with the application of the NC system the more common. NC curves, which are set out at intervals of 5, are illustrated in Figure 5.1. A

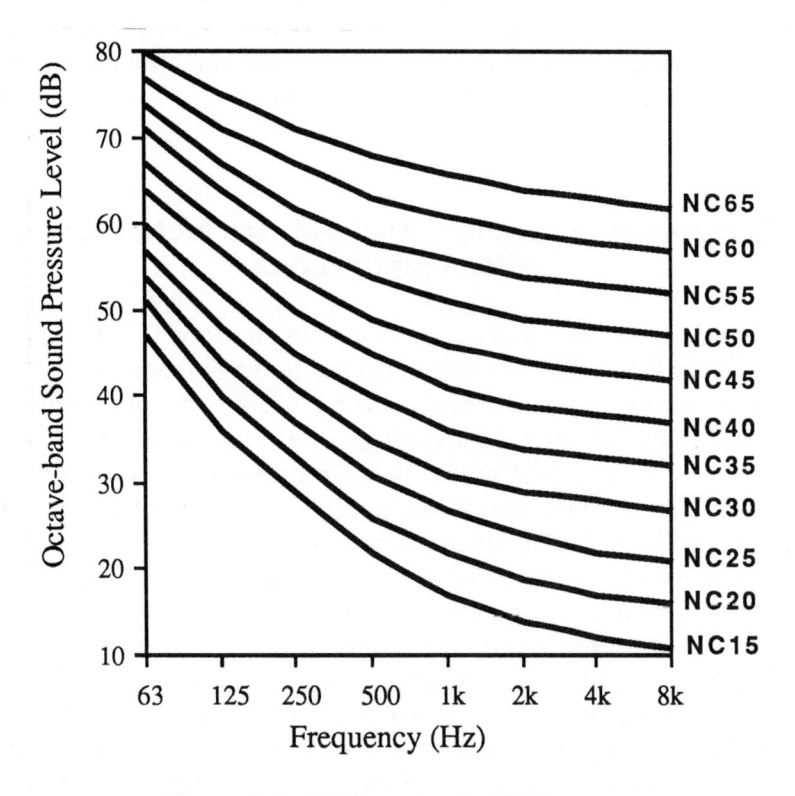

Figure 5.1 Noise criteria (NC) curves

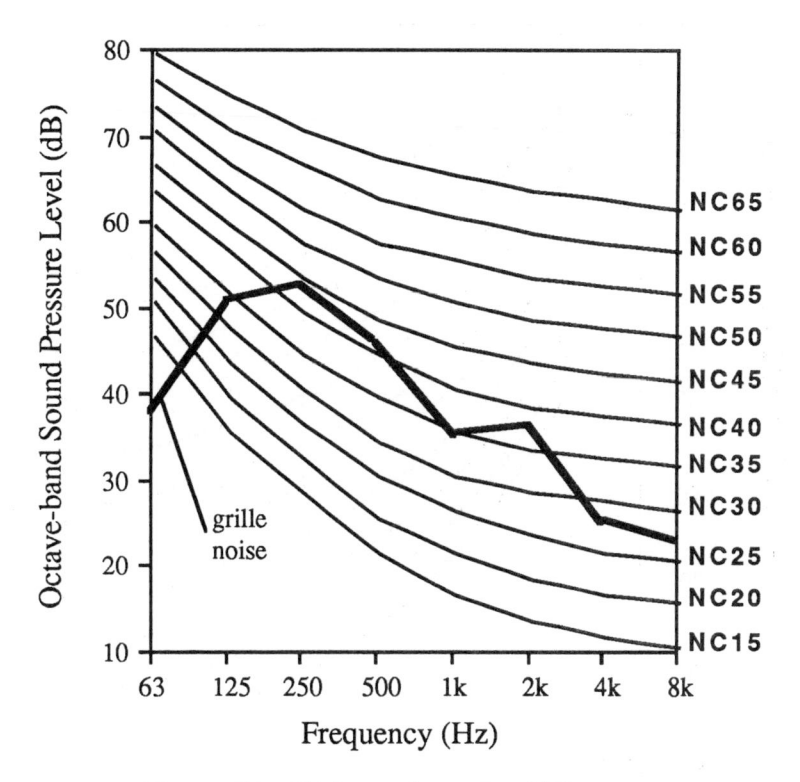

Figure 5.2 Noise rating using NC curves

given NC curve rating is 1 dB above the octave sound pressure level at 2 kHz, *e.g.* for NC 50 the sound pressure level at 2 kHz is 49 dB.

Figure 5.2 shows the method of rating noise by the NC system. The octave spectrum of noise from an air supply grille, measured at a reference point, has been superimposed on the NC curves. The spectrum is wholly below NC 45 and therefore an NC 45 design criterion has been achieved. More accurately, the maximum level by which any octave value in the next lower curve (NC 40) has been exceeded is 4 dB at 250 Hz. The noise rating could therefore be classified as NC40 + 4.

Noise rating (NR) curves are shown in Figure 5.3. They are used in the same way as NC curves. NR curves are more tolerant of low frequency noise and less tolerant of high frequency than

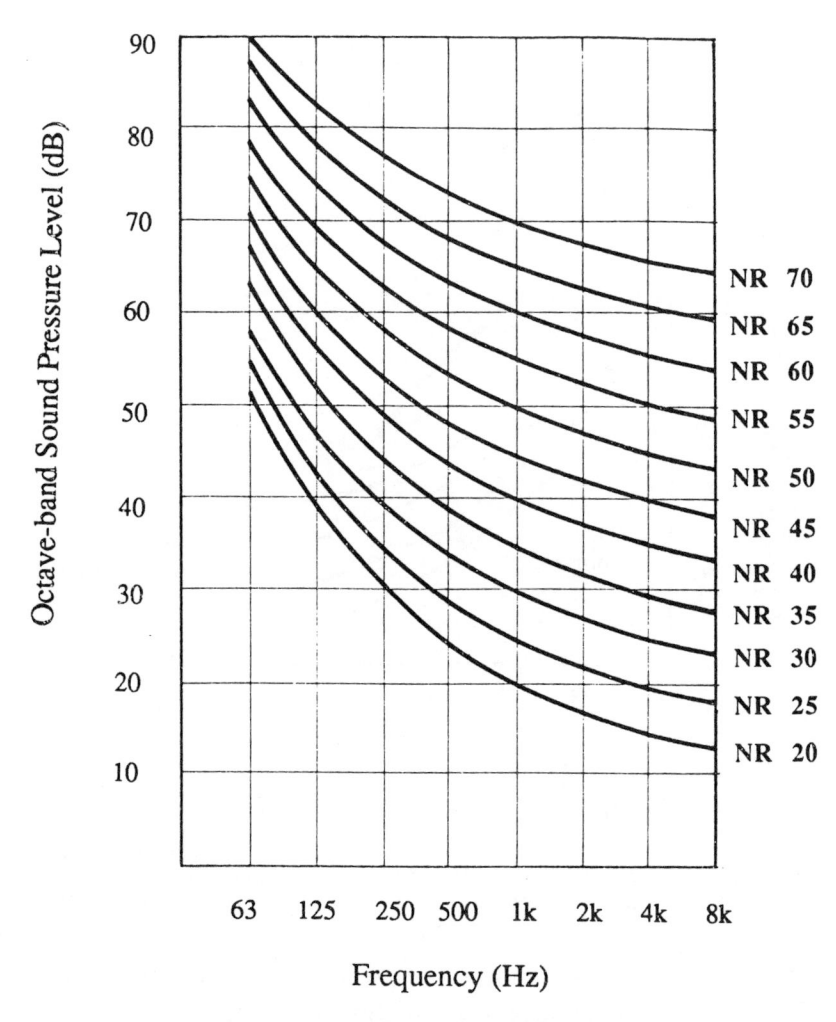

Figure 5.3 Noise rating (NR) curves

NC curves and are based on the relationship:

$$L = a + bN$$

where L is the octave-band sound pressure level for NR level N and a and b are constants depending on frequency band.

Noise Rating curves are based on 1 kHz. The NR value for a particular curve is equal to the octave-band sound pressure level at 1 kHz for that curve.

Preferred Noise Criteria (PNC) curves are illustrated in Figure 5.4. They are again used in the same way as NC and NR curves but are more demanding at the low and high ends of the spectrum.

NC/NR curves are used as design criteria for the control of noise from mechanical ventilation systems. Table 5.1 shows recommended NC/NR values for various types of buildings and rooms [1]. A more detailed list of criteria can be found in literature concerning noise control in building services [2], [3]. The appropriate criteria curve is selected to ensure that noise from mechanical ventilation systems is inaudible above other background noise sources and hence there is no advantage in

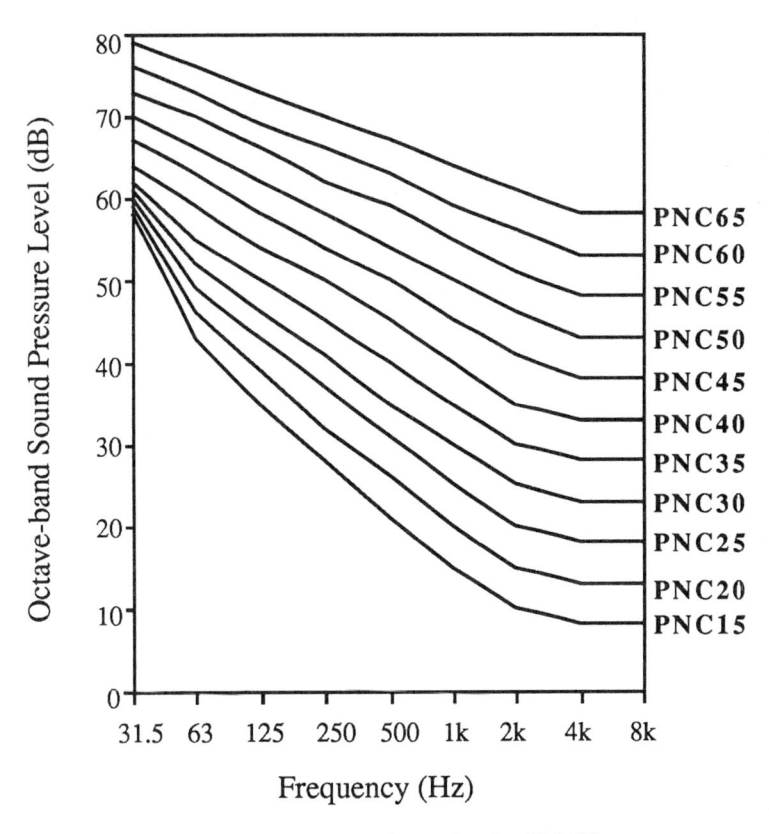

Figure 5.4   Preferred noise criteria (PNC) curves

selecting an inappropriately low criterion. For example, there would be no point in designing the ventilation system to produce NC 30 in a general office in which the noise from typewriters etc produces NC 45. This would involve a waste of money in excessive noise control measures, *e.g.* silencers, in the mechanical ventilation system. The selection of a higher criterion value, within the appropriate range, may have the benefit of the wide-band noise from the ventilation system masking out more intrusive noises and may also provide privacy for close-range speech. It is generally accepted that a ventilation system which is designed for an NC/NR value of 5 units below the background level will result in not more than 15% of people being aware of the noise from the system, *i.e.* a ventilation system producing NC/NR40 will be suitable for an environment in which the background noise is NC/NR 45 [4]. Although NC/NR curves are used most often as design criteria for mechanical ventilation systems, they are often used by Environmental Health Officers (EHO) to assess the degree of noise nuisance in houses and flats originating from some external noise source, *e.g.* noise from the cooling towers of a nearby industrial or commercial building.

An octave frequency analysis of the noise level in the house or flat would be carried out. The noise would normally be deemed a nuisance if the noise level from the external source exceeds NC 30 in living-rooms or NC 25 in bedrooms at night. Such values would apply to rural areas with higher values being acceptable in urban and industrial areas.

There is no unique relationship between the NC/NR value of noise and the noise level in dB(A). The actual correlation depends on the spectrum shape of the noise being rated, but the following rule of thumb relationship is often quoted:

$$dB(A) \approx NC/NR + 5$$

i.e. an NC/NR value of 30 would be approximately equivalent to a value of 35 dB(A).

It is emphasized that this relationship is very approximate and the addition factor of "5" can in fact vary between 0 and 11 depending on the spectrum shape.

Table 5.1 NC/NR design criteria

Situation	NC/NR value
Broadcasting/recording studios	20
Concert halls and theatres	20–25
Assembly halls and churches	25–30
Cinemas	30–35
Hospital wards and operating theatres	30–40
Homes, bedrooms	25–35
Private offices, libraries	35–45
General offices	35–45
Mechanized offices	40–55
Restaurants and bars	35–45
Department stores	35–45
Swimming baths, sports arenas	35–50

Speech Interference

It is important that in internal environments where verbal communication is essential, and where telephones are used, that speech can be heard clearly at relevant distances without masking effects from other noise sources. In such environments good speech intelligibility is a major influence on the acceptability of the interior. The concept of background noise interfering with speech intelligibility was quantified by Beranek in the USA [5] and the original speech-interference level (SIL) was defined as the arithmetic average of the sound pressure levels in the three octave bands : 600 to 1200 Hz, 1200 to 2400 Hz, and 2400 to 4800 Hz. These frequencies covered most of the speech range and hence background noise in the range 600 to 4800 Hz was likely to interfere with speech communication if the background sound levels were excessive. Following the change in preferred band-centre frequencies in 1962, speech interference was based on the three octave bands with centres 500, 1000, and 2000 Hz. The arithmetic average of the sound pressure level in the three bands was termed the preferred octave speech interference level (PSIL). It has long been known that consonants in speech contain frequencies as high as 8 kHz, and it has become increasingly accepted that the frequency range above 2 kHz is important for good speech communication, particularly in noisy environments. An ISO Technical Report [6], published in 1974, argued for the redefinition of PSIL to include the octave band centred on 4 kHz. Thus the new PSIL is defined as the arithmetic average of the sound pressure levels in the four octave bands centred on frequencies 500 Hz, 1 kHz, 2 kHz, and 4 kHz. The PSIL values shown in Table 5.2 have been suggested for good speech communication [7]. With PSIL values much above the suggested levels, normal speech will only be heard at very close distances.

In the design of interiors the use of NC/NR curves is now much more common than the use of PSIL values. The CIBSE Guide [8] gives the data shown in Tables 5.3 and 5.4 for sound levels for speech intelligibility and for telephone conversations.

Table 5.2 Suggested maximum PSIL values

Type of room	Maximum acceptable PSIL (dB)
Small private office	45
Conference room	30–35
Concert hall	25
Typing pool	60
Bedroom	30
Living-room	45
Classroom/lecture theatre	30

Sound Insulation Requirements

In terms of the Building Regulations for England and Wales, Scotland, and Northern Ireland, airborne sound insulation requirements are specified for separating walls and separating floors between dwellings. Requirements for the limitation of impact sound transmission are specified for separating floors between dwellings.

Table 5.3 Sound level / distance relationships for speech intelligibility

Background sound level (dB(A))	Background (NR)	Maximum distance for intelligibility (metres)
48	40	7
53	45	4
58	50	2.2
63	55	1.2
68	60	0.7
73	65	0.4
77	70	0.2
over 77	over 70	too noisy for speech

Distances are for normal speech. The distance is increased by raising the voice and is approximately doubled by raising the voice 5 to 6 dB.

Table 5.4 Background sound levels for telephone conversations

Quality of conversaton	Sound level (dB(A))	NR
Satisfactory	58	50
Slightly difficult	68	60
Difficult	82	75
Unsatisfactory	over 82	over 75

The sound insulation criteria also apply to walls and floors separating dwellings from non-residential buildings, *e.g.* shops. A full list of the building elements to which the regulations apply can be found in the appropriate regulations. There have been recent moves to harmonize the regulation requirements between the various parts of the UK, *e.g.* Approved Document E [9] in England and Wales deals with guidance to cover material change of use of a dwelling, such as the conversion of a large house into flats, an area which was not adequately covered in the previous regulations. The building regulations in Scotland have never made any distinction in the regulation requirements between conversions and new build.

The regulation requirements are such that noise from normal domestic activities in an adjoining dwelling or other building is kept down to a level that will not threaten the health of the occupants of the dwelling and will allow them to sleep, rest and engage in normal domestic activities in satisfactory conditions. This does not mean that one dwelling will be totally isolated from noise in adjoining dwellings, or other buildings, and anti-social behaviour, such as the playing of stereo systems at a high volume, may constitute a nuisance in neighbouring dwellings even though the separating walls and floors comply with the appropriate regulations.

The performance criteria are set out in terms of sound insulation tests carried out in accordance with BS 2750:1980 [10] and rating methods in accordance with BS 5821:1984 [11]. Although tests are not required for certain types of approved constructions, it is necessary to outline the test and rating procedures in order to understand the specified performance criteria.

Airborne sound insulation test

The equipment and method for carrying out airborne sound insulation tests are illustrated in Figure 5.5. Wide-band noise (pink noise) is generated in the source room (which should be the larger of the two rooms if they differ in size) and the sound pressure level is measured at each third-octave frequency in the range 100 Hz to 3150 Hz. To obtain the average sound pressure level at each frequency, a microphone on a rotating boom, or a number of fixed microphone positions (at least 6), is used. The measured data would be stored in the memory of a building acoustics analyser. The average corresponding sound pressure levels in the receiving room are then measured, again using a microphone on a rotating boom or a number of fixed microphone positions. Again the data would be stored in the memory of the building acoustics analyser. The level difference at each third-octave frequency is given by:

$$D = L_1 - L_2 \quad \text{dB}$$

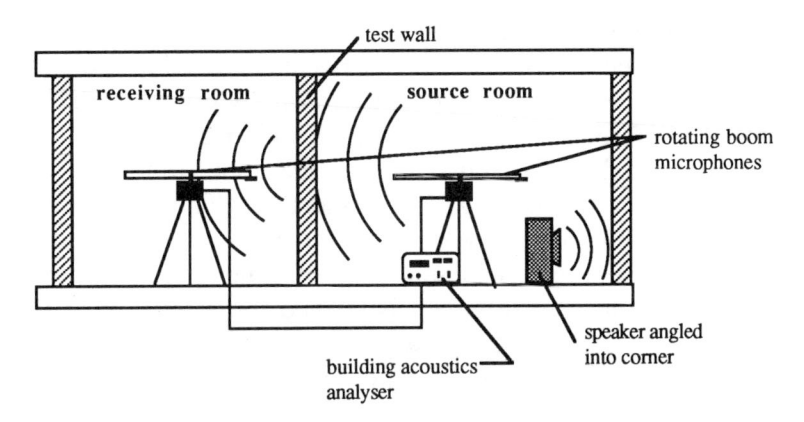

Figure 5.5 Measurement of airborne sound insulation

where L_1 is the source room average sound pressure level at a given frequency (dB) and L_2 is the receiving room average sound pressure level at the same frequency (dB).

The sound pressure levels measured in the receiving room are for sound energy which has passed through the test element (separating wall or floor) and which has then been modified by the acoustic conditions in the receiving room. If the receiving room were large and the surfaces reflective, the values of L_2 would be higher than if the receiving room were small with absorbent surfaces and the level difference, D, would be smaller. To eliminate variations in receiving room acoustic conditions the results are "standardized" in respect to a receiving room *reverberation time* of 0.5 seconds, which is typical of a furnished living-room. Reverberation time is the time taken for a 60 dB decay in sound energy level when a sound source is suddenly switched off. The reverberation time (T) varies directly with the size of receiving room and inversely with the amount of absorption in the receiving room. The relationship, known as *Sabine's formula,* is given by:

$$T = \frac{0.163 \, V}{A}$$

where T is the reverberation time (seconds), V is the volume of room (m^3) and A = amount of absorption in the room

(m^2 absorption units or m^2 sabins).

To enable the standardization of results a reverberation time analysis of the receiving room is carried out by producing narrow bands of noise centred on the frequencies 100 Hz to 3150 Hz, one at a time, and measuring the reverberation time for each frequency using the building acoustics analyser. The reverberation times for each frequency are stored in the memory of the analyser. The final parameter calculated for airborne sound insulation performance for a test element is termed the *standardized level difference* (D_{nT}). The value of D_{nT} is calculated for each of the 16 third-octave frequencies in the range 100 Hz to 3150 Hz from:

$$D_{nT} = L_1 - L_2 + 10 \log_{10} \frac{T}{0.5} \text{ dB}$$

where L_1 is the source room average sound pressure level at a given frequency (dB), L_2 is the receiving room average sound pressure level at the same frequency (dB), T is the receiving room reverberation time at the same frequency (seconds) and 0.5 is the reverberation time of "standard" receiving room (seconds).

Example: At 500 Hz the source room average sound pressure level, the receiving room average sound pressure level and the receiving room reverberation time are 102 dB, 54 dB and 0.9 seconds respectively. Calculate the standardized level difference, D_{nT}, for the test element at 500 Hz.

$$D_{nT} = 102 - 54 + 10 \log_{10} \frac{0.9}{0.5} \text{ dB}$$

$$= 50.6 \text{ dB}$$

This example shows the importance of the standardization factor. The apparent insulation value of the test element is ($L_1 - L_2$), *i.e.* (102 − 54) dB = 48 dB, but because the receiving room is more reverberant than a "standard" receiving room, the measured sound pressure levels in the receiving room are higher than they would have been if the receiving room reverberation time was 0.5 seconds. The sound insulation value for regulation purposes is therefore better than the measured 48 dB, *i.e.* 48 + 2.6 = 50.6 dB.

Note: (i) If the measured receiving room reverberation time is actually 0.5 seconds at a particular frequency, then the standardization factor becomes zero, and $D_{nT} = (L_1 - L_2)$ at that frequency. (ii) If the measured receiving room reverberation time at a particular frequency is less than 0.5 seconds, then the standardization factor becomes negative, and D_{nT} is less than $(L_1 - L_2)$ at that frequency.

Modern building acoustics analysers have the capability of measuring and storing all of the relevant data for the above type of calcalation, and will also calculate D_{nT} for each frequency from the stored data.

Impact sound transmission test

Impact sound transmission tests are carried out in accordance with BS 2750 : Part 7, 1980. The equipment and procedure are illustrated in Figure 5.6.

The test floor, which should not be covered with carpet or other non-permanent finish, is excited by the standard impact

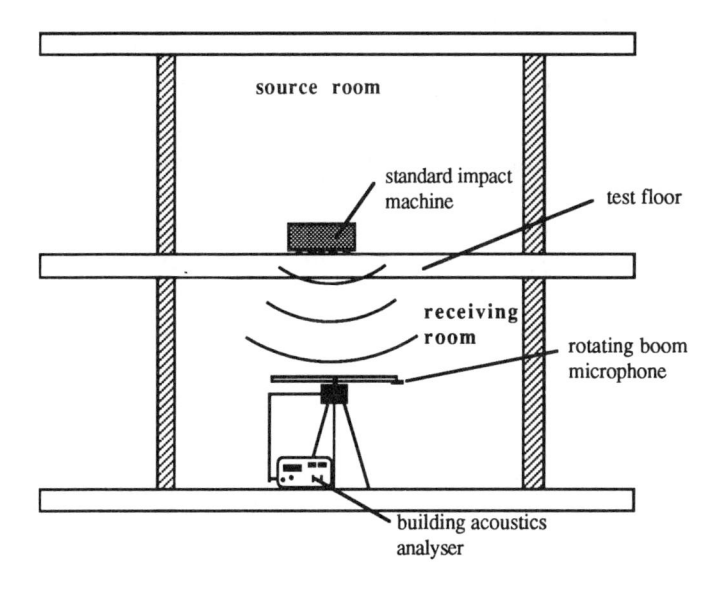

Figure 5.6 Measurement of impact sound transmission

machine. This machine comprises five metal hammers, each of which has a mass of 500g and drops freely through 40 mm when released from a rotating cam. The machine drives the hammers to give 10 impacts per second thus putting a standard amount of kinetic energy into the floor. The amount of sound energy transmitted from this kinetic energy is measured in the receiving room below. No measurements are carried out in the source room. Although the tests are often referred to as "impact sound insulation tests", what is actually measured is the impact sound transmission and not the insulation.

A third-octave analysis of the sound pressure levels in the frequency range 100 Hz to 3150 Hz is carried out in the receiving room using a building acoustics analyser and a microphone on a rotating boom. Alternatively the average sound pressure levels could be found by using at least six static microphone positions. To ensure an acceptable average performance for the floor, at least four floor positions are chosen for excitation by the standard impact machine for each test floor. This is particularly important for ribbed floors where the impact sound transmission through a rib may be significantly different to the transmission through the slab between ribs.

The receiving room sound pressure levels result from sound energy which has passed through the test floor and then been modified by the acoustic characteristics of the receiving room. As in the airborne sound insulation test, a standardization of the results is required for building regulation purposes. To enable this process to be carried out, a reverberation time survey is carried in the receiving room and the results are again standardized with respect to a standard receiving room reverberation time of 0.5 seconds. The parameter calculated is termed the *standardized impact level* (L_{nT}). The value of L_{nT} at each of the third-octave frequencies, is calculated from:

$$L_{nT} = L - 10\log_{10}\frac{T}{0.5} \text{ dB}$$

where L is the measured average sound pressure level in the receiving room at a given frequency, T is the receiving room reverberation time at the same frequency and 0.5 is the reverberation time of the "standard" receiving room.

Note that the standardization factor is negative. This is because of the fact that if the receiving room reverberation time at a particular frequency is greater than 0.5 seconds, the measured level "L" will be higher than for the standard receiving room condition. Again the standardization correction becomes zero for any frequency at which the receiving room reverberation time is equal to 0.5 seconds, and becomes positive for any frequency for which the measured receiving room reverberation time is less than 0.5 seconds.

Example: The measured average receiving room sound pressure level at 250 Hz is 66 dB in an impact sound transmission test. The receiving room reverberation time at the same frequency is found to be 1.1 seconds. Calculate L_{nT} at 250 Hz.

$$L_{nT} = 66 - 10 \log_{10} \frac{1.1}{0.5} \text{ dB}$$

$$= 62.6 \text{ dB}$$

It is important to realize that in the airborne sound insulation test a high value of D_{nT} indicates a high level of airborne sound insulation for a test element, but in the impact transmission test, which only deals with receiving room sound pressure levels, a high value of L_{nT} indicates a poor level of impact sound insulation, *i.e.* high impact transmission.

Rating criteria

The rating of elements for sound insulation performance is carried out in accordance with BS 5821 : Parts 1 and 2, 1984 [12]. In this method a reference curve (rating curve), one for airborne sound and one for impact sound, is moved up or down until the sum of the unfavourable deviations of D_{nT} or L_{nT} with respect to the appropriate reference curve, in the frequency range 100 Hz to 3150 Hz, is as close to 32 dB as possible without exceeding 32 dB. The value of the reference curve in dB at 500 Hz is then used as a single figure index for the test element. The airborne sound insulation index thus produced is termed the *weighted standardized level difference* ($D_{nT,w}$). The impact transmission index is termed the *weighted standardized impact sound pressure level* ($L_{nT,w}$).

Table 5.5 and Figure 5.7 show the results of, and rating procedure for, a separating wall subject to an airborne sound insulation test. The reference curve (rating curve) has been moved until the unfavourable deviations are as close to 32 dB as possible without exceeding 32 dB, in this case 29.9 dB. As can be seen from Table 5.5 and Figure 5.7, unfavourable deviations occur for frequencies between 125 Hz and 800 Hz, inclusive, *i.e.* in this range the calculated D_{nT} value is less than the rating curve value. The unfavourable deviation at each frequency is found by

Table 5.5 Results of an airborne sound insulation test

Frequency (Hz)	L_1 (dB)	L_2 (dB)	T (s)	D_{nT} (dB)	Rating curve (53 dB)	Unfavourable deviation (dB)
100	88.4	53.5	0.42	34.1	34	
125	96.5	60.7	0.31	33.7	37	3.3
160	96.9	59.6	0.38	36.1	40	3.9
200	91.8	55	0.36	35.4	43	7.6
250	91.3	48.4	0.29	40.5	46	5.5
315	94.1	47	0.38	45.9	49	3.1
400	93.4	44.1	0.38	48.1	52	3.9
500	92.4	40.2	0.37	50.9	53	2.1
630	93.7	40.7	0.59	53.7	54	0.3
800	93.9	38.6	0.45	54.8	55	0.2
1 k	89.8	30.2	0.38	58.4	56	
1.25 k	89.8	27.6	0.38	61	57	
1.6 k	88.5	23.7	0.4	63.8	57	
2 k	89.1	22.1	0.38	65.8	57	
2.5 k	89.7	21.6	0.37	66.8	57	
3.15 k	85	20	0.4	64	57	

Total unfavourable deviation = 29.2 dB
Rating $D_{nT,w}$ = 53 dB

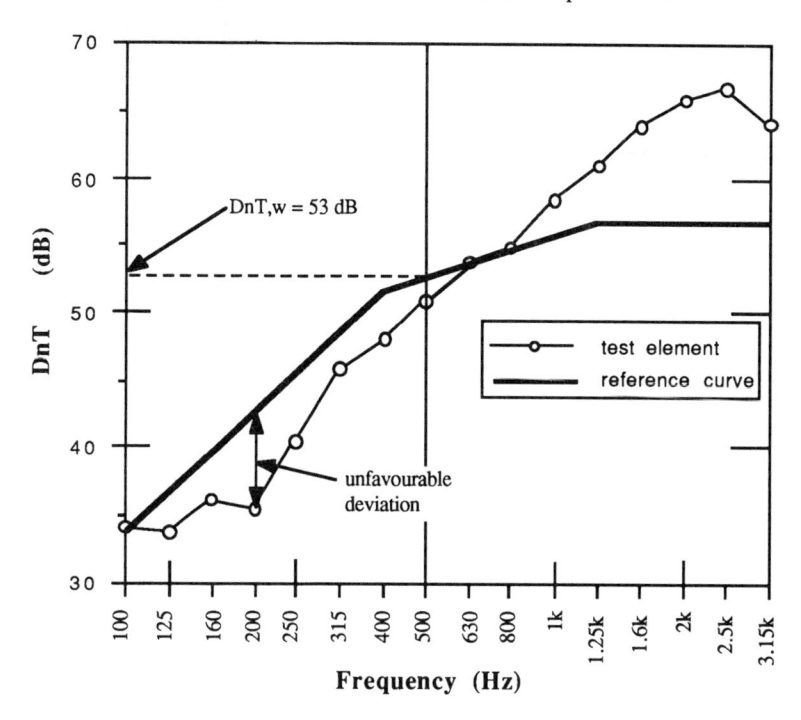

Figure 5.7 Graphical representation of airborne sound insulation performance and rating procedure using data from Table 5.5

subtracting D_{nT} value from the rating curve value, e.g. at 200 Hz the unfavourable deviation is (43 −35.4) dB, *i.e.* 7.6 dB. The value of the reference or rating curve at 500 Hz is 53 dB and hence the weighted standardized level difference for the test wall is $D_{nT,w}$ = 53 dB. Fortunately, modern building acoustics analysers can carry out all of the calculations and produce the $D_{nT,w}$ value automatically.

Table 5.6 and Figure 5.8 show the results of, and rating procedure for, a separating floor between dwellings subject to an impact sound transmission test. The reference or rating curve is again moved up or down as a unit until the sum of the unfavourable deviations is as close to 32 dB as possible without exceeding 32 dB. Since the impact test deals with sound levels and not insulation, unfavourable deviations occur where the value of L_{nT} exceeds the appropriate reference curve value. In

Table 5.6 Results of an impact sound transmission test

Frequency (Hz)	L (dB)	T (s)	L_{nT} (dB)	Rating curve (66 dB)	Unfavourable deviation (dB)
100	67.8	0.36	69.2	68	1.2
125	72.5	0.34	74.2	68	6.2
160	74.2	0.35	75.7	68	7.7
200	72.9	0.6	72.1	68	4.1
250	74.1	0.48	74.3	68	6.3
315	70.1	0.47	70.4	68	2.4
400	67.1	0.47	64.7	67	0.4
500	63.8	0.76	62	66	
630	65.5	0.36	66.9	65	1.9
800	60.4	0.62	59.5	64	
1 k	59.2	0.43	59.9	63	
1.25 k	52.7	0.63	51.7	60	
1.6 k	49.9	0.44	50.5	57	
2 k	45.3	0.43	46	54	
2.5 k	40.3	0.45	40.8	51	
3.15 k	38.2	0.42	39	48	

Total unfavourable deviation = 30.2 dB
Rating = $L_{nT,w}$ 66 dB

the example given, unfavourable deviations occur at frequencies between 100 Hz and 400 Hz, inclusive, and at 630 Hz. The total unfavourable deviation is 30.2 dB. When the reference curve has been moved to achieve this total unfavourable deviation, the value of the curve at 500 Hz is 66 dB. Hence the weighted standardized impact sound pressure level is $L_{nT,w}$ 66 dB. The manipulation of the reference curve, all calculations and the rating procedure can again be made automatically on a building acoustics analyser.

Building regulation performance criteria

The building regulations for the various parts of the UK are now

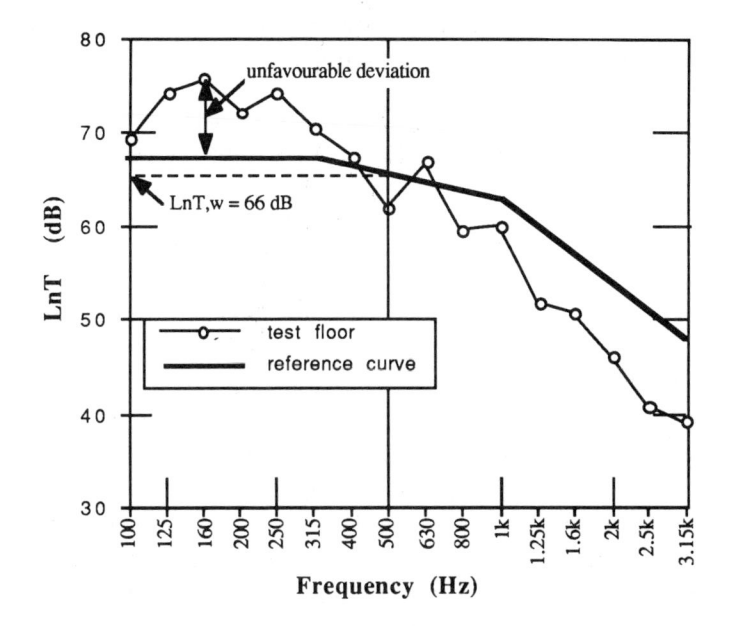

[Figure: Graph showing LnT (dB) vs Frequency (Hz) from 100 to 3.15k, with test floor curve and reference curve, annotated "unfavourable deviation" and "LnT,w = 66 dB"]

Figure 5.8 Graphical representation of impact sound transmission performance and rating procedure using data from Table 5.6

fairly uniform in terms of the acceptable sound insulation performance criteria for separating floor and walls to which the regulations apply. The performance criteria are set out in terms of the minimum acceptable standard for an individual test section and the minimum acceptable mean value for a group of sections tested. Tables 5.7 and 5.8 show the acceptable criteria for airborne and impact sound respectively.

Table 5.7 Airborne sound insulation requirements

Airborne sound tests in up to 4 pairs of rooms

Minimum values of weighted standardized level difference, $D_{nT,w}$

	Mean value (dB)	Individual value (dB)
Walls	53	49
Floors	52	48

Table 5.8 Impact sound transmission requirements

Impact sound tests in up to 4 pairs of rooms

	Minimum values of weighted standardized impact sound pressure level, $L_{nT,w}$	
	Mean value (dB)	Individual value (dB)
Floors	61	65

It is important to note that if the mean value has not been achieved, even though each individual test section has been satisfactory, the wall or floor construction, as a whole, will be deemed to have failed to meet the regulation requirements. For example, 4 test wall sections in a block of flats could reveal $D_{nT,w}$ values of 50 dB, 50 dB, 52 dB and 52 dB respectively. Although each individual section is satisfactory in that the $D_{nT,w}$ value is above the regulation requirement of 49 dB (Table 5.7) the wall construction, as a whole, has a mean performance of $D_{nT,w}$ 51 dB which is less than the acceptable value of 53 dB (Table 5.7). The wall construction is therefore unacceptable in terms of airborne sound insulation.

If less than 4 test sections are available the mean criteria have still got to be achieved. For example, two new semi-detached bungalows may have only one section of separating wall between them. That section has therefore got to demonstrate a $D_{nT,w}$ value of 53 dB.

Achieving the regulation performance requirements

Although the performance requirements in terms of airborne and impact sound insulation have been harmonized between the various parts of the UK, there are still differences in the methods for demonstrating compliance with the appropriate regulations. This is particularly the case when considering England/Wales and Scotland.

Noise Criteria and Insulation Requirements

The methods of complying with the Building Regulations 1991 in England and Wales are set out in Approved Document E 1992 [13]. This document deals with new work and building conversions. In terms of new work, three methods are available for demonstrating compliance with the sound insulation requirements.

(1) The adoption of the widely used forms of construction, including junction details, described in the document for separating walls and floors.
(2) The adoption of a form of construction which is similar to one that has been shown by field tests in an existing building to comply with the regulations.
(3) By testing part of the proposed construction in a specified type of acoustic chamber.

It is interesting to note that tests on the completed construction is not one of the methods listed for demonstrating compliance with the appropriate regulations, however, it states in the Approved Document E that there is no obligation to adopt any particular solution contained in the Document if it is preferred to meet the relevant requirement in some other way. Presumably tests on the completed construction would qualify as "some other way".

The Approved Document E gives guidance on "similarity" if method (2), above, is adopted. The new building and the existing construction tested must be substantially similar in respect to the masses of separating walls and floors, the size of rooms adjacent to separating walls and floors, the construction of elements adjacent to separating walls and floors, the provision of doors and windows in the external wall adjacent to separating walls and floors, and the extent of any steps or staggers in the buildings. Allowable differences between the existing and new building are listed in the Document.

Method (3), above, the test chamber method, has been introduced to encourage innovative forms of construction for separating walls. Combinations of separating wall and external wall are tested in a special two-storey test chamber with specifications relating to size of test rooms and the control of flanking transmission. LC Fothergill [14] identifies that a potential weakness of the test is that the test constructions may be built to an untypically high standard and thereby produce sound insulation test results which will be much higher than for the same type of construction when used in actual buildings. Field tests have shown that for most types of construction the best examples perform around 4 to 5 dB $D_{nT,w}$ better than the mean for each type. To ensure that the average performance of a tested form of construction is likely to prove satisfactory, the acceptable modified $D_{nT,w}$ from the test chamber method has been set at the comparatively high value of 55 dB.

The Approved Document E gives a number of approved methods for upgrading the sound insulation of separating walls and floors in building conversions, *e.g.* the conversion of a large house into a number of flats. Because it is more difficult to control flanking transmission in this type of building the Document gives lower acceptable standards of airborne insulation for separating walls and floors and a lower standard of impact insulation for separating floors compared to new buildings. The acceptable standards of airborne sound insulation from field tests are $D_{nT,w}$ 49 dB for walls and $D_{nT,w}$ 48 dB for floors. The accepted standard of impact transmission from field tests is $L_{nT,w}$ 65 dB. These values equate to the lower values acceptable for individual sections in the new building section of the Document and therefore have a basis in precedent as well as reflecting practical limitations.

In Scotland the requirements for sound insulation are set out in Part H of Technical Standards for Compliance with the Building Standards (Scotland) Regulations 1990 [15]. The performance standards used in Scotland are the same as given in the new building section of Approved Document E for England and Wales. The appropriate values are as shown in Tables 5.7 and 5.8. Two methods are specified for achieving the performance standards.

(1) By using "deemed to satisfy" constructions for separating walls and floors as detailed in the Technical Standards.
(2) By the results of field tests after construction.

The Technical Standards also state that it is envisaged that other ways of satisfying the regulations could be acceptable. For example, satisfactory field test results from an *identical* block of dwellings built elsewhere.

There is no mention of laboratory tests in terms of the Technical Standards in Scotland. Another important difference between England/Wales and Scotland is that the Scottish Regulations make no distinction between new buildings and building conversions. The same sound insulation requirements apply to both. The fact that building conversions in Scotland can achieve the same standard as new buildings may be an argument against the need to retain a distinction in terms of the Regulations for England and Wales.

The problem of using an "approved construction" or a "deemed to satisfy construction" is that although the construction may be acceptable technically, bad workmanship on site may lead to unacceptably low standards of sound insulation. This may only be discovered when the building is occupied. Attention to detail and close supervision of workmanship is therefore critically important in achieving satisfactory levels of sound insulation. Because of the workmanship problem, several district councils, certainly in Scotland, now insist on sound insulation tests on completed new buildings and building conversions. Building Control will not issue a completion certificate for the building until satisfactory field test results have been provided.

References

1 Atkins Research and Development, *Control of Noise in Ventilation Systems, a Designers Guide*, (E and FN Spon, 1972).
2 *Environmental Criteria for Design*, CIBSE Guide, Volume A, Chartered Institute of Building Services Engineers, (1986).
3 *Noise Control in Building Services*, Sound Research Laboratories Ltd, Pergamon Press, (1988).
4 Hay B "Design guide-lines for noise in landscaped offices", BSE (August 1972) 40, 105-106.
5 Beranek LL, *Acoustics*, (1954).

6 *ISO Recommendation R 3352, Assessment of noise with respect to its effect on the intelligibility of speech*, (ISO, 1974).
7 Duerden C, *Noise Abatement*, (Butterworth, 1972).
8 See n2, above.
9 *The Building Regulations Approved Document E. Resistance to the Passage of Sound*, 1992 ed, (DoE and Welsh Office, HMSO, 1992).
10 BS 2750 : 1980, *Measurement of Sound Insulation in Buildings and of Building Elements*.
11 BS 5821 : 1984, *Rating of the Sound Insulation in Buildings and of Building Elements*.
12 See n11, above.
13 See n9, above.
14 Fothergill LC, *Sound Insulation and the 1992 Edition of Approved Document E*, BRE Information Paper IP 18/92, Building Research Establishment, Watford, (October 1992).
15 *Technical Standards for Compliance with the Building Standards (Scotland) Regulations 1990, Part H : Resistance to the Transmission of Sound*, (HMSO, 1990).

Chapter 6
Environmental Noise

Introduction

This chapter investigates the main sources of environmental noise pollution, i.e. domestic noise, transportation noise, industrial and commercial noise, construction noise, entertainment noise and noise associated with leisure activities. It outlines the main health effects of environmental noise, the assessment, prediction and calculation techniques available for environmental noise, and the control of environmental noise by planning for land use close to sources of environmental noise.

Noise complaints statistics

Noise pollution from environmental noise sources has increased dramatically over the last twenty years in the developed countries and consequently complaints about excessive environmental noise have shown a significant increase. In the UK, for example, noise complaints received by the environmental health departments of the local authorities increased threefold in the ten year period from 1978 to 1988. Over the same period the number of complaints associated with domestic noise increased fivefold. Domestic noise complaints, two thirds of which are due to amplified music and barking dogs, have been shown by a recent survey [1] in England and Wales, carried out on 14 000 households between 1985 and 1987, to affect around 14% of the adult population. Eleven per cent were shown by the survey to be bothered by road traffic noise and around 7% by aircraft noise. Figure 6.1 shows the number of noise complaints received by environmental health officers (EHOs) in the period from 1971 to 1988. [2]. The figure shows that domestic noise sources have become, by far, the predominant source of noise complaints in recent years.

In 1991 local authorities in the UK received more then 100 000 complaints about noise. The increase in the number of complaints is due to the increased public awareness of entitlement to a quieter environment, and increased public knowledge of complaints procedures, as well as to an increase in environmental noise levels.

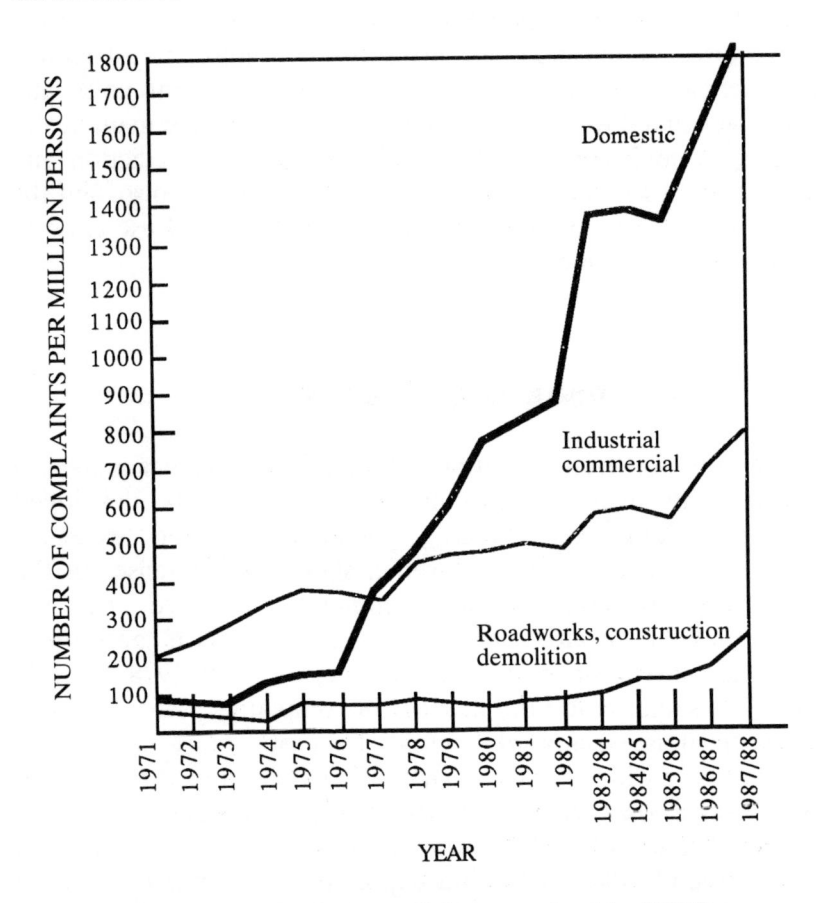

Figure 6.1 Noise complaints received by EHOs

Effects of environmental noise

The levels of noise relating to noise induced hearing loss have been discussed in Chapter 3. The levels of noise associated with environmental noise sources are unlikely to produce hearing defects (with the exception of amplified music and close proximity to construction plant and power tools) but can have secondary health effects arising from stress due to annoyance, sleep disturbance, and communication and task performance difficulties. Many studies have been carried out to investigate the effects of different types of environmental noise, *e.g.* road traffic noise, aircraft noise, rail noise. Most of the studies examine, using questionnaire survey techniques, the percentage of the people affected by the type, level and duration of the noise with respect to sleep disturbance, annoyance, speech interference, task performance difficulties etc. The problem of making definite conclusions from the surveys is that different types of noise have been assessed by different parameters, L_{Aeq}, L_{A10}, L_{DN}, and different measurement positions, some indoors and some outdoors, have been selected by different researchers. Also the type of questionnaire and the method of recording responses varies from one study to another. Some studies, *e.g.* sleep disturbance, have been carried out using a laboratory setting which, in itself, may influence the response of a subject. The one thing that can be concluded from all of the research is that the relationship between the measured noise level and the effect of that noise level is an extremely complex one that varies greatly from person to person. A large number of factors can influence an individual's opinions or feelings about noise. These include the person's general state of health, personality, social habits, social class, the type of community in which the person lives (urban or rural), the person's psychological state and any prejudice against the noise source. For example, a car owner who has difficulty in finding a parking space outside his house on a busy street may give a prejudiced answer to questions about road traffic noise on that street.

The various effects of environmental noise are interrelated, *e.g.* sleep disturbance may produce annoyance and may also lead to reduced efficiency in carrying out tasks at work the next day. For convenience, however, some of the aspects of the effects of environmental noise will be discussed under separate headings.

Annoyance

The World Health Organization (WHO) definition of annoyance is "a feeling of displeasure evoked by noise". Although it is comparatively easy to define annoyance due to noise it is an extremely difficult response to quantify mainly because of the wide variation in response from a number of subjects exposed to the same noise source. Work by Shultz in America [3] related annoyance due to environmental noise to the parameter day–night equivalent sound level, L_{DN} (see Chapter 4), using some 453 sites and 11 surveys. The results of the research are shown in Figure 6.2 Although it is possible to produce a best-fit

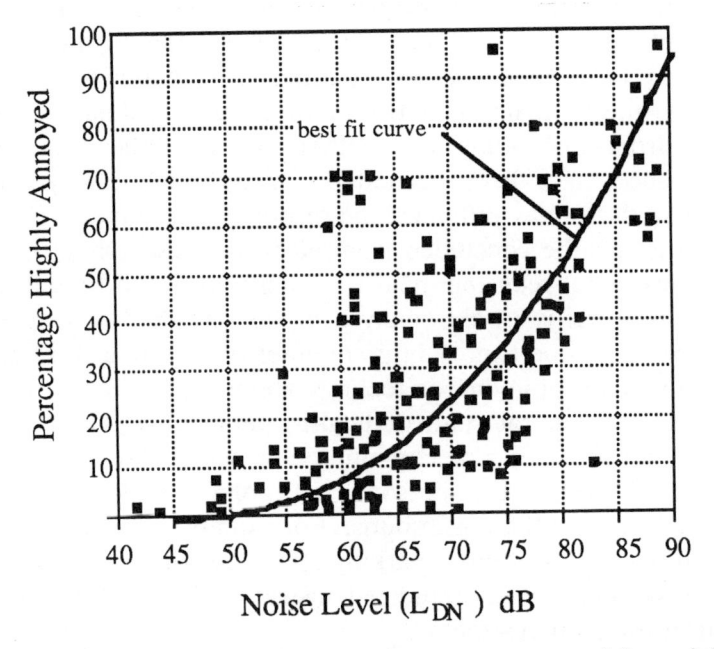

Figure 6.2 Relationship between annoyance and day–night equivalent noise level

curve through the data the important point illustrated by the figure is the vast scatter of results around the curve.

By using the curve the relationship between the percentage of the people likely to be highly annoyed and a given L_{DN} value is as follows:

$$\% HA = 0.8553\ L_{DN} - 0.0401\ L_{DN}^2 + 0.00047\ L_{DN}^3$$

where %HA is the percentage of people highly annoyed and L_{DN} is the day–night equivalent sound level (dB(A)).

Although best-fit curves with specific equations can be drawn up relating annoyance to a given noise parameter, their usefulness must be questioned in the light of the scatter of results about the curve. From the data in Figure 6.2 an L_{DN} level of 75 dB(A) should give a value of about 35% of the population highly annoyed, according to the curve. The actual range of values of percentage of people highly annoyed is from under 10% to over 90% for this L_{DN} value! Even when research relating annoyance to a single type of noise source, *e.g.* road traffic noise, is carried out there is still a considerable variation of responses and a wide scatter of results about any best-fit line or curve. This can be seen in Figure 6.3 which shows the results of a study [4] investigating the relationship between annoyance and road traffic noise using $L_{Aeq,24hour}$ as the noise parameter.

The results of numerous studies show that it is difficult to generalize on the scale of annoyance likely to be generated by a particular noise parameter, but it is useful to note that in terms of transportation noise very few people are annoyed at levels below L_{Aeq} 45 dB(A). As the outdoor noise level rises above L_{Aeq} 60 dB(A) the proportion of people annoyed increases sharply and at L_{Aeq} 65 dB(A) approximately 25% of the population will be "highly annoyed" [5].

The characteristics of the noise source have an important bearing on the relationship between annoyance and noise level. In terms of neighbourhood noise, intrusive music and barking dogs may cause annoyance at comparatively low noise levels because the type of noise attracts attention more so than, say, transportation noise at the same level.

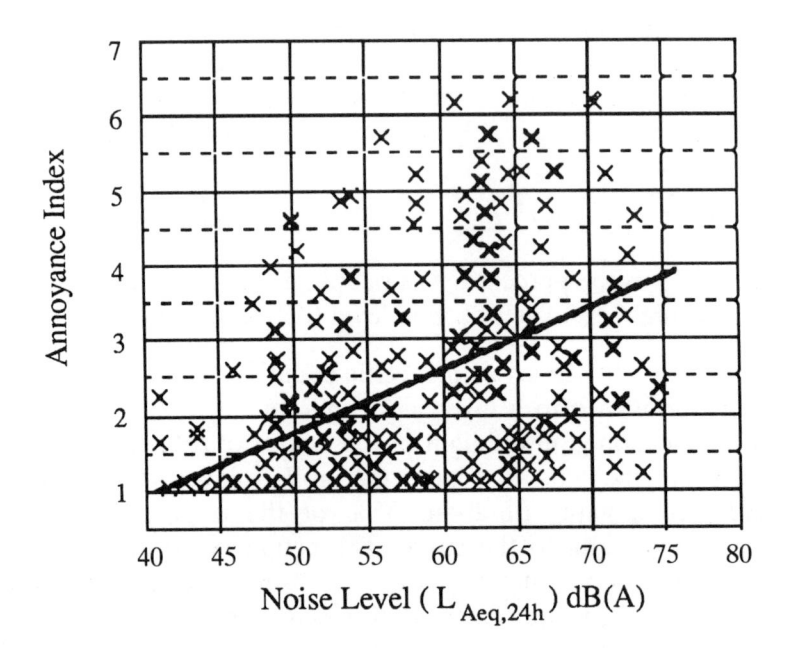

Figure 6.3 Relationship between noise level and annoyance for road traffic noise

Within the field of transportation noise, there is a different reaction of annoyance to road traffic noise, rail traffic noise and aircraft noise even when all have similar noise levels measured by the same parameter. Hall *et al* [6] showed in a very controlled survey of people living around Toronto International Airport that, for the same L_{DN} level, more people were annoyed by aircraft noise than by road traffic noise. This is shown in Figure 6.4.

An important study carried out by Fields and Walker [7] concluded that at high noise levels people in the UK report less annoyance from rail traffic noise than from either road traffic or aircraft noise of the same measured outdoor noise level. Fields and Walker found it difficult to quantify how much less annoying rail noise was, but also concluded from their work that, for railway noise, the degree of annoyance increased less rapidly with increase in noise level than for either road traffic or aircraft noise.

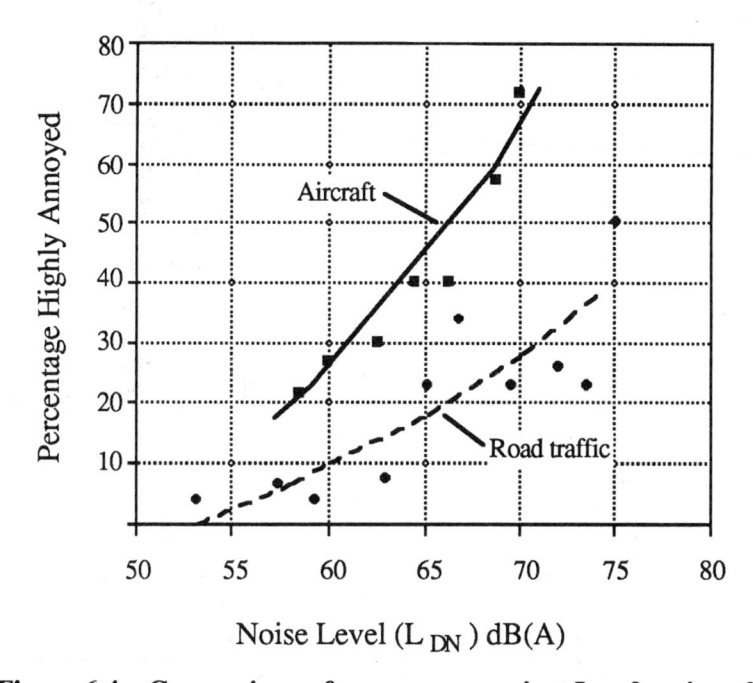

Figure 6.4 Comparison of annoyance against L_{DN} for aircraft and road traffic noise

Many types of industrial noise include tonal and/or impulsive characteristics and consequently tend to produce annoyance levels greater than would be indicated by using an energy based parameter such as $L_{Aeq,T}$. The traditional way of accommodating impulsive and/or tonal characteristics has been to add on a penalty value to the measured dB(A) noise level. The original 1967 (as amended 1975) and the new, 1990, BS 4142 *Method for Rating Industrial Noise Affecting Mixed Residential and Industrial Areas* [8] advocate the addition of a 5 dB(A) penalty to the measured noise level if the industrial noise contains distinguishable tonal and/or impulsive components. The 5 dB(A) penalty is highly empirical and may be inadequate for many types of industrial noise. Current and recent research has attempted to quantify, more accurately, the annoyance aspects of tonal and impulsive noise. [9].

Although the current simple 5 dB(A) penalty may be criticized for its empirical nature, it must be remembered that most environmental noise complaints are investigated by EHOs using, at best, simple integrating sound level meters, and hence complex formulae for quantifying tonal and impulsive characteristics may be of limited practical use in the overall estimation of the effects of industrial noise on the community.

Sleep disturbance

Disturbance to sleep is one of the most common forms of annoyance due to noise and of all of the forms of annoyance is probably the least tolerated. Consequently there has been a great deal of research carried out over the past 20 years into the influence of noise on sleep. Sleep itself is a very complex subject. Sleep is not a continuum but consists of at least six separate stages which can be classified as ranging from REM (rapid eye movement) sleep through deep sleep (delta sleep) to light sleep prior to wakefulness. The same noise level can have different effects of sleep disturbance depending on a subject's stage of sleep when exposed to the noise, *e.g.* a noise which may prevent someone from falling asleep, or which may wake someone from REM sleep, may not be disturbing during deep sleep. Much of the research which has taken place has therefore concentrated on the influence of noise on particular stages of sleep. The physiological effects are generally measured using three response parameters :

(1) Electroencephalographic (EEG) activity.
(2) Electromyographic (EMG) or chin muscle activity.
(3) Oculo-motor (EOG) activity measuring electrical potentials in the eye.

Other parameters such as blood pressure, heart and breathing rates, and sweat gland excretion can be measured.

Many studies investigating noise and sleep disturbance have been carried out in a laboratory environment which inevitably alters an individual's reactions. Care must be taken to allow a subject to become accustomed to sleeping in the new surroundings before any measurements are taken. This may take several nights. Surveys carried out by questionnaires are, like all psycho-social surveys, highly subjective and lead to a wide range of responses to the same noise exposure. Other problems which are encountered in research into noise and sleep disturbance are:

(1) Sleep disturbance is largely influenced by the age of the subjects, *e.g.* sensitvity to sleep disturbance is lower in children than in adults and the elderly tend to be disturbed to the highest degree.
(2) Many people have sleeping difficulties unrelated to noise. Langdon and Buller [10] found in a survey of sleep disturbance due to road traffic noise in Greater London that about 20% of people suffered from sleep disturbance for reasons other than noise. The main reasons were related to health, anxiety, discomfort and insomnia.
(3) Physiological habituation, *i.e.* people become adapted to sleeping with a certain degree or type of noise. It is generally accepted, however, that little or no adaptation occurs for internal noise levels above 60 dB(A).

Like other forms of noise annoyance, sleep disturbance is influenced largely by the nature of the noise source as well as the noise level. In terms of freely flowing road traffic the percentage of people annoyed and disturbed at night has a fairly linear relationship with the L_{Aeq} value averaged over the time period of 22.00 to 06.00 [11]. This is shown in Figure 6.5 which is based on German research.

Langdon and Buller's research [12] into sleep disturbance and night-time road traffic noise levels was a very comprehensive study worthy of reading in its entirety. They used the night time (22.00 to 06.00) L_{A10} as the noise parameter for a total sample of 2933 residents in Greater London. The summary of percentage undisturbed and percentage disturbed against night-time L_{A10} is illustrated in Figure 6.6.

Langdon and Buller concluded that there was a good correlation between measured noise level and the number of disturbances attributed to noise in the range of L_{A10} values of from 52 dB(A) to 79 dB(A) encountered in the survey.

Disturbance to sleep is often event dominated, *e.g.* aircraft

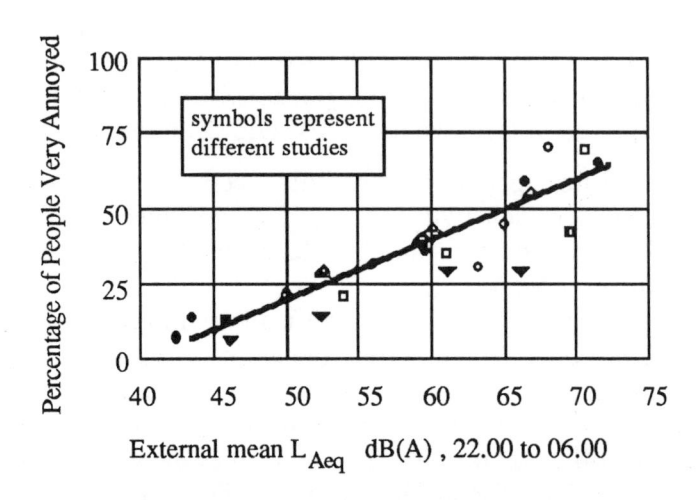

Figure 6.5 Summary of German studies of night annoyance and disturbance due to road traffic noise

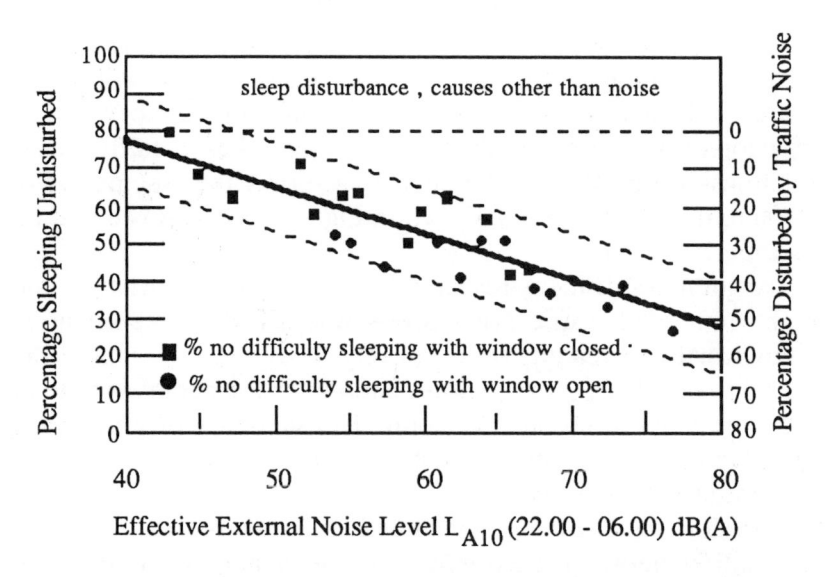

Figure 6.6 Summary of Langdon and Bullers' study of sleep disturbance with road traffic noise (regression line and 95% confidence limits)

noise, where the amount of disturbance is a function of the frequency of noisy events, *i.e.* how often the event occurs, as well as the noise level of the event. In such cases it has been suggested that the peak noise level of the event and even the rise time of the noise may be useful indicators of the disturbance due to the noise. Vernet [13] in a study of train noise and sleep disturbance concluded that for levels of L_{Aeq} 70 dB(A) the total number of individual sleep disturbances was three times greater for lorries than for trains. Vernet showed that there were no awakenings for indoor train peak noise levels of less than 50 dB(A). Griefahn [14] studied the effects of sleep disturbance in relation to the time interval between successive noise events. He found there was a maximum probability of an EEG effect when the time interval between noise events was 40 minutes. This shows that it may be less disturbing to group aircraft movements together, safety considerations allowing, than to spread the movements out over roughly 40 minute intervals. In terms of road traffic noise it has been demonstrated [15] that an average passing frequency of 1.8 vehicles per minute gives proportionally a greater EEG reaction than a higher vehicle passing frequency of 4.3 vehicles per minute.

The results of a study carried out by the Civil Aviation Authority into aircraft noise and sleep disturbance are currently being analysed. A description of the approach to the study and the experimental work has recently been published. [16].

Because of the variables in research studies, the methodology and parameters used, it is difficult to state with any degree of authority that a particular noise level will produce a specific reaction in terms of sleep disturbance. Various international organizations have, however, made recommendations about noise levels likely to be acceptable in terms of the prevention of sleep disturbance. Some examples are:

(1) The World Health Organization (WHO) recommends an internal noise level of about 35 dB(A) at night. [17]
(2) the EC considers that an internal L_{Aeq} of 30–35 dB(A) or below and peaks not exceeding 45 dB(A) do not affect sleep. [18].

(3) The Organization for Economic Cooperation and Development (OECD) recommends the adoption of the following L_{Aeq} levels in member countries : 35 dB(A) during the period of getting to sleep; 45 dB(A) during periods of light sleep ; 50 dB(A) during periods of deep sleep. [19].

It is interesting to note that as far back as 1963 the Wilson Report [20] made the recommendations shown in Table 6.1 for the maximum acceptable values of L_{A10} indoors.

Table 6.2 shows the summary of research into sleep disturbance and noise levels for transportation noise [21].

Minimum EEG and physiological responses are likely to be induced if noise levels can be kept to or below the table values.

Table 6.1

Situation	Day	Night
Country areas	40 dB(A)	30 dB(A)
Suburban areas	45 dB(A)	35 dB(A)
Busy urban areas	50 dB(A)	35 dB(A)

Table 6.2

Noise source	L_{Aeq} (dB(A))	Peak noise level (dB(A))
Continuous road traffic	35	50
Aircraft	40	52–55
Trains	40	50–55

Task performance and communication

The influence of internal noise levels on speech communication has been discussed in Chapter 5. Many laboratory studies have been carried out to assess the influence of noise on task performance. From the studies it can be concluded that there is no simple, consistent relationship between noise level and the various descriptors which have been used to assess task performance. Generally it is accepted that noise has an influence on an individual's state of arousal and as a consequence will affect a person's ability to carry out tasks. Noise is accepted to influence task performance in a number of ways :

(1) Noise may stimulate people, *e.g.* noise may increase a person's state of arousal and improve concentration and performance in relation to simple repetitive tasks.
(2) Noise, particularly loud, monotonous ambient noise, may decrease arousal and diminish task proficiency.
(3) Loud noise is inherently annoying and distracting.
(4) Loud noise interferes with the physiological mechanisms which are essential for the performance of complex or intellectual tasks.

If people have optimal states of arousal for performing particular tasks, the influence of noise on improving or degrading task performance will depend largely on that person's pre-existing state of arousal and the effect of noise on that state.

In terms of noise level and safety, it has been shown that fewer accidents occur when noise levels are reduced [22]. It has also been illustrated in American research [23] that children whose classroom looked out on to noisy railway lines performed less well in reading tests than children in the same school whose classrooms were on the quiet side of the school. Some studies have also concluded that levels of aggression are increased by noisy environments and that people who work in noisy industries are more likely to have domestic disputes than workers in quieter environments.

Studies into noise and task performance have, unfortunately, lacked consistency of findings and hence controversy has arisen regarding the study methods, paricularly with regard to the methods of assessing task performance. The methods vary from questionnaires through observations to measurement of physiological changes, *e.g.* cardiovascular and other autonomic changes. New theories and new parameters are currently being considered and this may eventually result in more definite conclusions about noise and task performance.

Transportation noise

It is not the intention of this publication to investigate the detailed engineering aspects of the noise producing mechanisms relating to the major forms of transportation, *i.e* road traffic, aircraft and railways, nor is it the purpose of this publication to examine the more engineering and technology based aspects of noise control such as improved engine design. Readers wishing a comprehensive treatment of all aspects of transportation noise are advised to consult the *Transportation Noise Reference Book* [24]. This publication seeks only to highlight the broader concepts of noise production, noise prediction and noise control with reference to the major forms of transportation.

Road traffic noise

In terms of transportation noise, there is no doubt that road traffic noise affects the greatest number of people and has, in fact, been shown to be the major contributor to dissatisfaction in terms of community noise. It is known that about 15% of the people in OECD countries (*i.e.* more than 120 million people) are currently exposed to road traffic noise levels which are judged by most authorities to be unacceptably high [25]. Road traffic has increased enormously over the last twenty years and with the increase in vehicle numbers has come increased traffic congestion and increased traffic noise.

The main sources of road traffic noise are the power and transmission units, *i.e.* engine and gearbox, exhaust noise and tyre noise. In general terms, heavy vehicles, *e.g.* lorries and buses, produce higher noise levels than do lighter vehicles such as cars and light vans ("heavy vehicles" are defined as vehicles with an unladen weight in excess of 1525 kg). The comparison of typical pass-by spectra for heavy and light vehicles is shown in Figure 6.7. The spectra are similar in shape with most of the noise occurring in the lower frequencies, with peaks around 125 Hz.

At low speeds, particularly in congested traffic, noise from the engine, gearbox, exhaust and brakes tend to dominate. As the traffic speed increases, tyre noise becomes more important and at high speeds, especially on wet roads, will become the major source of noise. Wet roads can increase traffic noise by up to 10 dB(A) depending on the nature of the road surface though the typical increase is around 3 to 4 dB(A). At high speeds aerodynamic noise is also important. The basic relationship between traffic speed and noise is shown on Figure 6.8. Very slow-moving traffic is noisy with many instances of gear changes and revving of engines. The noise level drops as the traffic speed picks up and the traffic becomes freely flowing, usually somewhere around 30 to 35 km/h. After this point the traffic noise level increases with increase in speed. The actual relationship between traffic noise and speed, and the speed at which traffic becomes freely flowing, depends on the percentage of heavy vehicles in the traffic flow.

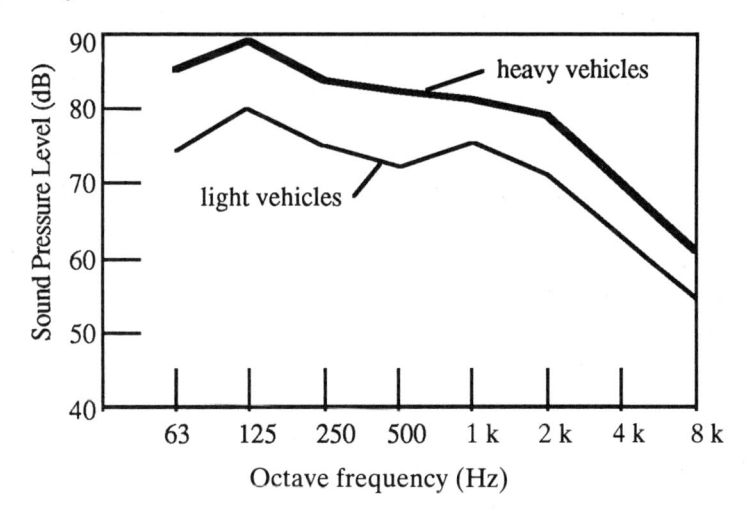

Figure 6.7 Typical pass-by noise spectra for freely moving vehicles

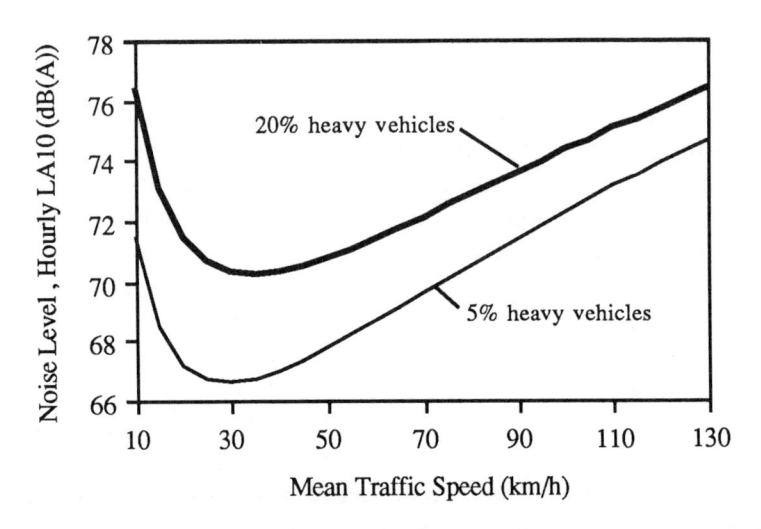

Figure 6.8 Noise level at 10m distance versus speed for a traffic flow of 500 vehicles/hour

The emission of noise from individual new vehicles is controlled by international agreements and incorporated in UK regulations. In 1964 the International Standards Organization (ISO) established ISO R 362 [26] as a method of measuring the noise emission from vehicles. Basically the test method attempts to simulate a driving condition similar to the most noisy type of urban driving. The test involves an acceleration with a "wide open throttle" over a 20 m zone from an approach speed, usually 50 km/h, and in second gear. A-weighted sound pressure level measurements are made with the microphone positioned 7.5 m to the side of the centre line of the track. The test method was adopted by most Western European countries and in the UK it became the basis of BS 3425 : 1966 [27]. Refinements to the test procedure and the test site were made under Council Directive 81/334/EEC [28]. Over the years the EC has been able to introduce progressively more stringent limitations to the noise emission levels of new vehicles. For example, in 1969 the permissible level for cars was 84 dB(A) and the permissible level for heavy lorries was 92 dB(A). The current limits are 77 dB(A) for cars and 84 dB(A) for heavy lorries [29]. This shows a 7 dB(A) reduction for cars and an 8 dB(A) reduction for lorries. Further significant reductions in power unit noise have recently been accepted by the EC. The reductions are planned to come into effect by the mid-1990s. Projects for quiet vehicle development, such as the Transport Road Research Laboratory (TRRL) Quiet Heavy Vehicle Project [30], have shown that quiet vehicles are technically feasible at realistic costs. The TRRL project has shown that it would be possible to produce heavy goods vehicles which are 5 dB(A) below current legislative noise emission limits.

In the past few years there have been particular problems related to noise from motorcycles fitted with non-standard or defective silencers and legislation is now in place which makes it illegal to sell a non-standard motorcycle silencer or exhaust. Existing vehicles (including motorcycles), as opposed to new vehicles, are simply required not to produce excessive noise. Noise emission is not part of the MOT test on existing vehicles. The problem of defective silencers is not likely to be resolved until a simple roadside vehicle noise test procedure is developed and introduced.

The test procedure used for new vehicles can not be carried out at the roadside due to the specification of the test site which must be free from reflecting objects, such as buildings, bridges, rocks and fences, within a 50 m radius of the middle of the 20 m long test stretch.

Much research is currently being carried out into the reduction of noise produced by the road/tyre interaction. Minimum noise is produced from smooth tyres on untextured roads but, unfortunately, this combination is the least desirable from the point of view of road safety. It would appear that the nature of the road surface has a larger influence on noise production than the tread pattern of tyres, and hence there are greater opportunities for reducing noise by concentrating on the re-design of road surfaces rather than on the re-design of tyre treads. Road surfaces which have an open or porous surface have been found to produce lower noise levels than conventional, non-porous, bituminous road surfaces. Porous surfaces also have the advantage of removing surface water quickly, thereby helping to reduce the incidence of skidding accidents, the tendency for ice formation on roads, and the amount of spray generated by traffic in wet weather.

Unfortunately, the benefits of reduced noise from individual vehicles and improved road surface design may be substantially reduced by the rapid growth in the number of vehicles using the roads. In the near future it is likely that the increase in noise due to increased traffic flows will balance the improvements in noise reduction.

In the UK many people living in houses adjacent to busy main roads are subject to traffic noise levels which would be deemed excessive. Unfortunately, if the noise level is due to a road on which the traffic flow has increased solely due to the natural, exponential growth of traffic, the residents in such houses have no entitlement to any compensation in terms of grants for improved sound insulation of the dwelling. If, however, the increase in noise is due to a new road, or a significantly altered, improved, or re-aligned road, then legislation provides powers for the road authority to offer sound insulation treatment to affected properties. The upgrading of the sound insulation normally involves the provision of acoustic double glazing and acoustically treated ventilation units. In the UK the treatment is carried out under the Land Compensation Act 1973. The conditions for entitlement are set out in the Noise Insulation Regulations 1973, modified in 1975 and 1988. Three conditions have got to be tested to assess entitlement when using the maximum traffic flow figures expected between 06.00 and 24.00 hours on a normal working day within a period of 15 years after opening the new or improved road to traffic.

(1) The $L_{A10,\ 18\ hour}$ value (relevant noise level), *i.e.* the arithmetic average of the hourly L_{A10} values in the period 06.00 to 24.00 hours (see Chapter 4) must not be less than 68 dB(A).
(2) The relevant noise level is at least 1 dB(A) more than the prevailing noise level, *i.e.* the total traffic noise level existing before the works to construct or improve the road were begun.
(3) The contribution to the increase in the relevant noise level from the new or altered road must be at least 1 dB(A).

The method used for calculating the traffic noise levels is given in *Calculation of Road Traffic Noise* (CRTN) [31] produced by the Department of Transport. The CRTN details the procedures for both the prediction of and measurement of road traffic noise. It is a widely used document which, as well as being the standard for calculating entitlement, is the basis for assessing the effect of traffic noise on properties in the Department of Transport's *Manual of Environmental Appraisal* (MEA) [32] and the Scottish Office's *Scottish Traffic and Environmental Appraisal Manual* (STEAM) [33]. The CRTN predicts $L_{A10,\ 18\ hour}$ values for reception points 1m in front of windows in relevant façades of buildings using a series of graphs and charts. The calculation consists of five stages:

(1) Dividing the road scheme into a number of segments such that the variation of noise within a segment is small, *i.e.* not more than 2 dB(A).
(2) Calculating the noise level at a reference distance of 10 m away from the nearside carriageway for each segment. This noise level depends on the traffic flow, the mean traffic speed, the composition of the traffic (percentage of heavy vehicles), the type of road surface and the gradient of the road.
(3) Assessing for each segment the noise level at the reception point taking into account the attenuation (noise reduction) between the 10 m reference distance and the reception point. This attenuation depends on the height and distance between the 10 m reference distance and the reception point, the ground absorption, the provision of noise barriers between the source and reception points, and any other screening between the source line and the reception point.
(4) Correcting the noise level at the reception point to take into account site layout features including reflections from buildings and façades, and the size of the source segment.
(5) Combining the contributions from all of the segments to produce the predicted noise level at the reception point for the whole road scheme.

It is important to appreciate that the accuracy of the noise prediction process is governed by the accuracy of the data available, *e.g.* predicted traffic flows for a period 15 years on, and the predicted percentage of heavy vehicles.

If the highway authority decides that it is inappropriate to use the prediction method, the CRTN sets out measurement methods for assessing future traffic noise levels. The CRTN describes a full measurement method for obtaining the hourly L_{A10} values for each hour in the period 06.00 to 24.00 hours and then averaging the values arithmetically to obtain the $L_{A10,\ 18\ hour}$ value. It also details a shortened measurement procedure whereby hourly L_{A10} values are measured for each hour over any 3 consecutive hours between 10.00 and 17.00 hours. The hourly L_{A10} values are then averaged arithmetically to give the $L_{A10,\ 3\ hour}$ value. The $L_{A10,\ 18\ hour}$ value can then be calculated from the relationship:

$$L_{A10,\ 18\ hour} = L_{A10,\ 3\ hour} - 1\ dB(A)$$

The limitations of the shortened method are specified in the CRTN.

From the measured existing levels, the future levels can be predicted provided data is available on the future traffic flow, the future traffic speed and the future percentage of heavy vehicles.

The qualifying $L_{A10,\ 18\ hour}$ value of 68 dB(A) has been in use since 1973. Social attitudes to noise have changed since then and research is needed to ascertain whether the current 68 dB(A) value is still appropriate. There is a strong body of opinion which suggests that the 68 dB(A) level is too high, particularly when considering rural areas crossed by motorways and busy trunk roads.

In terms of road traffic, noise exposure can be reduced by :

(1) Improved vehicle design.
(2) Improved road design, *i.e.* road surface, road alignment, the use of cuttings where the sides of the cut act as a screen to protect sensitve areas.
(3) The provision of noise barriers, screens and earth embankments between the source and reception points.

The effectiveness of any barrier is proportional to the path difference (δ) created between sound travelling over the barrier and sound travelling directly from the source to the reception point. This is shown in Figure 6.9. The greater the

path difference, the more effective the barrier.
(4) Traffic management schemes, *e.g.* banning lorries from roads in quiet areas, the provision of by-pass roads.
(5) Land use planning, *e.g.* using land beside busy roads for non-residential and non-noise sensitive developments such as industrial and commercial buildings, screening residential buildings behind non-noise sensitive development.
(6) Improved sound insulation of buildings close to busy roads.

Path Difference, $\delta = (SB + BR) - SR$

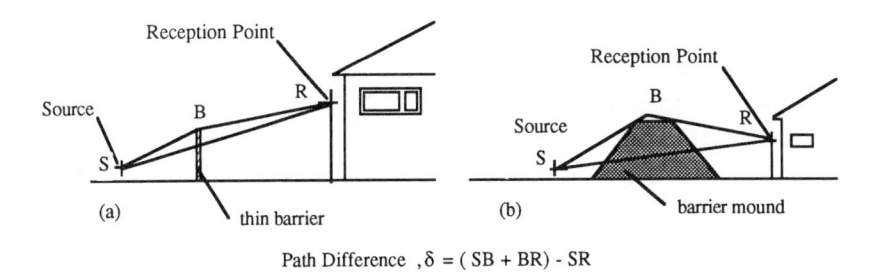

Figure 6.9   Path difference for obstructed sound propagation

Aircraft noise

A survey of 14 000 households published in 1990 [34] and carried out between 1985 and 1987 showed that in the UK some 7% of people are bothered by aircraft noise in comparison to 11% bothered by road traffic noise. Although the number of people bothered by aircraft noise is smaller, people living close to airports are exposed to much higher noise levels than the traffic noise levels to which people living beside busy roads are exposed. It is also accepted that, even at the same noise level, people find aircraft noise, particularly jet-aircraft noise, more annoying than road traffic noise. This is because of the fact that much more of the frequency content of aircraft noise is in the range of frequencies to which the ear is most sensitive. A comparison between the percentage of people annoyed by aircraft and road traffic noise, at the same noise level, is shown in

Figure 6.4. For people living close to airports, the nature and level of aircraft noise is likely to be distracting, and is likely to interfere with speech communication during an aircraft movement, *i.e.* take-off or landing. Noise levels around airports are determined by the type of individual aircraft using the airport as well as the frequency of aircraft movements.

Noise levels from individual aircraft are governed by the noise certification requirements for civil aircraft given in the Federal Aviation Regulations (FAR) Part 36 (USA) [35], and Convention on International Civil Aviation (ICAO) Annex 16 [36]. The UK noise regulations, British Civil Airworthiness Requirements (BCAR) Section N [37], are generally accepted as being equivalent to ICAO Annex 16. Since 1977 more demanding noise certification requirements, applicable to new aircraft, have been in force. Before 1977 the FAR regulations in the USA differed from the ICAO regulations. However, the latest requirements are basically the same and are referred to as *Stage 3* noise requirements in the USA and *Chapter 3* requirements within the ICAO. The parameter used to assess aircraft noise in terms of noise certification is the *effective perceived noise level* (EPNL) which is measured in EPN dB. This metric depends on :

(1) The annoyance perceived by the ear.
(2) The tonal content of the flyover noise spectrum.
(3) The time during which the aircraft noise remains within 10 dB of the peak noise at the measurement position.

The effective perceived noise level is defined by:

$$\text{EPNL} = L_{\text{EPN}} = 10 \log_{10} \left[\frac{1}{10} \int_{t1}^{t2} 10^{\text{PNLT}/10} \, dt \right] \text{ EPN dB}$$

where t_1 and t_2 are the times between which the noise level is within 10 dB of the peak and PNLT is the tone-corrected perceived noise level.

The idea of normalizing to 10 seconds is to penalize aircraft that make a lot of noise for a comparatively long time period. Ten seconds is thought to be a reasonable time for a typical fly-

Environmental Noise 113

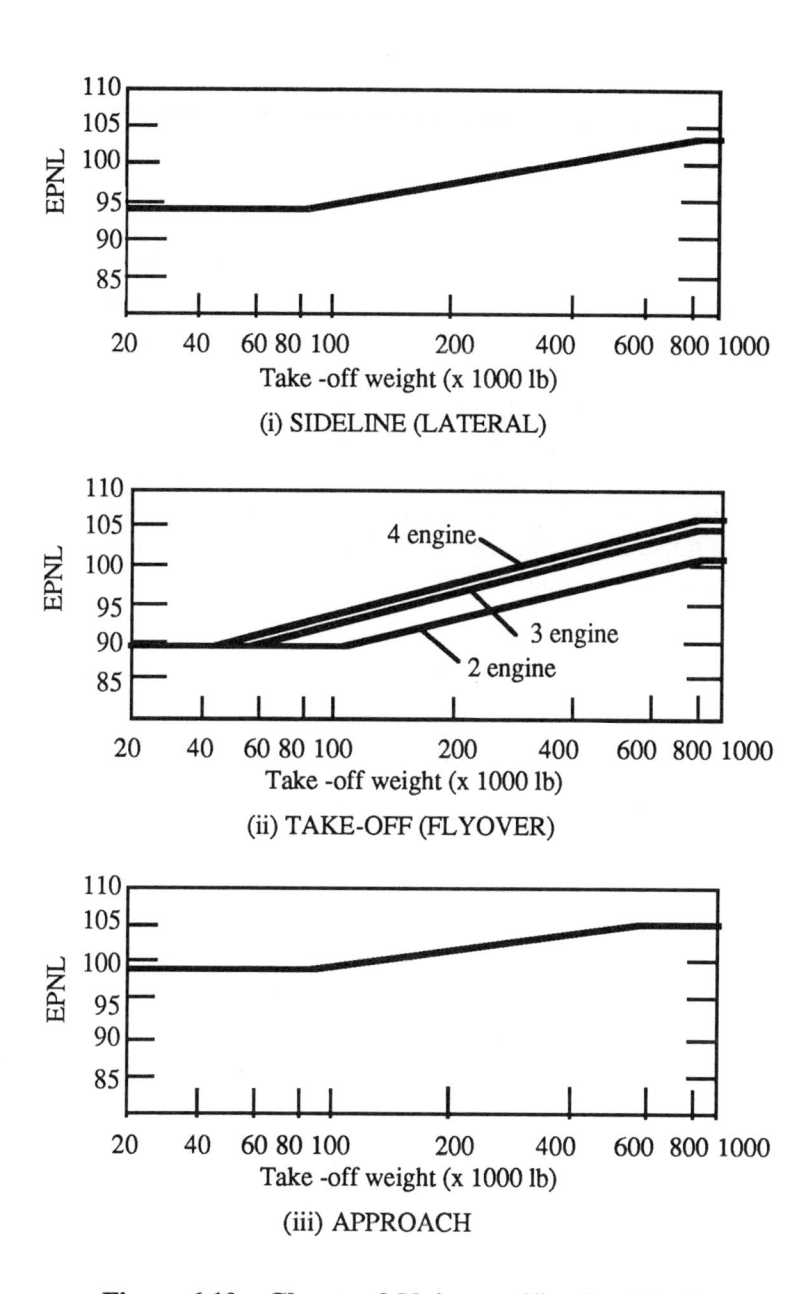

Figure 6.10 Chapter 3 Noise certification Limits

(i) SIDELINE (LATERAL)

(ii) TAKE-OFF (FLYOVER)

(iii) APPROACH

past. The parameter can be thought of as follows:

EPNL = peak perceived noise level (PN dB) + tonal correction + duration correction

The EPNL value is measured for (i) sideline noise during take-off, (ii) take-off noise and (iii) approach noise. The Chapter 3 requirements for each of the above are shown in Figure 6.10.

The noise limits required to be met by individual aircraft are based on maximum certificated take-off weights and, in the case of take-off noise, the number of engines. Ideally the noise levels produced by new aircraft should be at or below the appropriate curve values. However, in practice a noise limit can be exceeded by up to 2 EPN dB at any point, with a total exceedance of 3 EPN dB, provided the exceedances are offset by corresponding reductions at other points. The measurement positions for assessing noise levels are shown in Figure 6.11. The measurement positions can be summarized as follows :

Sideline: The peak noise received at a point along a line parallel to and 450 m from the extended runway centre.

Take-off: The noise received at a point directly beneath the aircraft take-off flight path and positioned 6.5 km from the point of brake release.

Approach: the noise received at a point directly beneath a 3 degree glideslope and positioned 2000 m from the runway threshold.

Measurement of aircraft noise for certification purposes is a very sophisticated and specialized process which can only be carried out under specified test environments. The tests are only valid within a range of meteorological conditions of wind velocity, relative humidity, sound attenuation rates, and with no precipitation. Topographical requirements demand flat terrain with no excessive sound absorbing characteristics such as tall grass, woodland or shrubs. There should be no obstructions such as buildings and earth banks between the aircraft and the microphone position. Environmental factors demand the exclusion of excessive ambient noise from from roads,

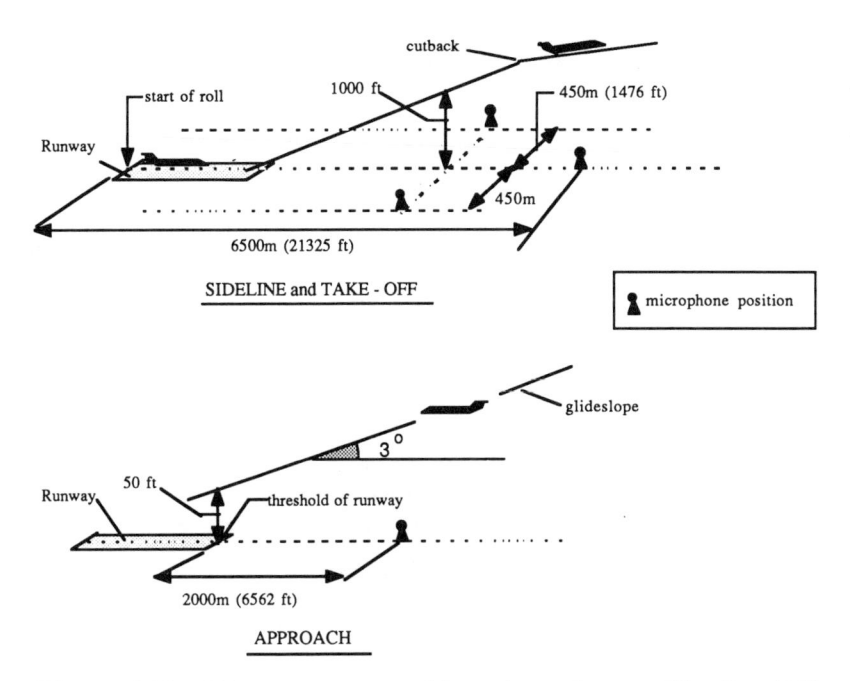

Figure 6.11 Measurement positions for noise certification [38]

agricultural machinery, low flying test aircraft etc.

Chapter 1 aircraft, which are the noisiest group, have been banned in UK airports since 1988 unless they have had noise reduction treatment to the engines (hush-kitted) to bring them into the less noisy Chapter 2 category. Manufacturers of new civil aircraft must meet the Chapter 3 requirements. Many Chapter 2 aircraft are still in use, but the long-term intention is to phase them out and replace them with new Chapter 3 aircraft. Fleet replacement is an ongoing process which is not based on noise alone, but also on fuel-efficiency, passenger capacity and operating cost.

Jet aircraft engines are very complex but consist basically of a fan, compressors, a combustion source and turbines. Noise is produced by the turbomachinery, the fan and compressors, the engine core, and the exhaust jets. Improved engine technology has given rise to significant reductions in engine noise over recent years. It is beyond the scope of this book to examine such

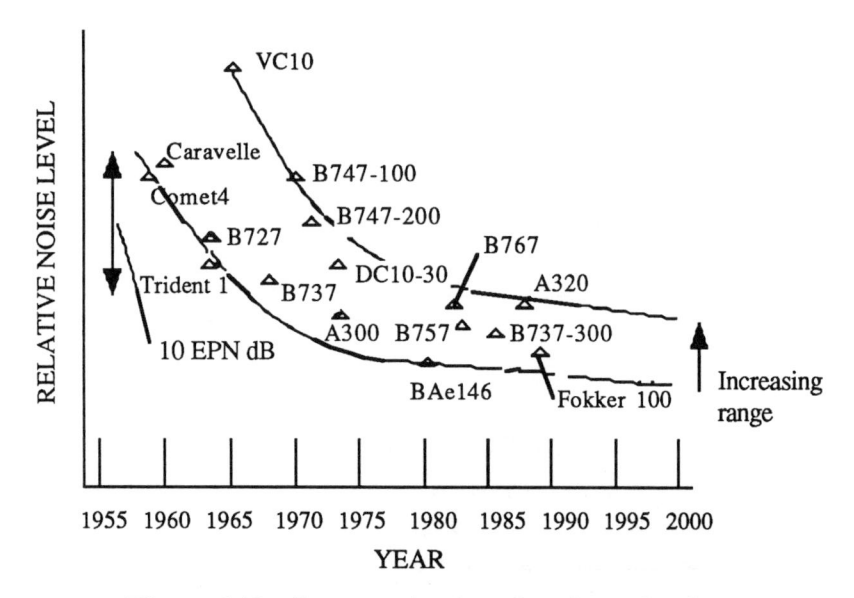

Figure 6.12 Progress in aircraft noise reduction

technology, but it can be stated that reductions in engine noise are due to improved fan design, improved efficiency, giving high thrust at lower jet velocities, the design of jet nozzles, the use of scooped inlets which throw noise upwards away from the ground, and by using absorbent liners and plugs within the engine. The downward trend in aircraft noise is shown in Figure 6.12. [39].

Noise from propeller aircraft tends to be lower than noise from jet aircraft but contains tonal characteristics which are annoying. The tones produced are due to harmonics of the propeller blade passing frequency.

The shape of the curve of the downward trend in aircraft noise shows that large reductions have been made, particularly in the period from about 1960 to 1980, but the fact that the curve is levelling off towards the present time indicates that a stage is being reached where the scope for further noise reduction, by improved engine design technology, is decreasing. Up to now improved fuel efficiency and noise reduction have been achieved simultaneously with the use of ultra-high bypass ratio engines (UHBPR). Super-fuel-efficient engine designs for the future do not appear to offer much opportunity for further noise reduction. With the demand for commercial air travel increasing at the forecast rate of 5 to 6% per annum, any further noise reductions produced by better engine technology are likely to be offset by the increased volume of aircraft using airports. Much care will therefore have to be taken with long term planning for land use around airports. Schemes to reduce the number of residential, hospital and school buildings in areas of high noise exposure will have to be implemented.

From the early 1960s until 1990 the impact of aircraft noise on people living near airports was assessed by a parameter termed the *noise and number index* (NNI). The NNI recognized that annoyance due to aircraft noise was a function of the peak noise levels produced during an aircraft movement, *i.e.* a landing or take-off, and the number of movements in a specified period of time. NNI was defined by:

$$\text{NNI} = L_{\text{APN}} + 15 \log_{10} N - 80$$

where L_{APN} is the average peak noise level of aircraft movements in perceived noise units, PNdB and N is the number of movements in the time period under consideration.

The suggestion was that noise levels of less than 80 PNdB were not significant in terms of annoyance and hence there was an 80 PNdB cut-off point for assessment purposes. From a knowledge of the types of aircraft using the airport, the typical noise "footprint" for individual aircraft, the number of flights and the operational use of runways, computer models were used to plot NNI contours around airports, generally using a 5 NNI contour interval. Typical NNI contours are shown in Figure 6.13. An NNI value of 35 was generally considered to represent the onset of annoyance and people living in an area between the NNI 35 contour and the airport represented the population deemed to be annoyed by aircraft noise. In terms of planning for land use around airports, *Planning and Noise Circular 10/73* [40] recommended NNI values above which certain types of new development should not be allowed. For example, for NNI 60 or above, planning permission should be refused for new dwellings, schools and hospitals. For NNI 50 to 59, no major new residential development should be allowed. Permission for new schools was undesirable at this level, but if a replacement school was necessary, planning permission could be granted provided the sound insulation of the school was sufficiently high (DES Guidelines). For NNI 50 to 59, new hospitals were undesirable, but office development would be permitted. For NNI, 40 to 49, no major new residential developments should be permitted, but schools and hospitals would be permitted if the appropriate standard of sound insulation was incorporated in the design. For NNI 35 to 39, planning permission would not be refused for any type of new development on noise grounds alone.

Most commercial airports in the UK operate noise insulation schemes for people living in residential areas which come within the NNI 50 contour, *i.e.* people living with an NNI level of 50 or above are normally eligible for a grant to upgrade the sound insulation of their dwellings.

NNI values are computed for noise exposure based on an average summer day between mid-June and mid-September. The contours have been updated annually on data describing noise levels, types of aircraft, height profiles and flight routings. It is

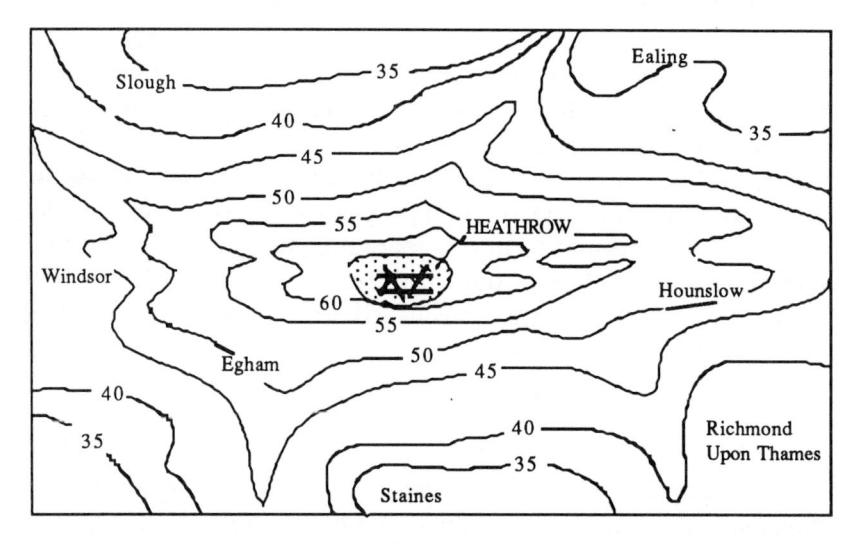

Figure 6.13   Approximate NNI contours for Heathrow airport around 1970

interesting to note that even though air traffic volume has increased, the use of improved, quieter aircraft, has resulted in the area within the NNI 35 contour (the area within which people are generally annoyed by aircraft noise) decreasing from 826 km^2 to 315 km^2, around Heathrow airport in the period from 1974 to 1989 [41]. This represents a reduction in the number of people living within the NNI 35 contour from 2 million in 1974 to about a quarter of that, *i.e.* 500 000, in 1989. This is an impressive reduction considering that the number of aircraft movements increased by 17% in the same period and the number of passengers carried increased by 55%. The fact that the number of passengers carried has increased by more than three times the number of aircraft movements in the 15 year period reflects the increased use of larger aircraft.

In recent years the use of NNI to describe annoyance due to aircraft noise has been subject to some criticism because of possible inaccuracies in the method of combining noise and number of events, and because of the 80 PNdB cut-off point for analysis purposes. The calculation of noise in perceived noise units is also a fairly cumbersome process. In the UK, the Aircraft Noise Index Study (ANIS) [42] was carried out in 1984 to investigate improvements in indices for quantifying the annoyance due to aircraft noise around airports. One very important conclusion of this study was that a good correlation exists between annoyance due to aircraft noise and the $L_{Aeq,24hour}$ value. This parameter is much easier to measure than NNI and has the added advantage that it is used for quantifying noise from other forms of transport and many other sources of environmental noise. $L_{Aeq,24h}$ received much support as an index to replace NNI but was criticized from the point of view that it did not give adequate recognition to the specific problem of disturbance in the evening or at night-time. After much consultation, the Department of Transport has adopted a daytime 16-hour L_{Aeq} (07.00 to 23.00) to assess aircraft noise and a separate 8-hour L_{Aeq} (23.00 to 07.00) to evaluate the effectiveness of restrictions on night operations at airports. $L_{Aeq,16h}$ was officially introduced as the UK aircraft noise exposure index in September 1990 [43]. The Aircraft Noise

Contour Model (ANCON) [44] is being developed to produce noise contours in terms of $L_{Aeq,16h}$. Such contours, published at 3 dB(A) intervals, will replace NNI contours around principal airports from 1990. There is no unique relationship between $L_{Aeq,16h}$ and NNI, but Table 6.3 [45] illustrates $L_{Aeq,16h}$ contours which approximate to NNI contours between NNI 35 and NNI 60. As can be seen from the table, an $L_{Aeq,16h}$ value of 57 dB(A) equates approximately to NNI 35 and thus represents the threshold of annoyance. $L_{Aeq,16h}$ 66 dB(A) equates approximately to NNI 50 and hence becomes the threshold for grant schemes to improve the sound insulation of dwellings. Figure 6.14 shows typical $L_{Aeq,16h}$ contours around an airport.

Large inroads have been made into noise reduction around airports by the improved design of aircraft engines, as previously discussed. Noise reduction can also be exercised through flight operations. Some of the techniques available may be summarised as follows :

(1) Thrust cut-back on take-off. This is effective for reducing noise in the region of the cut-back, but noise tends to be

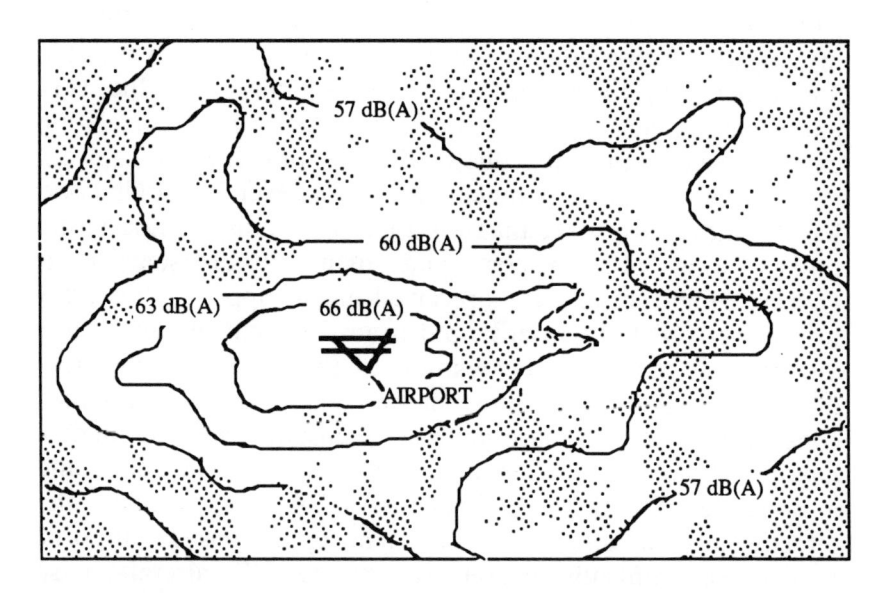

Figure 6.14   Typical $L_{Aeq,16h}$ contours around an airport

Table 6.3 $L_{Aeq,16h}$ **versus NNI**

$L_{Aeq.16hh}$ dB(A)	NNI	Annoyance
57	35	Low
60	40	
63	45	Moderate
66	50	
69	55	High
72	60	

increased further along the flight-path due to the decreased altitude of the aircraft. This is illustrated in Figure 6.15. It must be emphasised that there is no legal compulsion for the pilot to reduce thrust on take-off and that safety considerations will always over-ride noise reduction considerations.

(2) Two-segment approach. In this case the aircraft maintains a higher altitude than normal on the approach and makes a steeper descent close to the airport. This is illustrated in Figure 6.16. The noise reduction is greatest for people living under the approach path at a distance of 3 to 9 km from the airport.

(3) Planned preferred routing. As far as possible, take-offs should pass over the least populated areas thereby reducing the number of people exposed to the highest levels of noise. For most of the major airports in the UK, preferred routes are designated and termed "Preferred Noise Routes" (PNRs) or "Standard Instrument Departures" (SIDs).

(4) Reduced night-time operations. Many airports have night-time flying restrictions either in terms of a curfew or a limited quota of flights. Heathrow, for example, has fewer than 6000 night flights (23.30 to 06.00) allowed per year [46]. This represents less than 2% of the total flights. Such restrictions are always in conflict with the commercial development of airports. Airport managers maintain that airlines need the flexibility to fly at night due to world-wide scheduling

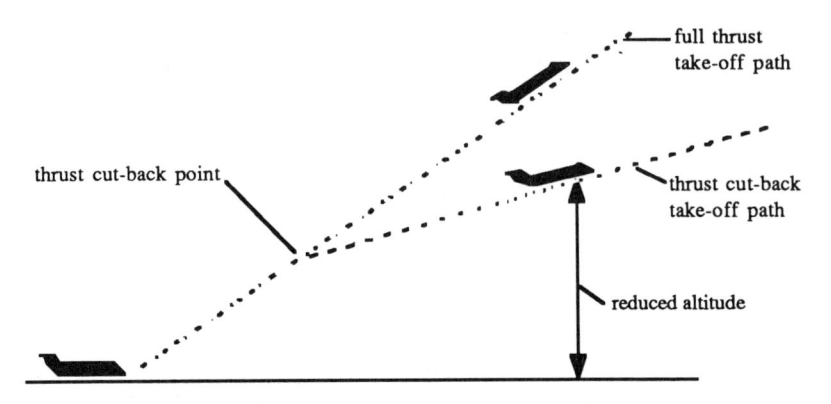

Figure 6.15 Thrust cut-back on take-off

considerations, long-haul flights crossing multiple time zones, and to cater for operational delays.

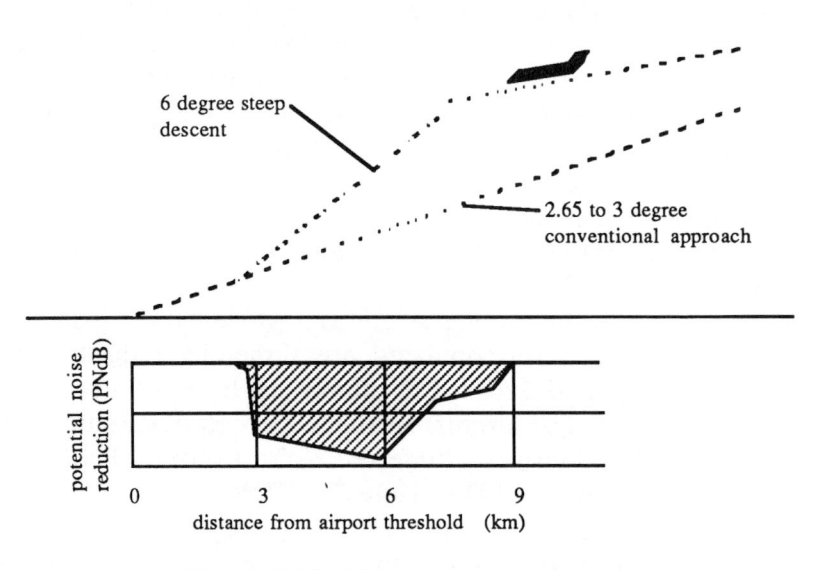

Figure 6.16 Two-segment approach

Military aircraft

The problem of noise annoyance due to military aircraft has increased over recent years. There are two main geographical areas subject to annoyance (i) areas around military airfields which are subject to very high noise levels due to continuous take-offs and landings and (ii) rural areas, usually hill, mountain or coastal regions, used for low-level flying exercises. The problem is increased due to the fact that such regions are almost invariably quiet areas with low background noise levels. The number of noise complaints associated with low-level flying exercises is currently around 8000 per year.

With civil aircraft there has been a continuous reduction in aircraft noise over the years due to more stringent noise certification requirements. The same cannot be said for military aircraft. It is currently impossible to apply the noise reduction techniques used for civil aircraft without an unacceptable loss of performance for military aircraft. The number of aircraft movements around military airfields is generally much smaller than around the large commercial airports but individual military aircraft are much noisier. Compensation for people living around the numerous military airfields in the UK would be unacceptably expensive if the criteria used for airports was applied. The Ministry of Defence operates its own criteria and has applied a compensation scheme since the early 1980s for people living close to military airfields. Since its introduction, the compensation scheme has cost about £15 million in double glazing, ventilation units and offers to purchase homes. The criterion used for grant aid is based on an $L_{Aeq,12h}$ of 70 dB(A). Where night-time flying (22.00 to 06.00) regularly occurs and exceeds 20 movements per night, an L_{Amax} 82 dB(A) contour is also defined. The outer limits of the 70 dB(A) contour and the 82 dB(A) contour become the extent of the compensation scheme. The National Physics Laboratory (NPL) has developed a computer model for producing noise contours for military aircraft. This software is termed AIRNOISE and some of its applications to military aircraft have recently been published [47]. Most of the work in quantifying military aircraft noise has been concentrated on areas close to military airfields, but now research by the NPL is concentrating on producing noise data for sites subject to constant low-level exercises. This will allow a model for such sites to be developed and permissible noise levels, in terms of the maximum A-weighted noise level, L_{Amax}, to be calculated. This research will prove to be of major importance since the number of low-level flying exercises in the UK is currently around 150 000 per year.

Helicopter noise

Between 1985 and 1992 the number of helicopters registered in the UK increased from 542 to 902 [48], *i.e.* an increase of 66%, and hence noise associated with helicopter movements is becoming an increasingly important environmental consideration. The number of bases from which helicopters operate has also increased. London, for example, has seen the number of helicopters based there increase from 34 in 1986 to 51 in 1992, and the number of bases increase from 5 to 11 in the same time period. Unlike fixed-wing aircraft, which can only operate from airports, helicopters can operate from almost anywhere, ranging from airports, roof-top helipads on city-centre hotels and commercial buildings to virtually unprepared locations in the countryside. The ability of helicopters to operate in close proximity to the ultimate embarkation and destination points brings them into much closer contact with people in a residential and work environment context than fixed-wing aircraft. Private landing sites in the commuter-belt are causing problems. Such sites can be used for up to 20 days per year without the need for planning permission. The Noise Review Working Party have recommended that provision should be made for local authorities to regulate the use of helicopters at private landing sites through a licensing system. Although helicopter noise is increasing in importance as an environmental problem, it must be stated that, in comparison with aircraft and road traffic noise, the number of people directly affected by helicopter noise is very small.

Helicopter noise differs in character from fixed-wing aircraft noise and is generally much lower in intensity, certainly in comparison to most jet-aircraft noise. The principal sources of noise are the main rotor system and engine. Rotor noise consists of both periodic noise, which includes "blade-slap", and broadband noise which is due to non-periodic aerodynamic interaction with the rotor. The periodic noise is a function of the blade tip speed (the higher the blade-tip speed, the higher the noise level) and, to a lesser degree, the number of blades. The higher the number of blades the greater the noise level, in general terms.

Although helicopter noise has different charateristics to fixed-wing aircraft noise, no separate or unique index has ever been used in its assessment. The CAA *Helicopter Disturbance Study* [49] concluded that, of all the exposure indices examined, NNI showed the greatest correlation between helicopter noise and annoyance, but that L_{Aeq} was only slightly inferior (and much easier to measure). Some studies into the comparison between helicopter and fixed-wing aircraft noise have concluded that, for the same exposure level, *i.e.* the same NNI or the same L_{Aeq}, helicopter noise annoyance is of the same order as that due to fixed-wing aircraft. In London, the CAA report showed that in areas which are exposed to noise from both helicopters and fixed-wing aircraft, helicopters were generally felt to be more annoying.

It is difficult to be absolute about acceptable limits for helicopter noise, but the now defunct Noise Advisory Council (NAC), as far back as the early 1970s, recommended that no residential area should be exposed to helicopter noise exceeding an $L_{Aeq,12hour}$ value of 62 dB(A) at the façades of buildings. Noise criteria for a proposed heliport for Milton Keynes in the mid-1980s proposed a maximum exposure at the facades of noise sensitive buildings of $L_{Aeq,15hour}$ 57 dB(A) (07.00 to 22.00) [50]. Now that the UK has adopted $L_{Aeq,16hour}$ as the metric for fixed-wing aircraft noise it is only a matter of time before it is applied to helicopters.

Exposure to noise from helicopters can be reduced by:

(1) Noise certification of helicopters.
(2) Planned routing, especially in built up areas. This would entail defining corridors through which flights should be

made and setting minimum altitude criteria during the flight.
(3) Licensing of private landing sites to control the number of permissible movements.
(4) Upgrading the sound insulation of noise-sensitive buildings in the vicinity of heliports and landing sites.

Railway noise

Of the three major forms of transportation, railway noise produces the lowest incidence of annoyance for a given exposure level. Currently railway operations are exempt from noise nuisance legislation and, unlike road vehicles and aircraft, there are no existing regulations to control noise emissions from individual railway vehicles at the design and manufacture stage. There are no regulations at present which give sound insulation entitlement grants to people affected by noise from new or existing railway lines. This will change in the immediate future since the Department of Transport has recently announced legislation to provide compensation for line-side residents exposed to high levels of noise from *new* railway lines. This will bring new railway lines into parallel with new highways. This is welcome legislation considering the implications of the new rail links associated with the development of the Channel Tunnel and the number of light railway transportation schemes which are at the advanced planning stage for many cities in the UK. The new legislation will protect people living beside new railway lines, but there is a strong body of opinion which believes that compensation should also apply to existing lines which become used more intensively as a result of the Channel Tunnel and Government policy to move freight off the roads and on to the railways. The south-east of England has seen the re-opening of lines which have been closed to passenger traffic for many years as well as large-scale proposals to construct new lines. There are proposals to re-open suburban lines throughout the country as roads become more congested. For example, studies are being carried out into the possibility of re-opening the suburban circle line in Edinburgh which has been closed to passenger traffic since 1963. Residents living next to such lines will not qualify for compensation under the new regulations as proposed.

Because railway noise is recognized as being less annoying than other forms of transport, there has been, historically, a lack of a standard for railway noise in the UK. The Greater London Council (GLC) looked objectively at railway noise and derived a standard façade level of $L_{Aeq,24hour}$ 65 dB(A) as being the maximum acceptable for noise sensitive buildings. This standard tended to be adopted locally and became the unofficial railway noise criterion from the mid-1980s until recent times. In the early 1980s British Rail commissioned the Institute of Sound and Vibration Research (ISVR), Southampton, to carry out a survey into the factors which influence the response of a community to railway noise. The results of this survey were published by Fields and Walker in 1982 [51]. The study found that there was very little annoyance for façade levels of less than $L_{Aeq,24hour}$ 50 dB(A). Above this exposure level annoyance rose smoothly with increase in noise level and above levels of 65 to 70 dB(A) there was a significant response of annoyance. This survey provided no evidence for the operation of a specific night-time criterion for railway noise. The Channel Tunnel links and associated railway development around London was recognized as demanding a strict regime of noise standards and criteria by Kent County Council and a consortium of London Boroughs. They recognized the fact that much of the freight traffic through the Tunnel may be moved at night and hence the necessity for a night-time criterion for controlling railway noise. Their suggestion was for a daytime L_{Aeq} of 65 dB(A), as adopted by the GLC, an evening L_{Aeq} of 60 dB(A), and a night-time L_{Aeq} of 55 dB(A).

The proposed new railway noise regulations do recognize the need for separate day and night criteria. The standards proposed as maximum façade levels are $L_{Aeq,18h}$ 68 dB(A) for day (06.00 to 00.00) and $L_{Aeq,.6h}$ 63 dB(A) for night (00.00 to 06.00).

The sources of railway noise can be summarized as follows:

(1) Traction systems. This includes motors gears and exhausts.
(2) Rail/wheel noise. The interaction between wheels and rail is

often the predominant source of noise for speeds of less than 80 km/h. This noise includes wheel resonances and noise at track joints. If rail joints are not aligned perfectly there may be a vertical step up or a step down at joints thereby producing more noise.
(3) Auxiliary equipment. This is made up mostly by compressors, ventilation and brake systems.
(4) Aerodynamic noise. This is due to turbulent boundary layer effects and may be the main source of noise at high speeds.
(5) Ground vibrations. Although not disturbing from a noise point of view, ground vibrations from railway lines are important with respect to buildings and bridges etc.

The spectra of noise from a diesel car set at a distance of 16 m, both for pass-by noise and propulsion noise, only, are shown in Figure 6.17. The difference between the two spectra is the contribution due to rail/wheel interactions and, to a lesser extent, aerodynamic noise.

When the proposed new legislation comes into force a refined technique for the calculation of railway noise will have to be available so that accurate predictions can be made for the façade noise levels at affected buildings. This will serve the same

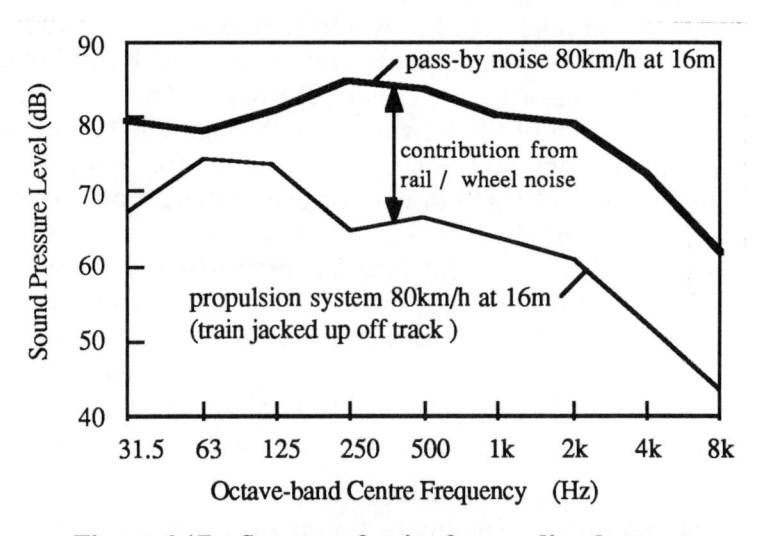

Figure 6.17   Spectra of noise from a diesel car set

Environmental Noise 129

function as the Calculation of Road Traffic Noise (CRTN) does for the establishment of entitlement with respect to new roads. The most comprehensive method of predicting railway noise to date is Chapter 15 of the *Transportation Noise Reference Book* [52]. The prediction methodology is similar to that used in the CRTN and can be summarized as follows :

(1) Calculation of the source noise from data on the types of locomotives or trains, the rolling stock, the train speed and the type and condition of the track.
(2) Calculation of the maximum noise, $L_{A(max)}$, at reception points at building façades taking into account propagation corrections, ground attenuations and the influence of cuttings and barriers.

Much of the data needed for the prediction of noise associated with particular types of locomotives and other railway vehicles still needs to be established for the production of a universal prediction document.

As well as the problem of noise from railways, the problem of vibrations transferred to line-side buildings needs to be considered. Techniques are available to predict vibration levels in buildings for comparison with tolerable levels in terms of building damage and the comfort of building occupants.

Railway noise and vibration can be controlled by :

(1) Improved locomotives and rolling stock.
(2) Improved continuous track.
(3) Isolating the track from the substructure with pads made from rubber or other resilient material.
(4) Isolating buildings from the supporting ground through which the vibrations are being transmitted.

Industrial noise and BS 4142

The trend in industrial noise appears to be ever upwards as illustrated by the increase in noise complaints associated with this type of noise. In 1988, local authorities received over 11 000 complaints relating to industrial and commercial premises. 7 500 of the complaints were confirmed as statutory nuisances requiring over 900 abatement notices. Most complaints were resolved without the need for court proceedings and only 56 convictions ensued from the magistrates courts [53].

The first standard to deal with the likely effect of industrial noise on residents living in mixed industrial and residential areas was BS 4142, 1967. The Standard was amended in 1975 and 1990 saw the introduction of the new BS 4142, *Method for Rating Industrial Noise affecting mixed Residential and Industrial Areas* [54]. To say that the new Standard received a mixed reception by EHOs, noise consultants and practitioners would be an understatement and the Standard has already been recalled for review. The 1990 Standard set out the measurement methods and the assessment criteria for industrial noise in terms of the likelihood of complaints resulting from the noise. In essence, the specific noise being rated is measured, corrected, and then compared to the background noise. The greater the value by which the measured, corrected, noise exceeds the background noise, the greater is the likelihood of complaints arising. The parameter used to measure industrial noise in terms of the Standard is $L_{Aeq,T}$. This is measured under permissible weather conditions at an outside position 1 m from the façade of an affected building and at a distance of at least 3.5 m from other reflecting surfaces. The reference interval, T_r, is 1 hour during the day and 5 minutes during the night. The Standard gives guidance on how to deal with specific noise of different duration characteristics, *i.e.* continuous or cyclic, with cycles equal to, greater than, or less than the reference time. For continuous noise, the reference value and the measurement value are the same, *i.e.* the measurement time, T_m, and the reference time are the same. This gives :

$$L_{Aeq,Tr} = L_{Aeq,Tm}$$

For intermittent noise where the on-time is less than the reference time interval the specific noise level is calculated from:

$$L_{Aeq,Tr} = L_{Aeq,Tm} + 10 \log_{10} (T_{on}/T_r) \quad dB(A)$$

where T_{on} is the on time of the noise.

Once the specific noise has been calculated, it is corrected by the addition of a 5 dB(A) penalty if the noise contains distinguishable tonal characteristics (whine, hiss, screech, hum), and/or the noise has a distinct impulsive character (bangs, thumps, clicks, clatter). For assessment purposes, the background noise to which the corrected specific noise is compared is the $L_{A90,T}$ value. Guidance is given on when to measure this background noise level. Essentially this background noise level should be measured during periods when the background noise is typical of that when the specific noise source is, or will be, operating. This to prevent low background noise measurements being made at 2 o'clock in the morning for rating purposes for a specific noise which only operates from, say, 3 o'clock to 5 o'clock in the afternoon. Section 8 of the Standard gives the method of assessing the noise for complaints purposes. The background noise, $L_{A90,T}$, is subtracted from the corrected specific noise level to give the level difference. Assessment is as follows:

(1) A difference of 10 dB(A) or more indicates that complaints are highly likely.
(2) A difference of around 5 dB(A) is of marginal significance.
(3) At a difference of less than 5 dB(A), the lower the value the less likelihood of complaints.
(4) A difference of −10 dB(A), *i.e.* the specific noise is less than the background noise, is positive indication that complaints are unlikely.

One of the problems of the new BS 4142, and the 1967 BS 4142, is that attention is not always paid to the limited scope for which the Standard is intended. The Standard is often manipulated to fit conditions where it is not intended to apply. This is not a fault of the Standard itself but in the people using the Standard. The Standard only applies to industrial noise, *i.e.* noise from factories, industrial premises, fixed installations, and sources of noise of an industrial nature coming from commercial premises. The Standard applies only to areas where the background noise level is not less than 30 dB(A), and is therefore inappropriate for rating any type of industrial noise in an otherwise quiet rural area. The Standard applies to measurements or predictions of noise outside buildings and therefore cannot be used to rate industrial or commercial noise affecting a house or flat in the same building as the noise source. For example, if a laundry at ground floor level caused noise nuisance to a flat above, the internal noise level in the flat cannot be rated by BS 4142. Another potential problem is the time period for the measurement of background noise. The measurement time is defined as being typical of that when the specific noise source is in operation and therefore contains all existing noise sources. If this is applied each time a factory wishes to install a new piece of machinery all previous machinery will be included in the new measurement of $L_{A90,T}$. The application of the Standard could therefore justify a steady increase in the prevailing noise climate. This is often referred to as "creeping background", *i.e.* each new assessment is made against an increased background noise level and hence the propensity of a new specific noise to elicit complaints, in terms of the assessment, may not increase. This problem has been highlighted and discussed by Horrocks [55]. The problem of steadily increasing background noise is not in the intended spirit of the Standard and is certainly at odds with *Planning and Noise Circular 10/73* which made specific mention of the need to avoid creeping background noise levels. The use of $L_{A90,T}$ as the base level against which the industrial noise is being assessed also has its critics in that it tends to be a parameter which suffers comparatively large fluctuations in level from day to day. Many EHOs now feel that BS 4142 is a hindrance rather than a help in the assessment of noise nuisance in relation to industrial noise. It is argued that an EHO investigating an industrial noise complaint need only address two issues [56]:

(1) Whether noise amounting to a nuisance exists, *i.e.* is there a material interference with a person's use or right over land arising from the noise?

Environmental Noise 133

(2) Is it reasonable to expect the perpetrator of the noise to implement a prescribed scheme of ameliorative works to remedy the problem? That is, to employ the best practicable means.

Such decisions can often be made without the need for a measurement of source and background levels. The existence of the Standard, however, may "strait-jacket" the assessment of industrial noise into a very defined procedure which may be inappropriate in many cases.

BS 4142 is often used as a prediction tool to assess the impact of new noise sources for planning purposes, but doubt has also been cast on its ability to do this. The Standard calculates the likelihood of noise complaints as the means of rating the affect of noise on the community. The 1987 BRE Survey showed that 5.5 million people were bothered by noise but the number of complaints received by local authorities numbered less than 100 000. This shows that a standard which uses the likelihood of complaints as the basis of assessment may be flawed in that its use may grossly under-estimate the affect of noise on the community as a whole.

It will be interesting to observe how the revised Standard addresses the issues raised by EHOs and noise consultants.

Construction and open-site noise

The increase in mechanization in the construction industry has led to an increase in noise levels associated with construction and open sites, *e.g.* open-cast mines. Large earth-moving equipment, pneumatic drills, piling operations, drag-lines, the delivery and handling of materials, are all potential sources of high levels of noise. The noise associated with increase in mechanization has been offset to some degree, however, by local authority control over site noise and by the influence of more stringent noise emission levels from plant introduced by various EC Directives. For example, there has been a substantial reduction in the noise output of compressors in recent years and it is becoming more common to find mufflers being used on pneumatic drills. The legal controls under the Control of Pollution Act 1974, and the Environmental Protection Act 1990, will be discussed in Chapter 7.

Because construction sites are of limited duration, annoyance due to construction noise is generally short term and there is evidence to suggest that people living near construction sites will accept higher levels of noise from these sites than they would from some fixed installation or permanent source of industrial noise. Nevertheless, all practicable means should be used to control construction site noise at source and to control the spread of noise to noise-sensitive buildings in the immediate neighbourhood. Control of construction site noise is also important in relation to the protection of hearing of construction site workers.

The first standard used specifically to control construction site noise was BS 5228, 1975, *Code of Practice for Noise Control on Construction and Demolition Sites* [57]. This Code was replaced in 1984 by a three part Code [58]. The parts are :

Part 1 : Code of Practice for Basic Information and Procedures for Noise Control.

Part 2 : Guide to Noise Control Legislation for Construction and Demolition including Road Construction and Maintenance.

Part 3 : Code of Practice for Noise Control applicable to Surface Coal Extraction by Open-cast Methods.

In 1992 Part 4 of BS 5228 was introduced : "Code of Practice for Noise Control applicable to Piling Operations". Also in 1992, Draft MPG11, Control of Noise at Surface Mineral Workings [59] was sent out to interested parties for comment prior to new guidance being published on the control and calculation of noise from surface mineral workings. Such workings are generally much longer term than construction sites and warrant separate consideration. Since the combined documentation in BS 5228 is extensive, it is only possible to give a brief summary of the aims and objectives of the Code. The basic aim of BS 5228 is to recommend procedures for noise control in respect of construction and open-site operators and to assist architects, contractors, site operatives, designers, engineers, EHOs and planners regarding the control of noise. The Code refers to the need to protect site workers and people living in the vicinity of the site. Various sections refer to hearing protection, noise and neighbourhood nuisance, project supervision, the control of noise at source and the spread of noise from the site. Methods are given for estimating noise from sites. To assist with this, extensive tables of the typical sound power levels of site plant and equipment are provided. In terms of the duration of site operations, the Code identifies the fact that the longer the site activities last, the more likely is the situation that site noise will be unsatisfactory with respect to the local community. It is therefore important that noisy operations are carried out according to schedule. Local authorities can set maximum permissible L_{Aeq} levels at parts of the site boundary close to noise sensitive buildings. For daytime working this is normally an $L_{Aeq,12hour}$ value of 75 dB(A) (07.00 to 19.00 hours) from Monday to Saturday. For sites working beyond this, evening levels should generally be 10 dB(A) lower than the daytime limit. The Code suggests that, for sites working 24 hours, during periods when people are trying to get to sleep, and just before awakening, a maximum $L_{Aeq,1h}$ of 40–45 dB(A), façade level, may be necessary. Many local authorities do not allow Sunday working but will generally give dispensation for work which must be carried out on a continuous basis, *e.g.* continuous pour concrete structures such as lift shafts and stairwells of high-rise buildings. For sites working 24 hours, site deliveries should be planned not to arrive between 19.00 and 07.00 hours if possible. This reduces traffic flow, and hence noise, on roads leading to the site during the night.

The Code instructs site personnel not to use excessively noisy equipment and to ensure that site equipment is properly maintained and therefore likely to produce less noise. Suggestions for the control of noise at source, by enclosures if necessary, and suggestions for controlling the spread of noise from the site by the use of earth bunds and by measures such as placing the site offices and buildings between noisy operations and noise sensitive buildings are given. The 1992, Part 4 of the code on piling operations outlines methods of calculating noise and vibration levels associated with piling operations. It also gives a list of case histories of vibration levels in buildings close to piling operations.

Noise control measures may have an effect on the duration of the site and on the type of plant used on the site. It is therefore likely have to have cost implications which must be taken into account by contractors at the tendering and planning stages of projects.

Other publications on the reduction of noise exposure in construction have been produced by the Construction Industry Research and Information Association (CIRIA) [60], [61].

Entertainment, leisure and sporting noise

Many types of entertainment, leisure and sporting activities have associated noise problems both from the point of view of hearing damage and environmental noise pollution. Obvious examples are pop-concerts, discotheques, game and clay pigeon shooting, motor sports, watersports and the flying of model aircraft. Much work is being carried out in the preparation of codes of practice to produce guidelines for the control of noise from many of the above activities.

Live and amplified music

The responsibility for the control of noise from venues which are used for live and amplified music, dancing and associated forms of entertainment lies with the local authorities through the licensing system. The local authority can therefore limit environmental noise from public entertainment by making noise reduction and noise control conditions of the operator's licence. Noise control conditions can also be placed on the licence required for the sale of alcohol. Many local authorities are now using "inaudibility" as a criterion for setting noise limits for live and amplified music, *i.e.* the music must be inaudible in the nearest residence to the premises used for music. A conference held by the Institute of Acoustics (IOA) in 1988 reported on the use of inaudibility as a noise criterion [62]. The inaudibility criterion requires great care in the sound insulation design of the building elements for venues hosting the music and also in the design of ventilation systems for such venues, *e.g.* silencers must be used in the extract system to prevent excessive sound propagation via this route.

The Greater London Council (GLC) was one of the first authorities to investigate noise from pop-concerts and published a Code of Practice for such concerts in 1976 [63]. In 1985 a revised, final version was produced and became adopted by many licensing authorities within the UK. The Code gave guidance on both audience exposure and environmental noise pollution to the surrounding area. Audience noise exposure limits were based on an L_{Aeq} of 93 dB(A) for an 8-hour event with equal energy principles applying to shorter or longer events, *e.g.* 96 dB(A) for a 4-hour event and 90 dB(A) for a 16-hour event. For outdoor events, the exposure was assessed at a distance of 50m from the sound system whereas for indoor events, assessment was made in terms of "any member of the audience" which usually implied the nearest audience position to the sound system, *i.e.* front barrier position. The environmental guidance was based on a 15-minute external L_{Aeq}. Results from the GLC studies [64] showed that for up to three concerts per year an increase of not more than 10 dB(A) above the background L_{Aeq} was likely to minimise complaints. The GLC guidelines were subsequently based on an increase of 10 dB(A) up to 20.00 hours, although in practice this was usually extended to 23.00 hours. For events which were more frequent than three per year, a 1 dB(A) increase in the L_{Aeq} up to 23.00 hours was defined as the acceptable criteria. After 23.00 hours the inaudibility criterion in the nearest residence became operative.

The Noise Council reviewed all relevant data and in March 1991 suggested guidelines to the Department of the Environment with a view to the establishment of a Code of Practice under the Control of Pollution Act. The Health and Safety Executive (HSE) at this time set up a working party to prepare guidance on all aspects of health, safety and welfare at pop-concerts. J. Griffiths of Travers Morgan carried out a study to assess audience exposure levels at a series of 18 concerts throughout the country [65]. A mean L_{Aeq} of 104.7 dB(A) was calculated for the front barrier position. The results obtained were very high and only one concert in the eighteen complied with the GLC exposure guidelines. An event L_{Aeq} of 104 dB(A), at first barrier position, has been suggested by the HSE in present draft guidance notes. A strong objection to this proposal has been made by the Concert Promotors Association. They suggest an exposure limit of L_{Aeq} 107 dB(A), *i.e.* twice the HSE limit in energy terms, based on an individual attending 25, two-hour concerts at most, at front barrier position, for ten years of the individual's life. Griffiths points out that this is equivalent in exposure terms to an individual exposed to a daily noise exposure at the "first action level", *i.e.* 85 dB(A), for 8 hours per day for 40 years of working life [66]. The concept of controlling audience exposure will always be contentious since some would argue that people are paying to hear pop-music and expect, and indeed demand, that it is at a high noise level. Promotors, however, have a duty to protect the hearing of workers, *e.g.* stewards, at such events. The draft proposals published by the HSE include guidelines on environmental noise control. The background level is based on L_{A90} rather than on background L_{Aeq} and hence the difference between the concert L_{Aeq} and background L_{A90} is increased by a 5 dB(A) compared to the original Noise Council report, *e.g.* an external L_{Aeq} being 10 dB(A) above the background L_{Aeq} will mean it is approximately 15 dB(A) above the background L_{A90}. After further discussions between the Department of the Environment, the Noise Council Working Party and the noise consultants involved, absolute levels have been suggested as the environmental criteria in relation to the number of events per year and the time of day. Maximum external 15-minute L_{Aeq} music noise levels (MNL) being proposed are :

(1) 75 dB(A) for 1 event per year.
(2) 70 dB(A) for 2 to 5 events per year.
(3) 67 dB(A) for 6 to 12 events per year.
(4) For more than 12 events per year it is proposed that the MNL should not exceed the background L_{A90} by more than 5 dB(A).
(5) After 23.00 hours the inaudibility criterion should apply within any noise-sensitive building with the windows open in a typical manner for ventilation.

Research is still being carried out with a view to the publishing of a final code of practice for pop-concerts in the very near future.

Noise exposure in discotheques is generally to levels which are not as high as those at live concerts but, nevertheless, concern is required since people, on average, attend discotheques much more frequently than they attend live concerts. A report in 1985 [67] estimated noise levels around 97 dB(A) at discos which are attended, on average, by about 6 million people for 4 hours per week for about 7 years. Exposure is for much shorter periods than typical exposure to noise at work, but the additional exposure at discotheques could be significant for people who are close to the maximum exposure at work.

Recently some information has been published on the assessment of disturbance caused by amplified music emanating from a neighbouring dwelling [68]. This research has been carried out by the Open University on behalf of the Department of the Environment. This adopts a BS 4142 type approach in that the suggestions are made for measuring the level of the intrusive music noise, measuring the background noise level at a time typical to that of the intrusive music but while the music is not playing, and correcting the intrusive noise for the time of day, the duration and the bass prominence. The rating is in terms of the justifiability of complaints, *i.e.* by how much does the corrected noise exceed the background noise. Bearing in mind the criticism levelled at BS 4142 in terms of industrial noise, it is debatable if this approach to music noise is a step forward. Many EHOs would prefer to declare intrusive noise a nuisance if it can be heard at all in a neighbouring dwelling and hence a rating system may be a disadvantage to complainants. There will always be conflict between subjective and objective assessment methods for this and many other types of noise.

Another cause for concern in terms of hearing risk is the extensive use of personal stereo systems. They are currently used by an estimated 5 million people in the UK [69]. Most sets are capable of producing over 90 dB(A) in the immediate vicinity of the ear and many sets are capable of levels in excess of 100 dB(A). The headsets do not cut out background noise and hence people using the sets in noisy environments, *e.g.* travelling on trains, the underground, and buses, tend to increase the volume of the personal stereo to the higher limits to compensate for the intrusion of background noise. The type of music listened to also has an influence on the level at which the system is played. Davis *et al* [70] found that the level selected was on average :

(1) 74 dB(A), music for background listening.
(2) 83 dB(A), if music was the main item of interest.
(3) 85 dB(A), if music was rock music.

The Royal National Institute for the Deaf has been very active in making public the possible dangers of high-output personal stereo systems, especially by young children, and has called for warnings to be printed on the packaging of personal stereo systems and personal CD players.

Sporting noise

Many sporting activities carry the danger of hearing risk as well as causing problems in terms of environmental noise. Davis *et al* [71] have concluded that exposure to noise during leisure activities can, in extreme cases, be equivalent to an occupational exposure of 80 dB(A) over a working lifetime. For those in jobs with a high noise exposure, already subject to noise around the first action level or more, leisure noise can effectively double the risk of developing hearing loss.

The shooting of guns for game or clay target purposes

produces very high levels of noise in the immediate vicinity of the shooter's ear. Studies [72] have shown significant hearing loss in one or both ears for many people with a history of long or frequent use of rifles, shotguns and pistols. Most people now, however, have the sense to use ear protectors while firing or while at a shooting range. The environmental impact of shooting is proportional to the number of shots fired in a particular time period. A few isolated shots in an afternoon in the countryside is unlikely to produce noise complaints, especially since the noise is in keeping with country activities. Much more of a problem, however, is the increasing number of commercial clay pigeon shooting centres and the increasing number of "war-games" centres, *e.g.* "paint-ball" games. The frequent use of such centres, which are almost invariably in otherwise quiet, rural areas, presents a considerable environmental noise problem and one which must be controlled by appropriate codes of practice and planning measures. A code of practice for clay target shooting is currently being produced which will address issues of minimum separation distance between centres and residential development, typical firing intervals, the definition of noise sensitive locations, noise control measures and the separate treatment of large scale commercial centres. The Noise Council Working Party are concerned to see effective licensing of war-game centres as part of noise control provisions.

The control of noise from motor sport activities is the responsibility of the Royal Automobile Club Motor Sports Association (RACMSA). Their role is to control the technical specification of competing vehicles which includes setting maximum permissible noise levels for vehicles used in different type of motor sports, *e.g.* hill climbs, track racing, autocross etc. Such noise regulations have been in effect since RACMSA was formed in 1979 and have been continually updated since then. The latest regulations in 1992 set out the maximum noise levels permitted from vehicles and the test procedures for establishing the noise levels [73]. The RACMSA technical committee licence some 20 trained noise inspectors who act as an auditing inspectorate and oversee the work of more than 100 noise test officials who, in turn, carry out noise measurements at events.

RACMSA have recognized the deficiency of the current regulations, which apply to vehicles only, to address the problem of the environmental impact of motor sport noise. In conjunction with the Association of motor Racing Circuit Owners (AMRCO), noise consultants have been employed to investigate the effects of motor sport noise on the community and methods of reducing environmental noise pollution from such events. The findings will assist with the preparation of a code of practice for the control of motor sport noise. The Noise Council Working Party have advocated the need for a similar code of practice for motor-cycle events including scrambling.

One form of sport or leisure activity which is already covered by a code of practice is the flying of model aircraft [74]. The frequency content of model aircraft is such that the noise produced is particularly annoying. The study by Davis *et al* surprisingly found cases of hearing loss in people associated with this pastime. This is due to owners of model aircraft running and tuning engines in confined spaces such as workshops, huts and garages. Noise levels as high as 114 dB(A) have been recorded in such situations.

Other forms of environmental noise control

Codes of practice have been or are in the course of preparation for the following sources of environmental noise: audible intruder alarms, automatic bird-scarers, ice-cream van chimes and car alarms. [75], [76].

Planning and noise

Environmental noise has been included in planning circulars since 1973. Correct planning is undoubtedly the best approach to controlling noise and, correctly applied, planning decisions can prevent situations developing where the potential for noise nuisance exists. Planning has two roles to play in terms of noise control:

(1) To prevent the development of noisy industry, transportation schemes, sporting, entertainment and other activities close to noise sensitive areas.
(2) To prevent the development of noise-sensitive buildings within areas which are already noisy due to industry, busy roads, aircraft, railway lines or some other noise source.

The 1973 Planning and Noise Circulars, 10/73 in England [77] and 23/73 in Scotland [78], are currently under review and are due to be replaced by a Planning Policy Guidance Note (PPG) on Planning and Noise [79] which has been sent out in draft form for comment. Comments have been returned by the interested parties and the PPG is now in the final stages of production. The PPG offers guidance on how the planning system can be used to reduce the impact of environmental noise on the community. The PPG describes new mechanisms and guidelines to be adopted by local planning authorities in considering the major transport, industrial, commercial, construction, sporting, recreational, and entertainment sources of noise.

The PPG proposes the use of $L_{Aeq,T}$ as the index for assessing noise, and the values which appear in tables refer to $L_{Aeq,T}$ measured or assessed at least 10 m away from any building. Traditionally, levels 1 m from the façade of a building have been used for road traffic and railway traffic assessment. The PPG suggests that façade levels are typically 3 dB(A) higher than levels measured away from buildings. The PPG refers to two time periods for noise consideration, *i.e.* daytime $L_{Aeq,16h}$ (07.00 to 23.00 hours) and night-time $L_{Aeq,8h}$ (23.00 to 07.00 hours). For road traffic most assessments have been are carried out using $L_{A10,18hour}$ as the parameter, but the PPG uses $L_{Aeq,T}$. The following approximation exists:

$$L_{Aeq,16h} \approx L_{A10,18h} - 2 \text{ dB(A)}$$

For aircraft noise, values in the PPG refer to contours.

In considering new noise-sensitive development near existing sources of noise, the PPG classifies areas into four exposure categories in increasing order of noise exposure:

Category A: For proposals in this category noise need not be considered as a determining factor in granting planning permission, but noise levels at the high end of the category should not be regarded as desirable levels.

Category B: For proposals in this category authorities should increasingly take noise into account when determining planning applications, and require noise control measures.

Category C: For proposals in this category there should be a strong presumption against granting planning permission. If permission is granted on the basis of no other alternative sites being available, conditions should be imposed to ensure an adequate level of sound insulation against external noise.

Category D: For proposals in this category planning permission should normally be refused.

The recommended limits for dwellings and schools for transportation and mixed noise sources are shown in Tables 6.4 and 6.5. The PPG states that the noise exposure categories

Table 6.4 Noise exposure categories for dwellings, $L_{Aeq,T}$.

Noise source	Noise exposure category			
	A	B	C	D
Road traffic (0.7.00–23.00)	<57	55–63	63–72	>72
Air traffic (0.7.00–23.00)	<57	57–66	66–72	>72
Rail traffic (0.7.00–23.00)	<55	55–65	65–74	>74
Mixed sources (0.7.00–23.00)	<55	55–63	63–77	>72
All sources (0.7.00–23.00)	<42	42–57	57–66	>66

Table 6.5 Noise exposure categories for schools, $L_{Aeq,T}$ (T = schoolday)

Noise source	Noise exposure category			
	A	B	C	D
All sources	<52	52–57	57–71	>71

should not be used for industrial noise sources which should be assessed on an individual basis (*e.g.* BS 4142). When industrial noise exists at a "mixed source" site, it should be included in the overall noise level used to establish the appropriate noise exposure category, provided it is not the dominant source of noise.

References

1. *Report of the Noise Review Working Party*, (DoE, HMSO, 1990).
2. *Environmental Health Reports*, (Institution of Environmental Health Officers, 1987/88).
3. Shultz TJ, "Synthesis of Social Surveys on Noise Annoyance", *Journal of the Acoustical Society of America*, 64, 377-405.
4. Bradley JS and Jonah BA, "A Field Study of Human Response to Traffic Noise", SV-77-2, Faculty of Engineering Science, University of Western Ontario, (1977).
5. Nelson P. (ed.), "Summary of the Effects of Noise on Man", *Transportation Noise Reference Book*, (Butterworths, 1987).
6. Hall FL, Birnie SE, Taylor SM, and Palmer JE, "Direct Comparison of Community Reaction to Road Traffic Noise and to Aircraft Noise", *Journal of the Acoustical Society of America*, (1981) 70, 1690-1698, .
7. Fields JM and Walker JG, "Comparing the Relationship between Noise Level and Annoyance in Different Surveys: A Railway Noise vs. Aircraft and Road Traffic Comparison", *Journal of Sound and Vibration*, (1982) 81, 51-80.
8. BS 4142 : 1990, *Method for rating industrial noise affecting mixed residential and industrial areas*.
9. Robinson DW, "Annoyance of Tonal Noise. A Parametric Study", *Acoustics Bulletin*, Institute of Acoustics, (1993) Vol. 18, No 2, 9-13. Berry BF, *The Evaluation of Impulsive Noise*. National Physics Laboratory Report, Ac 111 (1987).
10. Langdon FJ and Buller IB, "Road Traffic Noise and Disturbance to Sleep", *Journal of Sound and Vibration*, (1977) 50(1), 13-28.

11 Vallet M, "Sleep Disturbance", *Transportation Noise Reference Book*, (Butterworths, 1987).
12 See n10, above.
13 Vernet M., "Effects of Train Noise on Sleep for People Living in Houses Bordering Railway Lines", *Journal of Sound and Vibration*, (1979) 3, 66-74.
14 Griefahn B, "Long term Exposure to Noise. Aspects of Adaptation, Habituation and Compensation", *Waking Sleeping*, 1, 383–386 (1977).
15 Muzet A. and Metz B., "Direct Effects and Interactions of Increases in Noise Levels and Ambient Temperatures on Sleep", *Noise and Sleep, Collection Recherche et l'Environnement*, (1977) Vol. 3, la Documentation Francaise, 81-160.
16 Jones CJ, and Ollerhead JB,"Aircraft Noise and Sleep Disturbance : A Field Study", *Proceedings IOA*, (1992) Vol. 14, Part 4, 119-127.
17 World Health Organization. *Environmental Health Criteria 12–Noise*, (1980).
18 CEC, *Damage and Annoyance Caused by Noise*, (Eur.Report 5398e, 1975).
19 OECD Report, *Reducing Noise in OECD Countries*, (OECD Report, 1978).
20 Wilson, Sir Alan, Chairman. Noise, *Final Report of the Committee on the Problem of Noise*, Cmnd 2056 (HMSO, 1963).
21 See n11 above.
22 Broadbent D, "Human Performance in Noise", in Harris C. (ed.) *Handbook of Noise Control*, (McGraw-Hill, 1978).
23 Suter AH "Noise and its Effects", in Shapiro SA, *The Dormant Noise Control Act and Options to Abate Noise Pollution*, Washington DC, Administrative Conference of USA, (1991).
24 See n5 above.
25 Fothergill LC, Spring NC, Griffiths JET, and Nelson PM, " Noise Issues of 1992", *Acoustics Bulletin*, IOA, (1992) Vol. 17, No 5, 19-32.
26 ISO Recommendation R 362, *Measurement of Noise Emitted by Motor Vehicles*, (ISO, 1964).
27 BS 3425 : 1966, *Method for the Measurement of Noise Emitted by Motor Vehicles*.
28 Commission Directive 81/334/EEC on Adapting to Technical Progress, 70/157/EEC.
29 Commission Directive 84/424/EEC, amending 70/157/EEC.
30 Favre BM and Tyler J, "Quiet Vehicle Development", *Transportation Noise Reference Book*, (Butterworths, 1987).
31 *Calculation of Road Traffic Noise*, (Department of Transport, Welsh Office, HMSO, 1988).
32 *Manual of Environmental Appraisal*. Assessment Policy and Methods Division (Department of Transport, 1983).
33 *Scottish Traffic and Environmental Appraisal Manual*, the Scottish Office Industry Department, Roads Directorate, (1986).
34 See n1 above.
35 FAR Regulations, Part 36, Noise Standards : Aircraft Type and Airworthiness Certification – Amendment 13 (August 1981).

36 International Standards and Recommended Practices – Environmental Protection Annex 16 to the Convention on International Civil Aviation, (1981) Vol. 1. – Aircraft Noise.
37 *British Civil Airworthiness Requirements (BCAR)* CAP 469, (1988), Section N, Issue 4-1.
38 Mortlock AK, "Noise Certification of the BAe 146 and ATP", *Acoustics Bulletin*, IOA, (1989), Vol. 14, No 4, 5-11.
39 Ellis P. and Allin C., "The Airline Contribution to Noise Reduction", *Proceedings of IOA*, (1992), Vol. 14, Part 4, 137-151.
40 "Planning and Noise," *Planning and Noise Circular 10/73*, (DoE, 1973).
41 See n39, above.
42 Brooker P, Critchley JB, Monkman DJ and Richmond CG, *United Kingdom Aircraft Noise Index Study (ANIS) : Final Report*, CAA, DORA Report 8402, (January 1985).
43 Change Agreed to Daytime Noise Index for Aircraft Noise, Department of Transport, Press notice, No 304, September 1990.
44 Ollerhead JB, *ANCON : The CAA Aircraft Noise L_{eq} Contour Model – Version 1*, CS Report 9120.
45 Cadoux RE, "The Use of L_{eq} as an Aircraft Noise Index", *Proceedings IOA*, (1992) Vol. 14, Part 4, 41-48.
46 See n39, above.
47 Berry BF and Harris AL, "Military Aircraft Noise Prediction and Measurement", *Acoustics Bulletin*, IOA, (1991) Vol. 16, No 6, 13-16; Berry BF, "Environmental Impact of Military Aircraft", *Acoustics Bulletin*, IOA, (1993), Vol. 18, No 4, 22–24.
48 Simpson J. and Freeborn P, "Helicopter Noise the Public Perspective", *Noise and Vibration Worldwide*, (1992) 21-27, July.
49 Atkins CLR, Brooker P and Critchley JB, *Helicopter Disturbance Study : Main Report*, CAA DORA Report 8304, 1983.
50 Horrocks D, "A Heliport for Milton Keynes. Environmental Gain through Control", *Environmental Health*, (1985), Vol. 93, No 6, 143-149.
51 Fields JM and Walker JG, "The Response to Railway Noise in Residential Areas of Great Britain", *Journal of Sound and Vibration*, (1982) 85, 2, 177-255.
52 Hemsworth B., "Prediction of Train Noise", *Transportation Noise Reference Book*, (Butterworths, 1987).
53 See n2, above.
54 See n8, above.
55 Horrocks D, "BS 4142 : 1990 – An Evaluation of the Revised Standard and its Relevance to the Assessment of Community Noise", BSI Seminar, London, 18 April 1991.
56 *Ibid*.
57 BS 5228 : 1975, *Code of Practice for Noise Control on Construction and Demolition Sites*.
58 BS 5228 : Parts 1 to 3, 1984, Part 4, 1992, *Code of Practice for the Control of Noise on Construction and Open Sites*.
59 *Draft Mineral Planning Guidance Note MPG 11*, The Control of Noise at Surface Mineral Workings, (DoE, 1991).

60 Waller RA, *Planning to Reduce Noise Exposure in Construction*, Technical Note 138, CIRIA, (1990).
61 Waller RA, *A Guide to Reducing the Exposure of Construction Workers to Noise*, Report No 138, CIRIA, (1990).
62 "Inaudibility in the Assessment of Noise Nuisance", *Proceedings of IOA*, (1988) Vol. 10, Part 4.
63 *GLC Code of Practice for Pop-Concerts*, (1976).
64 Griffiths JET, " Noise Control Techniques and Guidance for Open-Air Pop-Concerts", IOA Autumn Conference, 1985.
65 Griffiths JET, *A Survey of Sound Levels at Pop-Concerts*, HSE Report 35/1991, (1991).
66 Griffiths JET, "Noise Issues of 1992", *Acoustics Bulletin*, IOA, (1992) Vol. 17, No 5, 23-26.
67 Davis AC, Fortnum HM, Coles RRA, Hagard MP and Lutman ME, *Damage to Hearing Arising from Leisure Noise : A Review of Literature*, (HMSO 1985, MRC and HSE).
68 Fothergill LC, "Assessing Noise Nuisance caused by Amplified Music", *Environmental Health*, 287-289, September 1993.
69 See n67, above.
70 *Ibid.*
71 *Ibid.*
72 *Ibid.*
73 Watson AE, "The Control of Motor Sport Noise", *Proceedings of IOA*, (1992), Vol. 14, Part 4, 473-476.
74 The Control of Noise (Code of Practice on Noise from Model Aircraft) Order 1981, SI 1981, 1830.
75 The Control of Noise (Code of Practice on Noise from Audible Intruder Alarms) Order 1981, SI 1981, 1829.
76 The Control of Noise (Code of Practice on Noise from Ice-cream Van Chimes) Order 1981 SI 1981, 1830.
77 See n40, above.
78 *Planning and Noise Circular 23/73* (Scottish Development Department, 1973).
79 *Draft Planning Policy Guidance Note PPGXX* (DoE, 1992).

Part II
The Legal Control over Noise

Chapter 7
Environmental Noise: Legal Control

Introduction

Noise has been a perennial environmental problem in the UK since the industrial revolution. However, unlike certain other forms of pollution, noise has tended not to be an emotive subject to the general public unless certain members of the population have become personally affected. In the development of environmental law, noise control is indeed the Cinderella. This is due to the very nature of the pollutant. Noise is invisible. Furthermore, noise seems to have been tacitly accepted as the inevitable consequence of modern life. More importantly, there seems to be a disinclination on the part of the public to recognise noise as potentially harmful to health. Indeed it was only as late as 1960, after effective pressure group action, that UK legislation expressly struck at the problem of environmental noise.

Whereas Parliament was relatively late in entering the war against noise, the common law since its earliest days has been able to offer some succour to those affected by noise, mainly by way of an action in the law of nuisance. Nuisance rapidly developed and crystallised in both England and Scotland during the nineteenth century. This was a period when Scottish private law, including the law of nuisance, came under strong English influence.

As far as the modern law is concerned, nuisance can be controlled either by action at common law or under statute. The statutory control of noise is a patchy affair, with a variety of unconnected statutes giving local authorities power to suppress environmental noise, and is considered in more detail below. The common law of nuisance is examined first since the main statutes dealing with noise all contain provisions relating to noise nuisance. In addition, the courts accord a similar meaning to the expression "nuisance" in its statutory context, as they do to its meaning at common law.

Nuisance

It is customary to divide common law nuisances into private nuisance and public nuisance. The first deals, in essence, with the unreasonable interference of the enjoyment of the plaintiff's land, whereas the latter deals with the interference of the comfort of the general public, there being no need for the relevant plaintiff to establish any proprietary right which has been undully prejudiced by the relevant adverse state of affairs. Private nuisance is discussed below with special reference to noise. The law of public nuisance is examined in relation to road traffic noise.

Private nuisance

The types of noise nuisances which have been the subject of litigation are varied and wide-ranging. Noise from building works (*Andreae* v *Selfridge and Co Ltd* [1938] Ch 1), cattle (*London Brighton and South Coast Railway* v *Truman* (1886) 11 App Cas. 45), a power station (*Halsey* v *Esso Petroleum Co* [1961] 1 WLR 683), an unruly family (*Smith* v *Scott* [1973] Ch 314) and the firing of guns (*Holywood Silver Fox Farm Ltd* v *Emmett* [1936] 2 KB 468) have all been the subject of litigation.

The law now discussed relates to nuisance in general. There are no special rules solely applicable to noise nuisance. It should also be noted here that there are few substantive differences in this area of law, between the law of England and Wales, and that of Scotland. The caselaw, therefore, is largely, but not entirely, interchangeable.

Elements of private nuisance

The occupier of land has a legal right to enjoy possession of that land. Such a right, in turn, places a reciprocal duty on others not to interfere with that enjoyment. The law of nuisance protects the enjoyment of land from unlawful interference emanating from a state of affairs situated outside the plaintiff's land (*NCB* v *Thorne* [1976] 1 WLR 543). In ascertaining if a nuisance exists, the courts take a variety of factors into account. None of the factors is *per se* conclusive and the various factors discussed below, furthermore, may not be exhaustive. New factors may be introduced by the courts in future, as judicial awareness of environmental matters increases. An example of such willingness on the part of the courts to add to the existing well recognised factors, is illustrated by the case of *Gillingham BC* v *Medway (Chatham) Dock Co Ltd* [1992] JPL 458 discussed below.

Social utility of the defendant's conduct

The court takes into account the social value of the defendant's conduct when considering if any given state of affairs constitutes a nuisance. The more socially useful such conduct is, the less likely the state of affairs will be regarded as a nuisance in law (*Harrison* v *Southwark and Vauxhall Water Company* [1891] 2 Ch 409). Unfortunately, from the point of view of the practitioner, the courts have scrupulously avoided constructing a clearly defined hierarchy of classes of activities in terms of social worth. While the courts certainly recognise the general public benefit which accrues from manufacturing activities (see eg *Bellew* v *Cement Co* [1948] IR 61), to what extent, if any, purely cultural and recreational activities are accorded any "weighting" for the purposes of this heading, is uncertain.

Motive of the defendant

The courts take into account the extent to which the relevant state of affairs is motivated by spite. If the defendant is motivated by spite, the court will readily incline to the view that a nuisance exists. The leading cases on the motive of the defendant all relate to noise being used as an instrument of retribution by the defendant. For example, in the leading case of *Christie* v *Davie* [1893] 1 Ch 316, the defendant became annoyed by the plaintiff's family playing musical instruments. The defendant, who lived next door, decided to retaliate by banging trays on the party wall which separated the respective properties. It was held that the cacophony created by the defendant constituted a nuisance in law. Similarly, in *Hollywood Silver Fox Farm Ltd* v *Emmett* [1936] 2 KB 468, the plaintiff's company bred foxes on its land, the defendant objected to this practice and proceeded to discharge shotguns along the boundary of the defendant's premises. This prompted the vixen to infanticide and detered mating. It was held that the relevant noise constituted a nuisance in law.

Locality

The nature of the locality in which the state of affairs exists is taken into account in determining if a nuisance exists. The courts are less likely to categorise a state of affairs as a nuisance if it is typical of the area in question (*Bramford* v *Turnley* (1862) 31 LJQB 286). The rationale of such an approach is based on the fact that the courts expect people who reside in areas where certain smells, sounds etc are endemic to have become habituated to them. However, the locality principle is only relevant in so far as the state of affairs in question affects physical comfort. The principle is redundant, therefore, if sensible or physical damage is occasioned to the property of the plaintiff by the relevant state of affairs (*St Helens Smelting Co* v *Tipping* (1865) 11 HLC 642, see also *Lord Advocate* v *Reo Stakis Organisation* 1982 SLT 140). Therefore if, for example, noise and vibration from a factory situated in an area of heavy industry were to occasion damage to the walls of a house in the vicinity, the nature of the locality would be quite irrelevant.

An interesting recent development is the extent to which planning permission in terms of town and country planning legislation can alter the nature of the relevant locality for the purposes of the law of nuisance. In the recent case of *Gillingham BC* v *Medway (Chatham) Dock Co Ltd* [1992] JPL 458 (which concerned an action in public nuisance) it was held that the grant of planning permission could change the nature of a locality for the purpose of determining if the state of affairs complained of was typical of the area concerned. It is suggested that the decision may be wrong, and that planning law can have no such effect on the nature of the locality.

Duration and intensity

The length of time the relevant state of affairs lasts, as well as its intensity, is relevant in determining if a nuisance exists (*Harrison* v *Southwark and Vauxhall Water Co* [1891] 2 Ch 409). The dissenting but authoritative judgement of Pollock CB in *Bramford* v *Turnley* (1862) 31 LJQB 286 at 346, phrased in the language of a bygone era, is worthy of repetition. The learned judge stated:

> A clock striking the hour or a bell ringing for some domestic purpose may be a nuisance, if unreasonably loud and discordant of which the jury alone must judge; but although not unreasonably loud if the owner for some whim or caprice, made the clock strike the hour every ten minutes or the bell ring continually, I think a jury would be satisfied in considering it to be a very great nuisance.

The longer the relevant state of affairs lasts, therefore, the more likely it will be categorised as a nuisance. However, even a state of affairs which lasts but a short period of time, can rank as a nuisance. Therefore noise which occasions loss of a single night's sleep, can be a nuisance (*Andreae* v *Selfridge & Co Ltd* [1938] Ch 1).

Time of day

The time of day the state of affairs exists, is relevant. On existing authority, it seems that the time of day is of significance, only in relation to noise nuisance. Noise which manifests itself during the night is therefore more likely to be to be categorised a nuisance, than noise which takes place during the day (*Bramford* v *Turnley* (1862) 31 LJQB 286).

Sensitivity of the plaintiff

A general theme engrained in the common law is that the courts are not indulgent to the oversensitive. In nuisance law this rule is well illustrated by the decision in *Heath* v *Brighton Corporation* (1908) 98 LT 718 where the plaintiff, who complained about the noise generated by the defendants, failed in his action since it was proved he was affected only by reason of his possessing hypersensitive hearing.

A state of affairs

The alleged nuisance must comprise a state of affairs for the plaintiff to succeed (*Spicer* v *Smee* [1946] 1 All ER 489). The circumstances complained of must, therefore, have a flavour of permanence before a nuisance can exist. This requirement is normally automatically satisfied in relation to noise nuisance.

Strict liability

As far as the law of England is concerned, nuisance is a tort of strict liability, that is to say that it is immaterial that the adverse state of affairs complained of has been caused by the defendant's negligence (see *Cambridge Water Co* v *Eastern Counties Leather plc* [1994] 2 WLR 53). Some degree of fault, however, is required if the adverse state of affairs has been foisted on the defendant by the act of a trespasser or by nature (see *e.g. Sedleigh-Denfield* v *O' Callaghan* [1940] AC 880; *Goldman* v *Hargrave* [1967] 1 AC 645 (see also *R* v *Shorrock* [1993]3 WLR 698) and *Leakey* v *National Trust for Places of Historic Interest and Natural Beauty* [1980] QB 485).

As far as the law of Scotland is concerned, however, *culpa* or fault is required (*RHM Bakeries (Scotland) Ltd* v *Strathclyde Regional Council* 1985 SLT 214). Fault in this area of law may have a broader meaning than that which exists in the law of negligence. The position is unclear and can only be clarified by judicial decision.

Who is liable?

The author

The person who creates the relevant nuisance is liable. He need have no proprietary interest in the land whence the nuisance arises (*Slater* v *McLellan*, 1924 SC 854). Persons who create unreasonable noise on a public highway, for example, could be liable in nuisance as could a group of musicians who occasionally use unoccupied premises for practice and disturb neighbours in the process.

The occupier

The occupier will normally be liable for a nuisance which exists on the relevant premises (*Sedleigh-Denfield* v *O'Callaghan* [1940] AC 880). In practice, the author and the occupier will be the same person.

The landlord

The general rule is that a landlord is not liable for every nuisance which is created during the appropriate lease (*Smith* v *Scott* [1973] Ch 314). The landlord is only liable for any nuisance, for example, a noise nuisance, which emanates from the relevant premises, provided such a state of affairs is the ordinary and necessary consequence of the granting of such lease (*Tetley* v *Chitty* [1986] 1 All ER 202). If, however, the source of the relevant nuisance is created by the landlord prior to the property being demised, the landlord is solely liable for the manifestation of that nuisance during the currency of the lease (*Metropolitan Properties Ltd* v *Jones* [1939] 2 All ER 202).

The licensor of the nuisance

The defendant will normally be liable if he authorises the commission of a nuisance on the premises he controls, especially if no attempt is made to abate the relevant nuisance. The leading Scottish case on this point is now *Webster* v *Lord Advocate* 1984 SLT 13 which, it is suggested, is also authoritative in England and Wales. There, it was accepted by the Outer House of the Court of Session, that the Secretary of State (the occupier of the Edinburgh Castle Esplanade) was liable in nuisance for authorising the performance of the Military Tattoo, the noise from the preparation of which, annoyed the pursuer. It was held irrelevant that the contract between the licencees, the Tattoo Policy Committee and the Secretary of State, contained a "no nuisance" clause, since no attempt had been made by the latter to monitor the activities of the licencees, or to enforce the clause. It is possible therefore, that a licensor would be absolved from liability in nuisance if the licensor was capable of, and did in fact take steps to enforce such a clause.

Defences etc

Statutory authority

It is possible for Parliament to sanction the existence of a state of affairs which would normally rank as a nuisance. While it is theoretically possible for a public general Act to licence the creation of a nuisance, the reported cases all concern the effect of private Acts of Parliament on the nuisance in question. The learning on this subject is derived mainly from the so-called nineteenth century "railway cases", which concerned the extent to which private Acts (which allowed railways to be built) negated potential suits in nuisance against the various railway companies. The law was reviewed in the leading case of *Allen* v *Gulf Oil Refining Ltd* [1981] AC 1001 where the appropriate private Act had authorised the establishment and operation of an oil refinery which gave rise to complaints from people residing in the locality. It was held that the defendant oil company had a complete defence in relation to a nuisance action against it, since the Act had sanctioned the existence and operation of the refinery, the necessary consequence of which was the creation of the nuisance. Whether a statute authorises the creation of a nuisance, therefore, depends on the construction of the relevant statute. The court in such circumstances would have to satisfy itself that the defendant conducted his activities without negligence and, furthermore, took all reasonable measures to mitigate the effects of the nuisance in question.

Prescription

The plaintiff cannot succeed in a nuisance action if he has acquiesced in the face of a nuisance for more than 20 years. Furthermore, the state of affairs complained of must have been a nuisance for the entire period of 20 years. It is insufficient, therefore, that the state of affairs complained of has simply existed for that period (*Sturges* v *Bridgman* (1879) 11 Ch D 852). The nuisance must have remained substantially constant over that period for the defence of prescription to apply. Minor differences in the nature and intensity of the relevant noise, however, can be ignored (*Webster* v *Lord Advocate* 1984 SLT 13; 1985 SLT 36).

Coming to a nuisance

It is no defence that the plaintiff has come to the nuisance and thereby, by implication, fully accepted its existence at the outset (*Sturges* v *Bridgman*; see also *Miller* v *Jackson* [1977] 3 All ER 338). This principle is well illustrated in *Webster* v *Lord Advocate* 1984 SLT 13 where the pursuer moved into a flat adjoining Edinburgh Castle in full knowledge that by doing so she would be able to hear the noise from the performance of the Edinburgh Military Tattoo. The Lord Ordinary accepted the view of both counsel that it was immaterial that the pursuer had come to the relevant nuisance.

Public benefit

It is no defence that the nuisance emanates from an activity which has social or economic value to the community in general (*Miller* v *Jackson* [1977] QB 966; see also *Bellew* v *Cement Co Ltd* [1948] IR 61; *Webster* v *Lord Advocate* 1984 SLT 13; 1985 SLT 36.

Remedies for nuisance

A very brief description is given below of the remedies which exist for common law nuisance. These remedies are general remedies which exist in law and are therefore not confined to nuisance.

Damages

Damages may be awarded to the plaintiff to compensate him for any physical damage caused to his property or discomfort caused to him, by the relevant nuisance. Such damage must not be too remote (*The Wagon Mound* [1961] AC 388).

Injunction

The court can grant an injunction (in Scotland, an interdict) to prevent occurrence or recurrence of the relevant nuisance. It is a discretionary remedy and the plaintiff does not have a right to be granted an injunction. No injunction will be granted to restrain simply slight interference with the plaintiff's rights (*Ankerson* v *Connelly* [1907] 1 Ch 678). The injunction, however, is a flexible tool and can be used to abate the relevant nuisance while still allowing the activity from which the nuisance emanates, to continue. For example, in the noise nuisance case of *Dunton* v *Dover District Council* (1978) 76 LGR 87, the plaintiff sought an injunction to combat the cacophony from a children's playground. The relevant injunction restricted the opening of the playground to between 10am and 6.30pm and then only to children under the age of 12. Another example is the interesting case of *Kennaway* v *Thompson* [1980] 3 All ER 329 where the plaintiff was affected by noise nuisance generated by powerboats on an adjoining lake. The Court of Appeal granted an injunction the effect of which prohibited the defendant boat club from holding more than one international event, two national events and three club events per racing season. In addition, no boat capable of creating more than 75 dB(A) was to be used on the club's water. The injunction also restricted the use of motorboats employed to pull waterskiers to the extent that not more than six could be used at any one time. As a general rule the terms of the relevant injunction are required to be precise (*Webster* v *Lord Advocate* 1984 SLT 13; 1985 SLT 36).

Declaration

The plaintiff may simply seek a declaration (in Scots Law, a declarator) that a given state of affairs constitutes a nuisance in law. The declaration, if awarded, has no mandatory force; it simply settles the rights of the parties to the dispute as from the date of the appropriate judgement.

Abatement

English law gives the plaintiff the right to abate a nuisance without first enlisting the help of the courts. Such a right extends to the plaintiff's entering the defendant's land to effect the necessary abatement. However, no unnecessary damage must be inflicted on such land.

Statutory control of noise

No single statute comprehensively deals with noise pollution. Indeed, this area of environmental law is a mosaic of legislative provisions. The first legislative controls expressly directed at noise took the form of local authority bylaws. During the course of the nineteenth century many local authorities, especially urban local authorities, made bylaws which dealt with noise nuisance. Such bylaws, in the main, gave local authorities power to suppress various types of noise which interfered with personal comfort. Bylaws certainly remained the main legislative source of noise control until Parliament, prompted by the then fledgling Noise Abatement Society, passed the Noise Abatement Act 1960. This Act, in essence, gave local authorities in the UK as a whole, power to suppress noise nuisances in their areas. The 1960 Act was repealed by the Control of Pollution Act 1974 (COPA) which in turn, was substantially amended by the Environmental Protection Act 1990 (EPA). The relevant provisions of these Acts are discussed below.

Environmental Protection Act 1990/Control of Pollution Act 1974

The relevant provisions of COPA and the EPA are examined below under the following headings:

— noise nuisance
— construction noise
— loudspeakers in streets
— noise abatement zones.

Noise nuisance

Generally speaking, statutory noise law in the UK is nuisance dominated. The most important powers local authorities have at their disposal to suppress neighbourhood noise, are nuisance based. This does have some disadvantages from the point of view of the local authority, as well as those affected by the relevant noise, in that normally the relevant authority is required to serve notice on the appropriate individual responsible for the removal of the relevant noise. It is only after the author of the nuisance fails to take relevant action, that punitive action follows. This *modus operandi*, as far as the removal of nuisances are concerned, has its foundations in the various Nuisance Removal and Public Health Acts which date from as early as 1848. We are to some extent therefore, victims of our own environmental history. Parliament thus far has scrupulously refrained from adopting a more draconian approach to nuisances in general and, for present purposes, noise nuisance in particular.

Noise in other jurisdictions

It is instructive, however, in this context to contrast the current position in the UK with statutory noise law in other jurisdictions. In Tasmania, for example, section 1 of the Environment Protection Act 1973 provides that:

> A person who emits or causes or suffers to be emitted onto land in other occupation, noise of a volume, intensity or quality, that is—
>
> (a) harmful to; or
>
> (b) offensive to the senses of human beings is liable to a penalty... .

Again, in Western Australia, under section 79(1) of the Environmental Protection Act 1986 (No 87), any person who, on any premises, uses, causes or allows to be used any equipment which allows unreasonable noise, commits an offence. In the state of Victoria, it is an offence for a person to emit or cause to be emitted, noise greater in volume intensity or quality, than the levels prescribed for tolerable noise without first obtaining a licence under the Environment Protection Act 1970. The concept of strict liability is also used by certain states in the United States in relation to noise control. For example, in Colorado, New Jersey and Illinois it is made an offence for noise to exceed prescribed noise levels.

England and Wales

As far as the present law of England and Wales is concerned, Part III of the EPA (as amended by the Noise and Statutory Nuisance Act 1993) deals with general statutory nuisances including noise nuisance. The relevant provisions are discussed below with special reference to noise.

Section 79(1)(a) of the EPA provides that any premises in such a state as to be prejudicial to health or a nuisance, ranks as a statutory nuisance in terms of the Act. In *Southwark London BC v Ince The Times*, 16 May 1989 the occupiers of dwelling houses successfully brought an action under section 92(1)(a) of the Public Health Act 1936 against the owners of the houses on the grounds that noise and vibration from passing trains and traffic was prejudicial to the health of the occupiers concerned. It was held that in considering whether the relevant premises constituted a statutory nuisance, it was legitimate to take external factors into account. Therefore, if the external walls of the relevant premises were so constructed that they could be easily permeated by noise, to the detriment of the health of the occupants, such premises would fall within the scope of the Act. Section 92(1)(a) which was repealed by section 79 of the EPA, corresponds to section 16(1) of the Public Health (Scotland) Act 1897.

Section 79(1)(g) of the EPA provides that noise emitted from premises so as to be prejudicial to health or a nuisance, ranks as a statutory nuisance in terms of the EPA. The word "noise" is defined as including vibration. In *A Lambert Flat Management Ltd v Lomas* [1981] 2 All ER 280, it was held that the expression "nuisance" in section 58 of COPA bore its common law meaning. It is suggested that the word "nuisance" as used in Part III of the EPA would be similarly interpreted. Therefore, in determining if a given noise source ranked as a nuisance in terms of section 79, one would apply similar principles to those discussed above. It is not necessary to prove that any occupiers of land were affected by the noise in question before the noise could rank as a statutory nuisance in terms of the EPA (*Wellingborough BC v Gordon* [1993] 1 Env LR 218).

By virtue of section 79(6) section (1)(g) does not apply to noise caused by aircraft other than model aircraft.

Car radios, stereos etc

Noise from car radios and stereos is a perennial problem for householders as well as those using roads and pavements. The

Noise and Statutory Nuisance Act 1993 introduces a new paragraph (ga) to section 79(1) of the EPA to the effect that noise which is prejudicial to health or a nuisance and is emitted from or caused by vehicle machinery or equipment in a street, ranks as a statutory nuisance. However, under the new section 79 (6A), section 79(1)(ga) does not apply to noise made—

(a) by traffic,
(b) by any naval, military or airforce of the Crown or by a visiting force (as defined in section 79(2) of the EPA), or
(c) by a political demonstration or a demonstration supporting or opposing a cause or campaign.

A duty is placed on the relevant local authority under section 79(1) to cause its area to be inspected from time to time to detect any statutory nuisances which ought to be dealt with under sections 80 and 80A (see below).

Abatement procedure for nuisances

Under section 80(1) of the EPA a duty is placed on a local authority if it is satisfied that a nuisance exists or is likely to occur or recur in its area, to take proceeding to abate the nuisance or to prohibit its occurrence or recurrence. The local authority may also order the execution of such works and the taking of such other steps as may be necessary for any of those purposes. As far as noise nuisance is concerned, relevant insulation work could be required to be carried out on the premises concerned.

Under section 80(2), the abatement notice must be served on the person responsible for the nuisance. The expression "person responsible" is defined in section 79(7) (as amended) as the person to whose act, default or sufferance the nuisance is attributable and, in relation to a vehicle, includes the person in whose name the vehicle is registered and any other person who is the driver of the vehicle. In relation to machinery or equipment the expression includes any person who is the operator of the machinery or equipment. Where the nuisance arises from any defect of a structural character, the notice must, under section 80(2), be served on the owner of the premises. However, where the person responsible for the nuisance cannot be found or the nuisance has not yet occurred, the notice must be served on the owner or occupier of the premises.

Under section 80(3) the person served with the notice may appeal against the notice to the magistrates' court. An offence is committed if a person on whom the notice is served, fails to comply with its terms without reasonable excuse (s 80(4)). In *Wellingborough BC v Gordon* [1993] 1 Env LR 218, it was held that the holding of a birthday party by the defendant did not provide a reasonable excuse for breach of a noise reduction notice in terms of section 58(4) of COPA. On the authority of *Stagecoach Ltd v Mc Phail* 1988 SCCR 289, which concerned a prosecution under Part III of COPA, the defendant cannot challenge the terms of a notice in the subsequent trial if the notice could have been challenged by way of appeal to the magistrates' court.

Statutory defences

Under section 80(7) of the EPA the defence of best practicable means (which is defined) is available in proceedings relating to the abatement of statutory nuisances under the Act. However, as far as noise is concerned, the defence only applies if the alleged offence arises on industrial, trade or business premises Furthermore, the defence does not apply in relation to a nuisance falling within the scope of section 79(1)(ga) except where the noise is emitted from or caused by a vehicle, machinery or equipment being used for industrial trade or business purposes (s 80(8)(a), as amended). The onus of establishing the defence rests on the accused (see s 101 of the Magistrates' Courts Act 1980). The defence must be established on a balance of probability: *Chapman v Gosberton Farm Produce Company Ltd* [1993] 1 Env LR 191. *Chapman* is also authority for the proposition that if the accused has taken all possible steps to secure planning permission for that which would reduce the effect of noise from the relevant premises, and thereby allow the provisions of the relevant abatement notice to be complied with, the defence of best practicable means could succeed.

Section 80(9) (as amended), provides for statutory defences in relation to proceedings taken by a local authority in respect of noise nuisances. It is a defence that the alleged nuisance was covered by relevant notices served by the local authority under sections 61 (construction sites), 65, 66 or 67 (noise abatement zones) of COPA (see below).

Power is given to the appropriate local authority to abate the relevant nuisance in the face of non-compliance on the part of the person on whom the notice is served (s 81(3)).

High Court proceedings

Mention should also be made of the provisions of section 81(5) of the EPA to the effect that if the relevant local authority is of the opinion that proceedings for an offence under section 80(4) would afford an inadequate remedy in the case of any statutory nuisance, the authority may take proceedings (normally an injunction) in the High Court to abate the relevant nuisance. It is a defence to such proceedings that the noise was authorised by a notice under either section 60 or 61 of COPA 1974.

Abatement of noise nuisance in the street

Street noise is now specifically dealt with by the new section 80A(1) of the EPA. As far as noise falling within the scope of section 79(1)(ga) of the EPA is concerned (see above), where the relevant nuisance—

(a) has not yet occurred, or
(b) arises from noise emitted from or caused by an unattended vehicle or unattended machinery or equipment,

the abatement notice must be served in accordance with section 80(2) of the EPA.

Under section 80(2) the notice must be served—

(a) where the person responsible for the vehicle, machinery or equipment can be found, on that person;

(b) where that person cannot be found or where the local authority determines that this paragraph should apply, by fixing the notice to the vehicle, machinery or equipment.

Under section 80(3) where the relevant abatement notice is served in accordance with section 80(2)(b) by virtue of a determination of the local authority in question, and the person responsible (see above for definition of "person responsible") for the vehicle, machinery or equipment can be found and served with a copy of the notice within an hour of the notice being fixed to the vehicle, machinery or equipment, a copy of the notice must be served on that person.

Where an abatement notice is served in accordance with section 80(2)(b) by virtue of a determination of the local authority, the person responsible for the vehicle, machinery or equipment may appeal against the notice under section 80(3) as if the appropriate person had been served with the notice on the date on which it was fixed to the vehicle, machinery or equipment (s 80(5)).

Section 81(1)(A) of the EPA provides that in the case of a statutory nuisance falling within the scope of section 79(1)(ga) for which more than one person is responsible, the notice under section 80(2) may be served on any one of the persons concerned.

In relation to a noise nuisance falling within the scope of section 79(1)(ga) the noise being emitted from or caused by an unattended vehicle or unattended machinery or equipment for which more than one person is responsible, section 81(1)(B) provides that the notice served under section 80A of the 1993 Act may be served on any of the persons responsible where such persons can be found.

Of practical importance are the additional powers conferred on local authorities by the 1993 Act to enter or open a vehicle, machinery or equipment, if necessary by force, or remove a vehicle, machinery or equipment from a street for the purposes of taking remedial action in terms of the nuisance removal provisions contained in the EPA.

Summary proceedings by private individuals

It may happen that a local authority for a variety of reasons may not wish to take statutory action to deal with a noise source which is the subject matter of a complaint. A private individual may also not wish to involve the local authority in question in his or her attempts to remedy a noise nuisance. Section 82 (as amended) of the EPA allows summary proceedings to be brought by a person aggrieved *inter alia* by a noise nuisance, including noise from vehicles or equipment etc on streets, before the magistrates' court. The defence of best practicable means applies in such proceedings (section 82(10)).

Audible intruder alarms

It is becoming increasingly common for occupiers of premises both domestic and commercial, to install burglar alarms. On some occasions such devices have the unendearing tendency to become activated and thereby cause a disturbance. Section 9 of the Noise and Statutory Nuisance Act 1993 makes specific provision for audible intruder alarms. A local authority (that is a district council in England and Wales and a district and islands council in Scotland) are given power under section 9, after consulting the Chief Officer of Police, to pass a resolution to the effect that Schedule 3 to the Act applies to the area. The schedule provides that an audible alarm which is installed in or on any premises must comply with any prescribed requirements (that is to say regulations made for the purpose by the Secretary of State) and that the local authority is notified within 48 hours of the installation of the alarm. It is an offence for a person without reasonable excuse to fail to comply with this provision.

A duty is placed on the occupier of any premises where an intruder alarm is installed not to permit the alarm to be operated unless the alarm complies with the prescribed requirements, the police have been informed *inter alia* of the names, addresses and telephone numbers of the current key holders and the local authority have been informed of the address of the police station to which the aforementioned notification has been given. Power is given to an officer of the local authority, authorised for the purpose, to enter any premises and turn off any intruder alarm which has been operating audibly for more than one hour after it was activated and the audible operation of the alarm is such as to give persons living or working in the vicinity of the premises reasonable cause for annoyance. The officer is empowered to apply to a justice of the peace for a warrant to enter by force, if need be, to inactivate an alarm if the alarm has been operating for more than one hour, is giving cause for annoyance, and the officer has taken steps to obtain access to the premises but has failed to gain access.

Scotland

As far as Scotland is concerned, noise nuisances still fall to be dealt with in terms of Part III of COPA. That Act places a duty on a local authority to deal with noise nuisances occurring in its area. A duty is imposed on the local authority to order the abatement of the nuisance (s 58). The person served with the notice can appeal to the sheriff within 21 days from the service of the notice. If the person on whom notice is served fails to comply with its terms, he commits an offence. Section 59 allows occupiers of premises affected by noise to take summary action before the appropriate sheriff court.

The Noise and Statutory Nuisance Act 1993 makes amendments to Part III of COPA analogous to those made by the 1993 Act to Part III of the EPA.

Construction noise

Noise from construction sites presents an obvious potential problem for those living in close proximity to the site in question. Such noise is generated usually by the carrying out of building operations (ranging from pile-driving to demolition) or the well recognised and indeed significant source of noise generated by site traffic. Construction noise in general may justifiably prompt complaints from neighbours: firstly, because those living in proximity to the site are not habituated to the noise in question (because the life of the site is normally quite short) and, secondly, by reason of the intermittent nature of noise commonly associated with building sites. It is an established fact that intermittent noise is more discomfitting than that which is of a constant nature. These factors combine to make construction noise worthy of special attention by Parliament. The relevant law is contained in Part III of COPA 1974 which is discussed below.

Section 60 of COPA gives local authorities both extensive and detailed powers in relation to noise from construction sites. The section applies to:

(a) the erection, construction, alteration, repair or maintenance of buildings, structures or roads;
(b) the breaking up, opening or boring under any road or adjacent land in connection with the construction, inspection, maintenance or removal of works;
(c) demolition or dredging work;
(d) (whether or not also comprised in paragraph (a), (b) or (c) above) any work of engineering construction.

Section 60(2) empowers the relevant local authority to serve a notice imposing requirements as to the way in which the works are to be carried out. The terms which the local authority can stipulate in the notice must be both practicable and precise (*Strathclyde Regional Council* v *Tudhope* 1983 SLT 22). It should be noted furthermore, that there is no requirement that a nuisance need exist before a notice can be served.

Section 60(3) provides that the local authority may, by appropriate notice, specify the plant or machinery which is or is not to be used, and the hours during which the works may be carried out. The notice may also specify the level of noise which may be emitted from the premises. Under section 60(4) the local authority must have regard to the provisions of any code of practice issued under Part III of COPA and the best practicable means to minimise the noise. The relevant notice must be served on the person who appears to the local authority to be carrying out, or going to carry out the works, and on other persons appearing to the local authority to be responsible for, or to have control over the works. Notice could, therefore, be served on the relevant building contractor as well as the person commissioning the works (if they are different persons) such as the owner or occupier of the land concerned. The notice may specify the time within which its terms are to be complied with and may require the person on whom the notice is served, to execute works as opposed simply to refrain from creating noise (s 60(6)). The person served with a notice under s 60 may appeal against the notice to either the magistrates' court or, as far as Scotland is concerned, to the sheriff court, within 21 days from the service of the notice (s 60(7)). It is a defence in relation to proceedings under section 58 (which deals with noise nuisances) to prove that the alleged offence is covered by a notice served under section 60 (s 58(6)(a)).

It is clear, therefore, that the possibility of the appropriate local authority serving notice under section 60 could act as constant threat to a building contractor, who requires to know at the very outset of the operations in question, how long the building operations will last, as well as the nature of machinery and plant which will be employed on site. Section 61 therefore allows a person who intends to carry out building works to apply to the local authority for consent. If, as normally will be the case, the building works require the approval of the relevant local authority in terms of the Building Regulations made under section 1 of the Building Act 1984, the application must be made at the same time as application for building works approval. The application must contain particulars of the works, the method by which they are to be carried out, and, perhaps more importantly, the steps proposed to be taken to minimise the noise resulting from the works. Section 61(4) provides that the local authority must give its consent to the application if it would not serve notice under section 60. When considering whether to grant consent, the local authority must address its mind to the provisions of section 60(4). If the local authority deems it appropriate to grant consent to the application, the annoyance potential of the site can be reduced by the local authority attaching relevant conditions to the consent in question and limiting or qualifying the consent to allow for any change of circumstances, and limiting the duration of the consent.

Environmental Noise: Legal Control 173

The applicant can appeal to the magistrates' court or in Scotland, to a sheriff court, against the refusal of a local authority to grant consent, or against any condition or qualification attached to the consent (s 60(7)). It would be prudent for any person who wishes to carry out building works to obtain consent under section 61, since, in any proceedings for an offence under section 60(8), it is a defence to prove that the alleged contravention amounted to the carrying out of works in accordance with a consent given under section 61. A further consequence of the giving of a consent in terms of section 61 is that such consent provides a defence in terms of both section 80(4) (which deals with statutory nuisances), and section 81(5) (which deals with High Court proceedings in relation to statutory nuisances) of the EPA (EPA, ss 80(9)(a) and 81(6) respectively.).

Loudspeakers in streets

While it is indisputable that street noise caused by loudspeakers has always troubled society, especially those living in towns, Parliament did not consider the problem sufficiently serious to warrant legislative intervention until 1960, when the Noise Abatement Act (now repealed) made special provision for loudspeaker street noise. This problem is now expressly dealt with by section 62 of COPA 1974, as amended by the Noise and Statutory Nuisance Act 1993.

Section 62(1)(a) makes it unlawful to use a loudspeaker in a street between nine in the evening and eight in the following morning, for any purpose. Section 62(1)(b) makes it an offence to use a loudspeaker in a street at any other time for the purpose of advertising any trade or business. Power is now given to the Secretary of State to amend the times specified in section 62(1)(a) by order (s 62(1A)). However, no order made may amend the times so as to permit the operation of a loudspeaker in a street (or road in Scotland) at any time between the hours of nine in the evening and eight in the following morning (s 62(1B)).

Section 62(2) exempts from the provisions of section 62(1) certain types of loudspeaker including those used by the police, fire brigade and ambulance. Also exempt is the use of a loudspeaker (*e.g.* a loudspeaker which is part of a car radio system) to entertain or communicate with the occupant of a vehicle provided the loudspeaker is not operated so as to give reasonable cause for annoyance to persons in the vicinity. Another important exemption in practical terms, is that made in respect of the operation of a loudspeaker between noon and seven in the evening of the same day, provided that the loudspeaker is fixed to a vehicle used for the purposes of sale of a perishable commodity (*e.g.* ice cream) for human consumption and is operated so as not to give reasonable cause for annoyance to persons in the vicinity (s 62(3)).

Under section 62(3A) power is given to the relevant local authority to give consent to the operation of a loudspeaker in terms of Schedule 2 to the Noise and Statutory Nuisance Act 1993 in which case the provisions of section 62(1) do not apply. However, the provisions of that schedule only come into operation if the local authority passes a resolution to that effect.

Noise abatement zones

Perhaps the most innovative provisions of COPA as a whole are those which deal with noise abatement zones. Section 63 allows a local authority to designate all or part of its area a noise abatement zone. The relevant order must specify the classes of premises to which it applies. Wide discretion is therefore given to local authorities as to the manner noise is to be controlled in its area. There is a tendency, however, for local authorities to confine relevant noise abatement orders to commercial premises, such as factories and places of entertainment.

Procedure for establishing zone

The procedure for setting up a noise abatement zone is set out in Schedule 1 to COPA. There is no legal obligation on the part of the local authority making the appropriate order to make a prior inspection of the relevant area (*Morganite Special Carbons Ltd* v *Secretary of State for the Environment* (1980) 256 EG 1105). However, the making of such an inspection would obviously be desirable. Provision is made in Schedule 1 to COPA for the relevant proposals to be adequately publicised to allow individuals who have a proprietary interest in property which could be affected by the order, to make objections to the local authority concerned. The local authority in turn, must consider objections prior to making the appropriate order under section 63.

Operation of zone

After the noise abatement zone has been established, the local authority is required to measure the level of noise emanating from the premises to which the order relates, and record the measurements in a register known as the noise level register, which must be kept by the authority (see the Control of Noise (Measurement and Registers) Regulations 1976, SI 1976/37). After recording the noise level in the register, the local authority must serve a copy of the record on the owner or occupier of the relevant premises (s 64(3)). Any person on whom a notice is served can appeal to the Secretary of State against the record. The latter has complete powers of review, and can give such directions to the local authority as he thinks fit. In turn, the local authority must comply with the relevant directions (s 64(4)).

Since the *raison d'etre* of a noise abatement zone is to prevent so called "creeping noise", that is to say noise which gradually increases with the passage of time, of prime importance is section 65(1) which provides that the level of noise recorded in the noise level register must not be exceeded except with the written consent of the local authority. The local authority's consent may be given conditionally (s 65(2)). The person applying for consent may appeal to the Secretary of State against the local authority's decision within three months of the date of the decision (s 65(4)). Again, the Secretary of State can review the local authority's decision, that is to say, he can substitute his own decision for that of the local authority concerned. It is an offence to emit noise from any premises in contravention either of section 65(1) or of a condition attached to a consent (s 65(5)). The magistrates' or sheriff court, when convicting a person of such an offence, if satisfied that the offence is likely to recur, may make an order requiring the execution of any works necessary to prevent it continuing or recurring. It is an offence to contravene such an order without reasonable excuse (s 65(6)). Default powers are given to the local authority if the order is contravened by the relevant individual failing to carry out the relevant works (s 69).

Reduction of noise levels in zone

It may happen that the area to which a noise abatement order applies changes character after the order is made. The area surrounding the noise abatement zone may have gradually encroached upon the relevant zone. Such circumstances may, therefore, render it desirable that the registered noise levels current in the zone, are reduced. Section 66(1) gives a local authority power to reduce the level of noise emanating from any premises situated in a noise abatement zone if the noise is of such a level that it is not acceptable having regard to the purposes for which the the order was made, and that a reduction would afford a public benefit. The noise reduction notice may specify particular times, or days, during which the noise level is to be reduced and may require the noise level to be reduced to different levels for different times or days. Whereas in Scotland the person served with a noise reduction notice can appeal to the sheriff against such a notice, in England and Wales the appeal can be made to the magistrates' court. It is an offence to contravene such a notice without reasonable excuse. There is no authority as to the meaning of reasonable excuse in terms of the section (but see *Wellingborough District Council v Gordon*). Section 69(2) gives a local authority power to carry out works in default of the person on whom a noise reduction notice is served.

New buildings in zone

It may happen that someone proposes either to construct a new building or to change the use of an existing building in an area which is already covered by a noise abatement zone. Section 67(1) provides that if it appears to a local authority that a new building is going to be constructed in a noise abatement zone or that the use of an existing building will be changed by reason of which in either case the terms of the noise abatement order will apply, the local authority may either on its own initiative or on the application of the owner or occupier of the premises or a person who satisfies the local authority that he or she is negotiating to acquire an interest in the relevant premises, determine the level of noise which would be acceptable from those premises. Appeal against this predetermined level can be made to the Secretary of State within three months of the date the applicant owner or occupier is notified of the decision of the local authority concerned (s 67(3)).

Miscellaneous provisions

Section 68 of COPA gives the Secretary of State power to make regulations for reducing noise from plant or machinery and limiting the level of noise which may be caused by any plant or machinery used in connection with building works. Under section 71 he can make codes of practice for minimising noise. To date codes of practice have been made for audible intruder alarms, ice cream van chimes, model aircraft, noise control on construction and demolition sites (BS 5228) and clay pigeon shooting.

Other statutory controls over noise

Bylaws

Prior to the passing of the Noise Abatement Act 1960, the main weapon in the armoury of local authorities in their battle against noise, took the form of byelaws. It was during the Victorian era, when the Industrial Revolution was at its zenith, that byelaws began to be made to a significant extent. Byelaws were generally directed at specfic types of noise, for example, street noise. The content of such byelaws often provides the historian with valuable primary evidence of the social, as well as the environmental conditions which were present during the period. For example, the byelaw which was challenged collaterally (that is, in legal proceedings) in the celebrated case of *Kruse* v *Johnston* [1898] 2 QB 91, purported to prohibit the playing of musical instruments or singing in any public place within 50 yards of any dwelling-house, after being ordered by any constable, or by an inmate of such house to desist.

As far as the current law relating to England and Wales is concerned, section 235 of the Local Government Act 1972 gives a district council or London borough council the power to make byelaws for the good rule and government and for the suppression of nuisances in all or part of its area. In Scotland, local authorities have similar power under section 201(1) of the Local Government (Scotland) Act 1973. Such power is ostensibly wide, and is indeed only circumscribed by the requirement of reasonableness (*Kruse* v *Johnston* [1898] 2 QB 91) and consistency with both the common and statutory law (*Powell* v *May* [1946] KB 330).

Town and Country Planning Act 1990

Planning legislation can be used by local authorities to reduce the capacity of various activities to cause discomfort (see generally, DoE Circular 16/73 "Planning and Noise" and Consultation Draft PPG XX "Planning and Noise" 1992). Firstly, structure, local and unitary development plans made under the Town and Country Planning Act 1990 can be employed to encourage the location of premises etc which generate noise a reasonable distance from houses. Secondly, when granting planning permission for the development of land in terms of section 55 of the 1990 Act, a planning authority can take into account *inter alia*, material considerations (s 70(2)). The authority could, therefore, take into account factors relating to noise from the development in question. Furthermore, under section 72(1), a planning authority, on granting planning permission, can impose conditions for regulating the development or use of land under the control of the applicant in question. Subject to the general requirement that such conditions be reasonable, relate to the permitted development, and are not employed for some ulterior motive (see *Pyx Granite Co Ltd* v *Minister of Housing and Local Government* [1958] 1 QB 554) the planning authority's powers are wide. By way of illustrating the type of condition a planning authority can impose to reduce noise from premises, it was held in *Penwith DC* v *Secretary of State* [1977] JPL 371 that a planning authority could lawfully impose, in relation to the extension to a factory, a condition that no machinery could be operated in either the existing factory or the extension between the hours of 6 pm and 8 am on weekdays or between the hours of 1 pm on Saturday to 8 am Mondays or on statutory holidays.

Planning permission is also required if a material change of use is made to land (s 55(1)). It sometimes happens that the occupier of land intensifies the existing use of land and thereby changes the use of the land in question, in terms of the section. The intensity of the use of the land can result in an unacceptable degree of noise being created. Enforcement action can therefore be taken in the absence of appropriate planning permission. Again, simply by way of illustration of the relevance of this aspect of planning control, in *Wallington* v *Secretary of State for Wales and Montgomeryshire District Council* [1990] JPL 112 the appellant increased the number of dogs in her dwelling house, to 41. The dogs created a noise. It was held that the increase in the number of the dogs constituted a change of use for which planning permission ought to have been sought. Furthermore, the enforcement notice served by the local authority to reduce the number of dogs on the premises to six, was valid.

Civic Government (Scotland) Act 1982

An interesting inclusion in the Civic Government (Scotland) Act 1982 (which applies only to Scotland) is section 54(1) which provides:

Any person who—

(a) sounds or plays any musical instrument;
(b) sings or performs; or
(c) operates any radio or television receiver, record player, tape recorder or other sound-producing device, so as to give any other person reasonable cause for annoyance and fails to desist on being required to do so by a constable in uniform, shall be guilty of an offence and liable on summary conviction, to a fine not exceeding £50.

Section 54(3) makes certain exceptions in relation to certain types of vehicles and loudspeakers, for example loudspeakers used by the police or fire brigade.

Liablity under the statute is strict. In practice, section 54 has been found to be particularly effective in relation to noise from hi-fi equipment etc used at all-night parties. The possibility of the police seizing such equipment for the purpose of evidence in relevant court proceedings has proved an effective deterrent to those who organise such events. The legality of such seizure, however, has not been judicially determined thus far.

Brief mention should also be made of section 49(1) of the Act which makes it an offence *inter alia* for any person to suffer or permit any creature in his or her charge to give a person reasonable cause for annoyance.

Health and Safety at Work Act 1974

Section 3 of the Health and Safety at Work Act 1974 places a duty of every employer and self-employed person to conduct their undertaking in such a way as to ensure, so far as is reasonably practicable, that persons not in their employment are not exposed to risks to their health or safety. The section, therefore, would protect occupiers of land in the vicinity of workplaces as well as the public in general from noise generated by activities which come within the scope of the Act, which could have an adverse effect on their health.

Public Health (Scotland) Act 1897

Under section 16(6) of the Public Health (Scotland) Act 1897 which applies exclusively to Scotland, any work, manufactory, trade or business injurious to the health of the neighbourhood or so conducted as to be injurious or dangerous to health ranks as a statutory nuisance and, therefore can be dealt with by the relevant local authority. This section, however, seems to have found little favour over the years with local authorities in Scotland, probably on account of the potential difficulty of proving a causal nexus between a given noise source and any alleged injury to health.

Licensing Acts

A perennial potential source of noise as far as the UK as a whole is concerned, are licensed premises, which in order to attract custom, are increasingly providing entertainment for their patrons, ranging from live music, karaoke and discotheques, to simple jukeboxes.

Under section 4 of the Licensing Act 1964, licensing justices granting a new justices on-licence other than a licence for the sale of wine alone, or British wine alone, may attach to it such conditions governing the tenure of the licence and any other matters as they think proper in the interests of the public. The appropriate justices could, therefore, attach conditions designed to reduce noise from licensed premises.

As far as Scotland is concerned, section 38(1)(f) of the Licensing (Scotland) Act 1976 allows a licensing board to make byelaws for the setting out of conditions which may be attached to licences, for the improvement of standards of, and conduct in, licensed premises. Under section 38(3) the board, when granting a licence, may attach to it any condition set out in a byelaw. Such powers could obviously be used to impose conditions to control noise from licensed premises. From the available evidence, it appears that some local authorities in Scotland have purported to invoke such power to impose conditions to the effect that no noise may emanate from relevant premises. It is suggested, in the absence of judicial authority, that such conditions may be *ultra vires* on the grounds of unreasonableness.

Aircraft noise

Aircraft noise poses an obvious and potentially serious environmental problem. The use of aeroplanes for civil and military purpose has rapidly increased since the Second World War. This trend is likely to continue. Aircraft noise from civil and military aircraft are examined separately below, since different legal regimes apply to each.

Civil aircraft

Aircraft can give annoyance to the community either while the aircraft is in flight, or, after the aircraft has landed at the appropriate airport. The relevant statutory controls over aircraft noise can be divided roughly into those which relate to the control of noise from the flight (or navigation) of aircraft, and those which specifically relate to the control of noise from aerodromes.

Flight noise

Section 76(1) of the Civil Aviation Act 1982 provides that that no action may lie in respect of trespass or in respect of nuisance, by reason only of the flight of an aircraft over any property at a height above the ground, which, having regard to wind, weather and all the ordinary incidents of flight, as long as the provisions of any Air Navigation Order and any orders made under section 62 (which allows the Secretary of State to control civil aviation during war and other emergency) have been complied with, and there has been no breach of section 81 (which proscribes dangerous flying).

Section 60(2) of the 1982 Act allows Orders in Council to be made *inter alia* to regulate air navigation. Under article 3(1) of the Aircraft Navigation Order 1989 (SI 1989/2004 as amended by SI 1990/2154 and SI 1991/1726) an aircraft may not fly over the UK unless it is registered in the manner prescribed by the Order. However, under para (6) of Schedule 2 to the Order, an unregistered aircraft may fly over the UK if its flight is in accordance with procedures which have been approved by the Civil Aviation Authority (CAA) in relation to the flight of aircraft over any congested area of a city or town. Under article 95(1) of the Order the CAA may direct the operator or commander of any aircraft not to make a particular flight etc, if the aircraft would be flown in such a way that article 3 would be contravened.

Of relevance also in relation to the control of flight noise is regulation 39 of the Rules of the Air Regulations 1991 (SI 1991/2439) which provides that an aircraft may not take off or land within the aerodrome traffic zone unless the aircraft has obtained the permission of the air traffic control unit. In practice this power is often used to regulate the flight of aircraft in such a way as to reduce the noise from aircraft to those living in the vicinity of the aerodrome.

Whereas the potential noise problems from aircraft can be reduced by controlling the flight of aircraft flying over Britain, much more important is the need to reduce the noise which emanates from aircraft at source, that is from the aircraft itself. Of prime importance in this respect is the Chicago Convention on International Civil Aviation (which deals with aviation in general) which was signed in 1944, to which the UK is party. Annex 16 to the Convention deals specifically with noise from aircraft. Volume 1, entitled "Aircraft Noise" sets out criteria in relation to aircraft noise. Chapters 2 and 3 lay down standards relating to noise from subsonic jet aircraft. Chapters 5 and 6 do likewise for propeller driven aircraft. Aircraft which meet such standards are generally referred to as "Chapter 2", "Chapter 3" aircraft etc. Furthermore, the EC (which has taken a progressively greater interest in this area of law) has made a number of directives based on agreements made under the aegis of the International Civil Aviation Organisation. As far as the UK is concerned, the relevant provisions of both the Chicago

Convention and the appropriate EC Directives are implemented by noise certification orders made under section 60(3)(r) of the Civil Aviation Act 1982. The general aim of such legislation is to gradually phase out the use of noisier aircraft.

Under such a policy, aircraft operators in the United Kingdom were first banned, in 1986, from operating non-noise certificated aircraft, that is to say aircraft which did not meet either the standards applicable for Chapters 2 or 3 in relation to subsonic aircraft, or Chapter 4 for supersonic jet aircraft, or Chapters 5 and 6 in relation to propeller-driven aircraft. Such a policy was instituted by EC Directive 80/51 and EC Directive 83/206, which were implemented by the Air Navigation (Noise Certification) Order 1984 (SI 1984/368) which came into force on 1 April 1984.

The second stage was banning the addition of Chapter 2 so called "first generation" and therefore noisier, subsonic jet aircraft to the UK register from 1 November 1990. This was effected by the Air Navigation (Noise Certification) Order 1990 (SI 1990/1514). The third stage consists of the phasing out of Chapter 2 aircraft from the register between 1 April 1995 to 1 April 2002 (see EC Directive 92/14). This is effected by the Aeroplane Noise (Limitation of Operation of Aeroplanes) Regulations 1993 (SI 1993/1409).

Aerodrome noise

It is obvious that noise from aircraft will pose a particular problem at aerodromes. It is hardly surprising therefore, that special legal controls should apply to aerodrome noise. The appropriate statutory law is set out in the Civil Aviation Act 1982 and the subordinate legislation made under the Act as well as that made under the Civil Aviation Act 1971, which is now repealed. Section 77(1) of the 1982 Act allows provision to be made by way of an appropriate Air Navigation Order, for regulating the conditions under which noise and vibration may be caused by aircraft on aerodromes. Under section 77(2) no action may lie in respect of nuisance by reason only of the noise and vibration caused by aircraft on an aerodrome, so long as the provisions of the Order are complied with. The appropriate current order is the Air Navigation Order 1989 (SI 1989/2004).

Section 78(1) of the 1982 Act allows the Secretary of State, by way of a notice published in the prescribed manner, to place a duty on the operator of an aircraft which is to take off or land at an airport designated for the purpose of the section, to secure that certain requirements specified in the notice are met, in order to reduce noise and vibration from the relevant aircraft. The Civil Aviation (Notices) Regulations 1978 (SI 1978/1303) makes provision for the relevant notification procedure. Publication is effected by way of a notice published in the CAA publication *United Kingdom Air Pilot* (which has been renamed, *United Kingdom Aeronautical Information Publication*; however it is correct to still cite the latter publication under its former title).

Under section 77(2) if it appears to the Secretary of State that any requirement specified in the relevant notice has not been complied with as respects any aircraft, the Secretary of State may, after giving the operator of the relevant aircraft a hearing, direct the person managing the aerodrome that, until he revokes his direction, facilities at the aerodrome are to be withdrawn from the operator in question to the extent specified in the direction.

Furthermore, if the Secretary of State considers it appropriate for the purpose of avoiding, limiting or mitigating the effect of noise and vibration connected with the taking-off or landing of aircraft at a designated aerodrome, he is empowered (under s 77(3)), to prohibit aircraft from taking off or landing at the aerodrome, or limit the number of occasions on which aircraft in general, or aircraft of a special description, may take-off or land at the aerodrome during certain periods, for example, during the night. In the recent case of *R* v *Secretary of State for Transport, ex p Richmond upon Thames LBC* [1994]1 WLR 74, it was held that it was not lawful for the Secretary of State to limit the number of night flights from a designated aerodrome by means of a quota system based on the noise generated by the aircraft using the designated aerodrome, in contradistinction to the number of aircraft using the aerodrome.

To date, only Heathrow, Gatwick and Stansted have been designated for the purposes of section 78. This was effected by the Civil Aviation (Designation of Aerodromes) Order 1981 (SI 1981/651) which was made under section 29 of the Civil Aviation Act 1971. The 1981 Order remains in force by virtue of the saving provisions contained in Schedule 14 to the 1982 Act.

While the reduction of noise at source is the most desirable form of noise control, a substantial benefit can be achieved by insulating premises exposed to noise from aircraft. Under section 79 of the 1982 Act, the Secretary of State may, by statutory instrument, in respect of designated aerodromes, make a grant towards the cost of insulating buildings or part of relevant buildings, against noise emanating from the aerodrome (see *e.g.* Gatwick Airport-London Noise Insulation Grants Scheme 1980, SI 1980/154, and Heathrow Airport-London Noise Insulation Grants Scheme 1980 SI 1980/8).

No aerodromes have been designated for the purposes of either section 78 or section 79 as far as Scotland is concerned.

Planning law and aerodrome noise

Planning law has an important role to play in relation to the control of ground noise associated with aerodromes. The role of planning law in noise control is discussed above. However, brief mention should be made here of the power which a planning authority possesses under section 70 of the Town and Country Planning Act 1990 to attach conditions on the grant of planning permission (as far as Scotland is concerned, section 26 of the Town and Country Planning (Scotland) Act 1972). Under general principles of planning law, conditions can only be imposed when a new aerodrome is being constructed, an existing aerodrome is being extended, or a new terminal constructed. In addition to being applicable to the regulation of the parts of premises which are being developed, conditions can be used to impose restrictions on the use of parts of the appropriate premises, other than those which are being developed. Such restriction is permitted as long as the relevant condition relates to the development for which permission is sought (*Kingston upon Thames Royal LBC* v *Secretary of State for the Environment*

[1973] 1 WLR 1549) and furthermore, the condition is not imposed for any ulterior motive (*Peak Park Planning Board* v *Secretary of State for the Environment* [1980] JPL 114). For example, it would not be permissible for a planning authority, in granting planning permission for the extension to an aerodrome runway, to impose conditions governing the use of a part of the aerodrome which could not reasonably be affected by the relevant proposals. Nor could a condition be made relating to the reduction of noise from the aerodrome as a whole, simply because the planning authority considered such a reduction in noise desirable.

Proposed reforms

The Government has proposed reform of the law relating to aerodrome noise (see *Review of Aircraft Noise Legislation* (1993)). At present the Government is currently responsible for noise mitigation measures for landing and taking-off. It is proposed to devolve responsibility for noise control on a day-to-day basis in respect of Heathrow, Gatwick and Stansted and also to encourage them to be directly accountable. Furthermore, it is proposed to introduce legislation giving aerodromes powers to prepare noise amelioration schemes. Operators which failed to comply with the relevant scheme would be penalised. The Government also proposes to repeal sections 78-80 of the Civil Aviation Act 1982. New legislation would give the Secretary of State power to compel an aerodrome to adopt a noise amelioration scheme. The aerodrome would be required to consult locally about the scheme and to seek agreement from the relevant local authority. In the event of agreement not being reached the Secretary of State would determine the dispute. The Government intends the power to compel the adoption of an amelioration scheme to be used only if voluntary arrangements have been shown not to be effective. As far as the enforcement of the new legislation is concerned local authorities would be given power to act against the operator of a designated aerodrome which did not take reasonable steps to ensure an agreed scheme was being operated effectively.

Military aircraft

Noise from military aircraft, especially low flying aircraft, presents a particular problem. The problem is aggravated by the fact that the design of military aircraft is such that they have more capacity to create noise than civil aircraft. Furthermore, the legal controls which are discussed above are largely inapplicable to military aircraft.

The Crown is generally immune from civil action in respect of noise from military aircraft (see the Crown Proceedings Act 1947, s 11). The Ministry of Defence, however, keeps noise from military aircraft under constant review by its Noise Panel which has no statutory status. The Ministry also provides noise compensation schemes for those living in the vicinity of military air fields. These *ex gratia* compensation schemes are comparable to those in operation for aerodromes designated by the Secretary of State under section 78 of the Civil Aviation Act 1982 (see above). Furthermore, the Ministry also is prepared to financially compensate owners of dwellings which have depreciated in value as a result of noise and other physical factors resulting from the creation of new airfields or the extension of existing airfields.

Traffic noise

An obvious source of environmental noise is that which emanates from motor vehicles. The problem associated with such noise has steadily increased throughout the twentieth century, especially in built-up areas. Indeed, the Noise Review Working Party considered road traffic noise as the most serious of all the transportation noise problems (*Report of the Noise Review Working Party* (1990) p 13).

Nuisance

Vehicle noise which unreasonably interferes with the enjoyment of land can constitute a nuisance at common law. It is also possible, as far as the law of England and Wales is concerned, that noise from a vehicle using a public road could constitute a public nuisance, provided that a sufficient number of people were affected by such noise and that the adverse effect of the noise was so widespread that it would not be reasonable to expect one individual affected by the noise, to take the necessary remedial action (*Attorney-General* v *PYA Quarries Ltd* [1957] 2 QB 169). However, if an individual affected by a state of affairs which constitutes a public nuisance could show that he or she has suffered personal injury or damage or inconvenience, substantially more serious than that suffered by others exposed to the same nuisance, the plaintiff would be able to succeed in a private action (*Rose* v *Miles* (1815) 4 M and S 101*).* A public nuisance is also a criminal offence.

Statutory controls

As far as the statutory control of noise from vehicles is concerned, section 41(1) of the Road Traffic Act 1988 allows the Secretary of State to make regulations governing *inter alia,* the use of motor vehicles on roads and the conditions under which they can be used. Power is also given to make regulations relating to the construction and equipment of vehicles. Under section 41(2)(c) such regulations can make provision *inter alia* for noise. Section 42 makes it an offence for a person to fail to comply with regulations made under section 41. The main regulations presently governing the construction and use etc of vehicles are the Road Vehicles (Construction and Use) Regulations 1986 (SI 1986/1078, as amended). Under reg 54 every vehicle propelled by an internal combustion engine requires to be fitted with an exhaust system including a silencer, both of which require to be maintained in good and efficient working order. Regulations 56 to 58 inclusive, make provision in respect of noise limits which vehicles must not exceed. Furthermore, under regulation 97, no motor vehicle may be used in such a manner as to cause any excessive noise which could have been avoided by the exercise of reasonable care on the part of the driver.

Of importance also in the context of noise is section 54 of the 1988 Act which gives the Secretary of State power to make regulations requiring the type approval of vehicles with regard to their design, construction and equipment. If the Secretary of State approves a vehicle as a type he must issue a certificate stating that the vehicle complies with the relevant type approval. A plethora of type approval regulations have been made. The vast majority of the regulations have no bearing at all on noise. However, the Motor Vehicles (Type Approval)(GB) Regulations 1984 (SI 1984/981) make provisions relating to noise and silencers in respect of vehicles.

Location and design of roads

The location and design of roads has an obvious bearing on the capacity of vehicles to discomfit the public by noise. The design of new roads, therefore, is of great importance. The Department of Transport designs major new roads in such a way as to reduce the impact of noise from vehicles. The practices adopted by the Department in so far as the design of roads is concerned, are generally followed by highway authorities in respect of new roads which they are responsible for. Reference should be made, in this context, to the memorandum, *Calculation of Road Traffic Noise* (1988), published by the Department of Transport and the Welsh Office. The memorandum describes the procedures for calculating noise from road traffic. While the procedures described in the memorandum simply provide guidance as to the eligibility for sound insulation grants in terms of the Noise Insulation Regulations 1975, made under the Land Compensation Act 1973 (see below) the memorandum also provides guidance as to the calculation of road traffic noise for more general application, such as the design of new roads and highways.

Role of planning law

Planning law also has a role to play in relation to noise from roads. In the preparation of local plans and urban development plans, the relevant planning authority can take into account the effect of noise from road traffic on noise sensitive developments. A local planning authority can, furthermore, take into account noise from road traffic when determining whether planning permission should be granted in respect of any new development. Appendix 1 to PPG XX (Consultation Draft) (1992) (issued by the Department of Environment and intended to supercede Circular 10/73, Welsh Office Circular 16/73) lays down recommended limits for dwellings and schools exposed to noise from, *inter alia,* road noise. Furthermore, an environmental assessment must be made for new local roads in terms of the Town and Country Planning (Assessment of Environmental Effects) Regulations 1988 (SI 1988/1199) before development consent is granted.

Noise in National Parks

Finally, mention should be made here of section 13(2) of the Countryside Act 1968 which allows a local authority to make byelaws, amongst other things, for the prevention of nuisance from excessive noise in National Parks. Such byelaws may require the use of effectual silencers on boats or vessels propelled by internal combustion engines, and also prescribe rules with a view to imposing limits on the noise and vibration which may be caused by any boat or vessel in a National Park.

Railway noise

Noise from trains can constitute a significant environmental problem. Such noise may emanate from the action of trains travelling on rails as well as from shunting operations. Approval for the building of new railway lines is obtained under a private Act of Parliament and not under the normal planning procedures. Since the power to construct the railway derives from an Act of Parliament, the defence of statutory authority would be applicable. Therefore, it would not be possible to take any action under nuisance law in relation to noise from the relevant railway, provided the creation of the relevant noise was the inevitable consequence of that which was authorised by the relevant Act *(Allen v Gulf Oil Refining Ltd* [1981] AC 1001).

When granting planning permission for new houses or schools, PPG XX (Consultation Draft) (1992) lays down noise exposure categories in relation to noise from railways (pp 34-35). Thus, local planning authorities can ensure that such premises are placed a suitable distance from the relevant railway.

It should be noted that at present noise insulation grants (see below) may not be awarded under the Land Compensation Act 1973 in respect of railway noise. This position may however be shortly changed.

Noise from household appliances

Many household appliances can generate noise which is capable of discomforting others. While there is, at present, no relevant statutory requirement, certain manufacturers of household appliances now adopt the policy, when marketing such products, of indicating the level of noise the product in question, is capable of generating. The Household Appliances (Noise Emission) Regulations 1990 (SI 1990/2179) regulation 3, prohibits the manufacturer or importer of an appliance manufactured or imported by him or her, on, or after 28 February 1990, from marketing any such appliance unless the provisions of regulation 4 are complied with. Regulation 4 provides that where a manufacturer or an importer of an appliance takes any steps to inform any person to whom the appliance is to be, or may be marketed, of the level of noise emitted from the appliance, that level requires to be determined in accordance with Article 6(1) of EC Directive 86/594 set out in the schedule to the Regulations.

Land Compensation Act 1973

As has been seen, most of the legislation which has been discussed thus far, is aimed at suppressing noise at source.

However, the problem of discomfort from environmental noise can be dealt with to some extent by insulating the premises occupied by the potential recipient of noise. Section 20 of the Land Compensation Act 1973 allows the Secretary of State to make regulations imposing a duty or conferring a power on responsible authorities, to insulate buildings, or to make grants in respect of the cost of such insulation, against noise caused by the construction or use of public works. The expression "public works" is defined by section 1(3) as any highway, aerodrome or works on land (not being a highway or aerodrome) provided or used in the exercise of statutory powers. Regulations made to date under the 1973 Act relate solely to noise from roads. Under reg 3 of the Noise Insulation Regulations (SI 1975/1763 as amended by SI 1988/2000; see also reg 3 of the Noise Insulation (Scotland) Regulations (SI 1975/460) made under s 18 of the Land Compensation (Scotland) Act 1973) where the use of a highway first open to the public after 1972 (or in respect of which an additional carriageway has been or is about to be constructed since that date) causes or is expected to cause noise at a level not less than the level specified in the regulations, then the appropriate highway authority is required to carry out insulation work itself or make the appropriate grant in respect of the carrying out of insulation work. Such grant is only available, subject to certain exceptions, in respect of dwellings and other buildings used for residential purposes. See the Department of Transport memorandum *Calculation of Road Traffic Noise* (1988).

Building Regulations

An important preventative measure against external noise consists of ensuring that buildings are adequately insulated. The construction of new buildings is governed by the Building Regulations 1985 (SI 1985/1065 as amended by SI 1989/1119) made under the Building Act 1984. Under Schedule 1 to Part 5 of the Regulations, walls and floors of houses must have reasonable resistance to both airborne and impact noise. The importance of the schedule is severely circumscribed in relation to noise control however, by the fact that the schedule only relates to houses in buildings (for example flats) or semi-detached property, in relation to noise transmitted from other parts of the relevant building. The schedule does not apply to wholly detached property.

As far as Scotland is concerned, Part H of the Building Standards (Scotland) Regulations (SI 1990/2179) deals with noise. Again, the Regulations are intended to protect the occupants of dwellings solely from excessive noise transmitted from other parts of the building. External noise sources are not dealt with.

Entertainment legislation

The vast bulk of the legislation now discussed has no bearing on noise, the various Acts being primarilly concerned with the protection of public health and safety as well as public morals etc. However, certain sections of the relevant legislation, can be employed by local authorities to reduce noise from premises to which the various Acts relate.

Under section 12 of the Theatres Act 1968, which applies to the United Kingdom as a whole, a licence is required for the performance of any play. The section also provides that music played by way of introduction, during the interval, or at the conclusion of the play, or the music played in the interval between two plays, is to be treated as forming part of the play, if the total time taken by the music so played amounts to less than a quarter of the time taken by the performance or performances of the play or plays given at the premises on that day. The relevant licence may be granted subject to conditions. A licensing authority could, therefore, impose conditions governing noise from either the performance of the play or the music at the relevant premises.

The Cinemas Act 1985 establishes a special licensing regime for cinemas in the United Kingdom. Under section 1 no premises may be used for a film exhibition unless the premises are licensed by the appropriate licensing authority. The relevant authority can grant a licence on such conditions as it thinks fit. The authority could therefore impose conditions relating to noise from the relevant premises.

Commercial amusements have undergone a veritable revolution over the last 15 to 20 years, as far as the nature of the various games made available to the public is concerned. The proliferation of electronic amusement machines which can generate noise, often of a disagreeable nature, presents an obvious environmental problem. Under section 16 of the Lotteries and Amusements Act 1976, commercial amusements require a permit from the appropriate licensing justice as far as England and Wales is concerned, and the local authority (*i.e.* the relevant district or islands council) in Scotland. The grant or refusal of such a licence is at the discretion of the appropriate licensing body. The appropriate licensing body could, therefore, take into account considerations of noise, when granting a licence.

Section 1 of the Local Government (Miscellaneous Provisions) Act 1982 permits local authorities in the United Kingdom to licence various forms of public entertainment (such as public dancing, music or other entertainment) mentioned in Schedule 1 to the Act. Such a licence may be granted conditionally. Conditions could therefore be imposed relating to noise from the premises.

Noise in the workplace

A worker's health and welfare can be seriously prejudiced unless appropriate measures are taken to ensure that the relevant employee is not unduly exposed to noise and vibration. As far as the legal controls over noise are concerned, the relevant controls take the form of common law and statutory controls. Each is now dealt with in turn.

Common law

Place of work
Every employer is under a duty at common law to take

reasonable measures to ensure that his or her employee has a safe place of work (*Naismith* v *London Film Productions Ltd* [1939] 1 All ER 794). This general duty obviously embraces an obligation to ensure that the employee does not sustain injury as a result of exposure to noise and vibration in the workplace. The duty incumbent on the employer to provide a safe place of work for the employee, remains when the employee is sent to work away from the premises which are under the control of the employer (*Wilson* v *Tyneside Window Cleaning Co* [1958] 2 QB 110). The duty owed by the relevant employer in such circumstances is much lower, however. Each situation requires to be decided on its own facts in determining the extent of the duty owed.

In some circumstances the law will require the employer to carry out an inspection of the relevant premises to which his or her employee is sent, to ascertain its condition. If the premises to which the relevant employee is sent presents an obvious potential risk to the employee in question, the employer is under a duty to inspect the relevant premises to ascertain its safety (*Wilson* v *Tyneside Cleaning Co* [1958] 2 QB 110). There is no relevant caselaw however, on the application of this general principle to a situation in which the relevant danger emanates from noise. However, in most situations in which noise could present a risk to the employee's health, the relevant state of affairs would be readily identifiable, normally by virtue of the existence of the relevant plant etc, capable of creating the noise, or, by virtue of the nature of the operations being carried out on the premises. In such a case, the law would, it is suggested, impose a duty on the part of the employer to ensure that the employee did not suffer injury by way of noise.

System of work

The employer is under a duty to ensure that all systems of work which the employee is required to perform within the scope of his or her employment are, as far as is reasonably practicable, safe (*Speed* v *Thomas Swift and Co* [1943] KB 557). The significance of such an obligation in the current context is that the various systems of work must be of such a nature that the employee suffers no injury by reason of being exposed to noise or vibration. The expression "system of work" has never been comprehensively defined and is somewhat elusive. It is however wide in scope. In *Speed* it was held that the phrase included the physical layout of the job, the sequence in which the work is to be carried out, as well as the provision, where necessary, of warnings, notices and instructions.

The appropriate precautions the employer is obliged to take, under general principles of the law of negligence, must be proportionate with the relevant risk (*Bolton* v *Stone* [1951] AC 850). Of practical significance in the present context is the extent to which the employer is under a duty to give warnings to the employee about the risks inherent in the relevant system of work. If the risk is insidious, which would seem from decided cases to be a question of fact and degree, there would be a duty to warn the employee of the relevant danger (*Pape* v *Cumbria County Council* [1991] IRLR 463). The risk presented to the employee by noise is often not readily apparent. Therefore, the employer would, in most cases it would seem, be under a duty to warn the employee of the relevant danger.

Another important issue in practical terms, is the extent to which an employer is required to ensure by affirmative action, that his or her employee indeed takes the relevant prophylactic measures in relation to his or her own safety, for example, by wearing earplugs. Again, as explained in the last paragraph, the requisite measures must be commensurate with the risk involved. The law requires the employer to ensure that the relevant preventative measures are taken by the employee if the risk of an accident occurring is small, but any injury, if such an accident were in fact to occur, would be grave (*Nolan* v *Dental Manufacturing Co* [1958] 2 All ER 449). Furthermore, in determining the precautions which must be taken, the ramifications of any accident to any particular employee must also be taken into account (*Paris* v *Stepney Borough Council* [1951] 1 All ER 42).

Finally, in the present context, it is well worth citing the judgement of Lord Denning in *Qualcast (Wolverhampton) Ltd* v

Haynes [1959] AC 743 at 759 where he stated that when considering if a particular employer has breached his or her duty of care at common law (including the duty to give appropiate warnings to the employee) one must guard against elevating decisions based on the facts of the relevant decided case, into propositions for general application. Therefore, the conclusion should be avoided that in relation to certain types of work, the employer is bound to provide the employee with specific safety measures.

Plant and machinery

Every employer has a duty under common law to take reasonable measures to provide his employees with plant and equipment which is safe (*Lovell* v *Blundells and Crompton and Co* [1944] 1 KB 502). The duty encompasses ensuring that the relevant plant etc is kept in a safe condition while it is available for use by the employee. The duty the common law imposes in relation to plant and equipment would cover injury to the employee by noise from plant and machinery etc used at work.

Statute

Statutory law has also a role to play in relation to noise in the workplace.

Health and Safety at Work etc Act 1974

Section 2(1) of the Health and Safety at Work Act 1974 provides:
 It shall be the duty of every employer to ensure so far as is reasonably practicable, the health, safety and welfare of all his employees.

Noise which affects the relevant employee's health, safety and welfare, would therefore come within the scope of the Act. The duty to ensure the employee's welfare is of practical importance, in that noise which is simply annoying to the employee, could also be dealt with under the Act. Therefore, it is suggested in the absence of authority, the sound of "piped" music could come within the scope of the section if it proved to be annoying to the staff of (say) a shop or licenced premises.

The Noise at Work Regulations 1989 (SI 1989/1790)

These important regulations implement EC Directive 86/188, which relates to the protection of workers from the risks related to exposure to noise at work. The regulations, which extend throughout the entire United Kingdom, place relevant duties in relation to noise, on all employers with the exception of those involved with sea-going ships and aircraft.

Duty to make noise assessment

Regulation 4 requires every employer, when any of his employees are likely to be exposed to the first action level (defined as a daily personal exposure of 85 dB(A) exposure) or above, or to the peak action level (defined as a level of peak sound pressure of 200 pascals) or above, to ensure that a competent person makes a noise assessment which is adequate for the purposes of, *inter alia*, identifying which of his employees are so exposed and providing the employer with such information as will facilitate the employer's compliance with the provisions of the regulations.

Duty to reduce noise

Regulation 6 imposes a general duty on every employer to reduce the risk of damage to the hearing of his employees from exposure to noise to the lowest level reasonably practicable. In many cases this requirement would be satisfied by the provision of ear protectors.

Under regulation 7 a duty is placed on every employer, when any of his employees is likely to be exposed to the second action level (which is defined as a daily personal noise exposure of 90dB(A)) or above, or to the peak action level or above, to reduce, so far as is reasonably practicable (other than by the provision of personal ear protectors) the exposure to noise of that employee. In practical terms the regulation requires, in the main, the relevant noise to be reduced at source.

Under regulation 8 a duty is placed on every employer to ensure so far as is reasonably practicable, that when any of his employees is likely to be exposed to the first action level or above, in circumstances where the daily personal noise exposure of that employee is likely to be less than 90dB(A), that employee is provided, at his request, with suitable and efficient personal ear protectors. In other words, there is a duty to provide personal ear protectors to those who ask for them.

Duty to provide ear protectors

However, an employer is placed under a duty to provide his employees with personal ear protectors, so far as is reasonably practicable, when they are likely to be exposed to the second action level or above or to the peak action level or above.

Ear protection zones

Regulation 9 is concerned with ensuring that employees are made aware, by means of appropriate notices, of the location of areas where the likelihood of injury by way of noise is greater. Each such ear protection zone (that is to say, any part of the premises where the employee is likely to be exposed to the second action level or above, or to the peak action level or above) must therefore be drawn to the employee's attention. The appropriate text must indicate that the zone is an ear protection zone, and that employees require to wear personal ear protectors whilst in the zone and, furthermore, that the employees must not enter the zone unless the employee is wearing ear protectors.

Duty to ensure ear protectors worn etc

Under regulation 10, a duty is imposed on every employer to ensure so far as is reasonably practicable, that anything provided by him to or for the benefit of an employee, in compliance with the employer's duties under the 1989 Regulations, other than personal ear protectors provided in terms of the provisions of regulation 8 (which simply place a duty on the employer to provide the employee with personal ear protectors at the request of the employee) is fully and properly used. It should be noted that a duty remains to ensure that ear protectors which must be provided by the employer under regulation 8 are properly used. Furthermore, a duty is placed on the employer by regulation 10 to ensure, so far as is reasonably practicable, that anything provided by him in compliance with his duties under the regulations is maintained in an efficient state, in efficient working order, and in good repair. A duty is also placed on every employee, so far as is reasonably practicable, to fully and properly use personal ear protectors when they are required to be provided by his employer in terms of regulation 8 whether requested or not by the employee.

Duty to provide instruction and training

It is fundamental to the well-being of the employee that he is made aware of the potential danger arising from noise at work.

Regulation 11 therefore provides that:

Every employer must, in relation to any premises under his control to provide each of his employees who is likely to be exposed to the first action level or above or to the second action level or above, with adequate information, instruction and training on—

(a) the risk of damage to that employee's hearing that such exposure may cause;
(b) what steps that employee can take to minimise that risk;
(c) the steps that that employee must take in order to obtain the personal ear protectors referred to in regulation 8(1) (that is, when the employee is likely to be exposed to the first action level or above, but likely to be less than 90dB(A)) and
(d) that employee's obligations under these Regulations.

The intention of the regulation is to ensure that those exposed to greater risks from injury of noise, are adequately informed. The regulation does not specify what form the information takes. Whether the information is adequate would be a question of fact, which would vary with the relevant circumstances. In some cases, where the risk of injury is slight, simple verbal instructions may be sufficient, whereas if the potential risk to injury is great, it would be necessary to provide detailed written instructions, films etc.

Duty of designers, manufacturers, etc

Regulation 12 relates to the duties imposed by section 6 of the Health and Safety at Work Act 1974. Section 6(1) essentially imposes a duty on the designers, manufacturers, importers or suppliers of any article to ensure, as far as is reasonably practicable, the safety of articles for use at work. The section also requires such persons to carry out appropriate examinations as may be necessary to allow compliance with the duties imposed by the section. The section also imposes a duty on designers etc, to take the necessary steps to ensure that there will be available in connection with the use of such articles, adequate information about the use for which it is designed and has been tested. Regulation 12 modifies section 6(1) to the extent that any duty imposed on any person by subsection (1) includes a duty to ensure that, where any article is likely to cause any employee to be exposed to the first action level or above or to the peak action level or above, adequate information is provided concerning the noise likely to be generated by that article.

Exemptions

Finally, regulation 13 empowers the Health and Safety Executive to exempt any employer from certain requirements of the 1989 Regulations, namely regulations 7 and 8(2). The Excutive may not, however, grant any exemption unless it is satisfied that the health and safety of persons who are likely to be affected by the exemption will not be prejudiced by it.

Index

Note: Page references in *italics* refer to Figures; those in **bold** refer to Tables.

Accidents, noise and, 103
Acoustics analyser, 76
Aggression, noise and, 103
Airborne sound insulation index, 82
Airborne sound insulation test, 76-9, 77, **82**, *83*
Aircraft noise,
  aerodrome noise, 184-6
  aircraft movements and sleep disturbance, and, 100, 101
  annoyance, 96, *97*
  changes in flight operations, 120-2
    thrust cut-back on take-off, 120, *122*
    two-segment approach, 121, *122*
  civil, 111-22, 182
  complaints about. 91-2
  flight noise, 182-4
  helicopter, 124-6
  jet-aircraft, 111, 115-16, 183
  legislation, 182-7
  measurement, 114-15, *115*
  military, 122-4, 188
  model, 136, 142
  night flights, 119, 121-2, 123
  NNI, 117-20, *118*
  noise certification limits, *113*, 114
  noise insulation schemes in residential areas, 118
  planned preferred routing, 121
  planning law and aerodrome noise, 186-7
  propeller aircraft, 116, 184
  proposed law reforms, 187
  reduced night-time operations, 121-2
  reduction in, 115, *116*, 120
  sleep disturbance, and, 99-101
  supersonic jet, 184
  take-off and landing, 185
  ultra-high bypass ratio engines (UHBPR), 116
Aircraft Noise Contour Model (ANCON), 120
Aircraft Noise Index Study (ANIS), 119
AIRNOISE, 123

Amusement machines, 195
Annoyance, 94-8
  day-night equivalent noise level, and, *94*
  studies of effects, 93
Association of Motor Racing Circuit Owners (AMRCO), 142
Audibility, threshold of, 12
  for young people, aged 18-25, *26*
Audience noise exposure limits, 137-8
Audiogram, 44, *45*, 46
Audiometer, 44-6
  automatic (Bekesy), 45
Audiometry, 44-7
  industrial, 46-7
Automatic (Bekesy) audiometers, 45

Background noise, 130, 131, 132
Bird-scarers, automatic, 142
British Civil Airworthiness Requirements (BCAR), 112
Building conversions,
  Scotland, in, 89
  sound regulations, 88
Building regulations, 193-4
  sound insulation, and,
    achieving regulation performance requirements, 86-9
    methods for demonstrating compliance with requirements, 87-8
    performance criteria, 84-6, *85*, **85**
Burglar alarms, 142, 169-70
Byelaws, 161-2, 177-8

Calculation of Road Traffic Noise (CRTN)(1988), 109-10, 129, 190, 193
Car alarms, 142
Car radios and stereos, 164-5
Cattle as nuisance, 152
Central deafness, 39
Channel Tunnel rail links, 126, 127
Chicago Convention on International Civil Aviation, 183-4

203

Civil aircraft, 111-22, 182
Civil Aviation Authority (CAA), 183
Clay pigeon shooting, 136, 140-1
Cochlea, 38
Communication, 102-4
Community noise equivalent level, 64-5
Compressors, 134
Concert Promotors Association, 138
Conductive deafness, 39
Constant bandwidth filters, 31-2
Constant percentage bandwidth filters, 30-1
Construction Industry Research and Information Association (CIRIA), 136
Construction site noise, 55, 133-6
  BS 5228 (1975), 134-6
  nuisance 152
Creeping background, 132
Cycle, one, definition, 6

Day/evening/night level, 64-5
Day/night equivalent sound level, 64
  annoyance, and, 94
Deafness, 39
Decibel values,
  addition of, 16-18
  scales, 12
  subtraction of, 18-19
Delta sleep, 98
Denning, Lord, 197
Digital filters, 32
Discotheques, 136, 139, 181
Dogs,
  annoyance, 95
  complaints about, 91
Domestic noise complaints, 91
Double glazing, acoustic, 57, 108
Dwellings, noise exposure categories, **144**

Ear, 37-9
  disease or deformity, 53
  frequency response of, 25
  hearing components, 37-8, *38*
  inner, 37
  middle, 37
  outer, 37
Ear drum, 37, 38
Ear protection zones,
  requirement to provide at work, 50-1, 200
Ear protectors,
  duty of designers, manufacturers, etc, 202
  requirement to provide at work, 50, 200
  requirement to wear, 51
  on shooting range, 141
Effective perceived noise level (EPNL), 112, 114
Entertainment legislation, 194-5
Entertainment noise, 136-40
Environmental Health Officers (EHO), 72, 92, 139-40
Environmental noise,
  complaints statistics, 91-2
  effects of, 93-102
  studies, 93
Environmental Protection Act (1990), 162-7
  abatement of noise nuisance in the street, 167-8
  abatement procedure for nuisances, 165-6
  audible intruder alarms, 169-70
  car radios, stereos etc, 164-5
  construction noise, 170-3
  England and Wales, 163-4
  High Court proceedings, 167
  loudspeakers in streets, 173-4
  miscellaneous provisions, 177
  noise abatement zones, 174
  new buildings in, 176-7
  operation of, 175-6
  procedure for establishing, 174-5
  reduction of noise levels in, 176
  noise in other jurisdictions, 163
  noise nuisance, 162-3
  Scotland, 170
  statutory defences, 166-7
  summary proceedings by private individuals, 169
Equivalent continuous sound pressure level, 48, 58-61
European Commission (EC),
  proposed Directive on Physical Agents, 52-3
  on sleep disturbance, 101

Filter shape, 28-9, *29*
Frequency, 7
Frequency analysis, 25, 28-32
  octave analysis, 28, 29-30, *30*
  straight line representation, 30, *31*
  third-octave analysis, 28, 29-30, *30*
Future developments, 52-3

Greater London Council (GLC), 127, 137
Griffiths, J, 138

Health and safety,
  noise, and, 103
  pop-concerts, at, 138
  workplace, in the, 196, 198
Health and Safety Executive, 137
Helicopter Disturbance Study, 125
Helicopter noise, 124-6
Hemispherical radiation, *21*
Household appliances, 192

Ice-cream van chimes, 142
Impact sound transmission test, 79-81, *79, 84,* **86**
Impedance, 10-11
Impulsive noise, 97
Inaudibility criterion, 137, 139
Incus, 38
Industrial noise, 55
  annoyance, 97
  BS4142, and, 129-33
  common law, 195-8
    place of work, 195-6
    plant and machinery, 198
    system of work, 196-8
  daily personal exposure, 48-9
  legislation, 195-202
  statute, 198-202
    designers, manufacturers, etc, duty of, 202
    ear protection zones, 200
    exemptions, 202
    ensure ear protectors worn, etc, duty to, 200-1
    instruction and training, duty to provide, 201-2
    make noise assessment, duty to, 199
    provide ear protectors, duty to, 200
    reduce noise, duty to, 199-200
Infra-sonic frequency, 7
Institute of Acoustics (IOA), 137
Institute of Sound and Vibration Research (ISVR), 127
Integrating sound level meter (ISLM), 65
International Civil Aviation Organisation, 183
International Organisation of Legal Metrology (OIML), 46
Intruder alarms, audible, 142, 169-70
Inverse square law, 20-2, *21*

Jukeboxes, 181

Karaoke, 181

Leisure noise, 136-42
Licensed premises, 181
Line sources, 22-3, *23*
Loudness, 26-8, *27*
Loudspeakers in streets, 173-4

Malleus, 37
Manual of Environmental Appraisal, 109
Military aircraft noise, 122-4, 188
Model aircraft, 136, 142
MOT test, noise emission in, 107
Motor sports, 136
Motorcycles, 107, 142
Music,
  annoyance, 95
  complaints about, 91
  inaudibility criterion, 137, 139
  indoor events, 137
  live and amplified, 136-40, 181
  neighbouring dwelling, from, 139-40, 154
  outdoor events, 137
Music noise levels (MNL), 138-9

Narrow band analysis of machine noise, *32*
National Parks, noise in, 191
National Physics Laboratory (NPL), 123
neighbourhood noise, 1
Noise, normal distribution, percentile parameters, *56*
Noise abatement notice, 168
Noise abatement zones, 174
  new buildings in, 176-7
  operation of, 175-6
  procedure for establishing, 174-5
  reduction of noise levels in, 176
Noise Abatement Society, 162
Noise Advisory Council (NAC), 125
Noise analyser, 65
Noise and Number Index (NNI), 117-20
Noise at Work Regulations (1989), 48, 49, 199
  action levels, 49-50
  requirements of employees, 51
  requirements of employers, 50-1
  requirements of makers, designers and suppliers of machines, 51-2, 53, 202
Noise certification orders, 184
Noise complaints statistics, 91-2, *92*
Noise Council, 137
  Working Party, 141, 142
Noise criteria (NC) curves, 67-9, *68, 69*

Noise criteria/noise rating (NR) values, 71-2, **73**
Noise immission level (NIL), 47
Noise induced hearing loss,
  assessing and controlling, 47-52
  percentage of population suffering, 47, *48*
Noise induced permanent threshold shift (NIPTS), 40, 43
Noise level register, 175
Noise parameters, 55-65
Noise pollution level, 61-2
Noise rating (NR) curves, 69-70, *70*
Noise Review Working Party, 188
Nuisance, 151, 152-61
  defences, 158-60
    coming to a nuisance, 159
    prescription, 159
    statutory authority, 158
    public benefit, 160
  liability, 156-8
    author, 157
    landlord, 157
    licensor of the nuisance, 158
    occupier, 157
  private, 152
    duration and intensity, 155
    elements of, 153-7
    locality, 154-5
    motive of the defendant, 153-4
    plaintiff, sensitivity of, 156
    social utility of defendant's conduct, 153
    state of affairs, 156
    strict liability, 156-7
    time of day, 155-6
  remedies for, 160-1
    abatement, 161
    damages, 160
    declaration, 161
    injunction, 160-1

Occupational hearing loss, 43
Oil refinery, 158-9
Open-site noise, 133-6
Organization for Economic Co-operation and Development (OECD), 102
Ossicles, 37
Ototoxic substances, 53

Pain, threshold of, 12
Paint-ball games, 141
Particle motion, 6-7, *7*
Particle velocity, 6

Percentile parameters, 55-8
  18-hour, 57
Period of vibration, 6
Permanent threshold shift (PTS), 40, 42-4
Personal stereo systems, 140
Phon, 26
Pitch, 7
Planning and noise, 142-5
Planning and Noise Circular 10/71, 132
Planning and Noise Circular 10/73, 117
Planning permission, 179
Planning Policy Guidance Note (PPG) on Planning and Noise, 143-5
Playground, children's, 160
Pneumatic drills, 134
Point sources, 19-22
Pop-concerts, 136, 137, 138
Power station as nuisance, 152
Powerboats, 161
Preferred noise criteria curves (PNC)
  curves, 71-3, *71*
Preferred octave speech interference level (PSIL), 73, **74**
Pregnancy, 53
Presbycusis, 44

Railway noise, 126-9
  annoyance, 96, *97*
  diesel car set, 128, *128*
  legislation, 191-2
  nineteenth century cases, 158
  proposed new regulations, 127
  sources, 127-8
Rapid eye movement (REM) sleep, 98
Rating criteria, 81-4
Rating curve, 81, 82
Reference curve, 81, 82
Reverberation time, 77
RMS sound pressure, 9-10, *10*
Road traffic noise, 55, 104-11
  complaints about, 91-2
  legislation, 188-91
  levels of traffic, 108
  location and design of roads, 190
  main sources, 104-5
  measuring, 106-7, 109-10
  new vehicles, 106
  noise barriers, 110, *111*
  noise level and annoyance, *96*
  noise reduction, 110
  nuisance, 188-9
  one hour sample, 56-7, *57*
  road/tyre interaction, 107-8
  role of planning law, 190-1

sleep disturbance, and, 99, *100*, *101*
statutory controls, 189-90
traffic speed, and, 105, *106*
Royal Automobile Motor Sports
  Association (RACMSA), 141-2
Royal National Institute for the Deaf, 140

Sabine's formula, 77-8
Safety. *See* health and safety.
Schools,
  airports, near, 117
  noise, and, 103
  noise exposure categories, **144**
*Scottish Traffic and Environmental
  Appraisal Manual* (STEAM), 109

Scrambling, 142
Sensory neural deafness, 39
Shooting, 136, 140-1, 152
Silencers, defective, 107
Simple harmonic motion, 6
Single event noise exposure level, 62-4
Sleep disturbance, 98-102
  effects, studies of, 93
  physiological effects of noise on, 98
  prevention of, 101-2
  research, problems with, 99
  transportation noise, and, **102**
Sound and distance, 19-24
Sound insulation requirements, 74-81
  airborne sound insulation test,
    76-9, 77
  buildings (Scotland) in, 88
  impact sound transmission test,
    79-81, *79*
Sound intensity, 11
Sound intensity level, 12-13
Sound level designator, 56
Sound power level, 12, 14-15
Sound pressure, 8-9
Sound pressure level, 12, 13-14, *15*
Sound waves, propagation in air, 5-8, *6*
Speech intelligibility, sound
  level/distance relationships,
  74, **75**
Speech interference, 73-4
  effects, studies of, 93
Speech-interference level (SIL), 73
Speed of sound, 7-8
Spherical radiation, *19*
Sporting noise, 140-2
Standardised impact level, 80
Standardised level difference, 78
Stapes, 38

Statistical noise parameters,
  measurement of, 65

Task performance, 102-4
  difficulties, studies of effects, 93
Telephone conversations, background
  sound levels, 74, **75**
Temporary threshold shift (TTS), 40
  exposure and recovery time, 40-2
Threshold shifts, 39-40
Tinnitus, 43
Tonal noise, 97
Toronto International Airport, 96
Traffic noise index (TNI), 57-8
Train noise, sleep disturbance, and,
  100
Transport Road Research Laboratory
  (TRRL) Quiet Heavy Vehicle
  Project, 107
Transportation noise, 104
  annoyance, 95
Travers Morgan, 138
Tympanic membrane, 37

Ultra-high bypass ratio engines (UHBPR),
  116
Ultra-sonic frequency, 7
Unattended machinery, 168
Unattended vehicle, 168
*United Kingdom Aeronautical Information
  Publication*, 185
United Kingdom Air Pilot, 185
Units of sound, 8-24

Velocity, 7-8
Ventilation systems, 71-2
Ventilation units, acoustically treated, 108

War-games centres, 141
Watersports, 136
Wavelength, 7-8
Weighted standardised impact sound
  pressure level, 82
Weighted standardised level difference,
  82
Weighting analysis, 25
Weighting networks, 33-6, *34*
  conversion of octave to A-weighted
    levels, **36**
  octave bands, **35**
  third-octave bands, **35**
Wide-band noise (pink noise), 76
World Health Organization (WHO),
  101